GREENWOOD
GUIDES

The Team

Simon Greenwood

Jamie Crawford

Ed Chivers

First published in 2000 by Greenwood Guides,
46 Lillie Rd, London SW6 1TN, UK.

Fourth edition

Copyright (c) June 2005 Greenwood Guides

ISBN 0-9537980-7-0 printed in China.

THE GREENWOOD GUIDE TO
SOUTH AFRICA
hand-picked accommodation

Including a section on Mozambique, Phophonyane
Lodge in Swaziland and Malealea Lodge in Lesotho.

fourth edition

www.greenwoodguides.com

Acknowledgements

A big thank-you to Marie McEvoy who was only supposed to be our estate agent, but turned out actually to be a saint!

Series Editor Simon Greenwood

Writing collaboration and inspections Simon Greenwood, Jamie Crawford and Ed Chivers

Maps created by InformAge, using ArcView GIS

Digital typographic contour and road data sourced from South African Chief Directorate: Surveys and Mapping

Production Jo Ekin

Printing, Colorcraft, Hong Kong

UK Distribution, Portfolio, London

SA Distribution, Quartet Sales and Marketing, Johannesburg

All incidental photographs were taken by Jamie Crawford, except the intro page for Mozambique which is courtesy of Nkwichi Lodge.

The cover image is of Sycamore Avenue Treehouse Lodge in KwaZulu Natal, entry number 224. Cover design and digital manipulation Tory Gordon-Harris.

Symbols

and what they mean

 No credit cards accepted.

 Meals can be provided, often by prior arrangement.

 Rooms all have TVs.

 Stocked wild game can be seen. This does not include naturally occurring wild animals like springbok and waterbuck.

 Children are welcome without proviso.

 Working farm.

 Off-street car parking.

 Access only for wheelchairs.

 Full wheelchair facilities.

 Swimming available in pool, sea, dam or river.

 No smoking inside the buildings.

 Good hiking or walking direct from the house.

 They have their own horses for riding.

Contents

Introduction
Maps

 WESTERN CAPE

EASTERN CAPE

MOZAMBIQUE

Introduction

The standard of accommodation in South Africa just keeps on climbing year after year and we have had to invest in new crampons, ice picks and ropes to keep up. Each book we have produced has represented a considerable step up from its predecessor and this is no exception. A quick thumb through the photos will tell you all you need to know. You are in for a treat.

There are one or two GG news items that I would like to highlight right at the start:

Firstly we are in the process of researching and producing a brand-new companion guide that will give you the Greenwood Guides take on things to do and places to eat in South Africa. The surprise title of the new book is to be The Greenwood Guide to South Africa, Hand-Picked Things to Do and Places to Eat. Well, at least you know where you stand….

The new guide will contain somewhere between 500 and 1000 restaurants, cafés, bars, wineries, gardens, walks, bird-watching sites/tours/guides, golf courses, activities, things to do with the kids, nature reserves and loads of one-off things to do that may or may not coincide with your trip. We are also including tour guides who offer very friendly expertise to help you find the best birding sites, to organise you on boat trips and walking tours etc. We have applied the same sort of likes and dislikes to the new book as we have to the accommodation guide. Thus:

Things we like: *natural, unstuffy, humorous guides and hosts, smiley service, cherished gardens, good food, untouristy spots, dirt roads, the lived-in look, the artistic, the unusual, the down-to-earth, hidden places.*

Things we don't like: *tourist traps offering little individual experience; megalithic conference centres; tour guides that treat you like cattle; the bland and the boring; falsely friendly service and bad value for money.*

Much of the new book has been personally recommended by owners from this book, who have spilled the beans on the absolute best that their area has to offer. You might not be able to find these eateries or activities any other way. Among the better-known establishments or things to do we have only included those that are truly worthy. It is hard not to mention Table Mountain, for example. But rather than tell you about the cable car, we will lead you up Skeleton Gorge from Kirstenbosch to the top, which is a fabulous walk but needs a little guidance. For example….

Anyway, I thought you might be interested. The new book is due for publication around the end of 2005. There is an order form at the back of the book if you would like to buy this or any of our other guides to accommodation: Canada, Australia and New Zealand.

Also new this year a small but sumptuous section on Mozambique. There are not many places that yet suit the GG model in Mozambique but those that we have found are among the best places to stay in the whole book.

Also there's a useful new index of activities at the back of the book. You can look up all the places that are fully child-friendly, do self-catering, organise history tours, cook gourmet cuisine, have lovely gardens etc. In case these are important criteria for you in choosing your place to stay.

THE GREENWOOD GUIDES APPROACH

There are essentially three types of place to stay. There are those that fulfil their obligations in a commercial way and leave you feeling throughout your stay like the paying customer that you are. And there are those few great places where you are welcomed in and treated as a friend, cliché though this may now have become, and where paying at the end of your visit is a pleasurable surprise. And of course there is a third category where paying for your stay is a disagreeable inevitability!

It is a particular irony of the accommodation world that no price is ever put on the essential qualities of a place – people, atmosphere, charm. These ideas are too woolly perhaps to quantify, but this is where one's real enjoyment of a place to stay stems from. You are asked to pay instead for tangible facilities like marble bathrooms and en-suite showers.

This is a fallacy that we try to dismantle in all our guides, which is why you will find places at all reasonable price levels. Expensive does not mean good. And nor does cheap (however appealing the word may sound!). If a place costs plenty then it will probably offer facilities in keeping with the price. But that does not mean you will have any fun. Some very expensive places forget that they are providing a service and look down their noses at their own guests. At the other end of the spectrum, the very cheapest places are often cheap for good reasons. Sometimes for spectacular reasons!

Character and genuine hospitality, the extra qualities we search for, are found spaced evenly across the price spectrum. Nowhere in this guide cuts corners at the risk of your displeasure. We give equal billing to each place we choose, no matter if it is a gorgeous lodge or a home-spun B&B.

At the top end, the most jewel-encrusted, nay 'boutique' places may drip with luxurious trimmings, but have retained their sense of atmosphere and humour, are friendly and informal and nearly all are still owned and managed by the same people. ('Boutique' always used to mean a 'small clothes shop in France', but it has sneaked into accommodation vocab somewhere along the line.)

Equally, there are places in the book that do not have much in the way of luxury, but easily compensate with unique settings, wonderful views and charming hosts.

We are hoping that those of you who normally only plump for luxury at a price will use this guide to vary their holiday a little and stay at a few of the wonderful family-run farms and B&Bs. And that those who usually go cheap as possible will splash out once in a while on a more luxurious option. This book allows for great flexibility in terms of price and style of accommodation. We do not wish to divide the world into budget and luxury, only great and not great enough.

It is the quality of experience that draws us in and this is not determined by how much you pay. In the end I know that you will really like the owners in this book, many of whom we now count as friends. And you will certainly make friends yourselves if you stick to the Greenwood trail.

DRIVING
There is nowhere in South Africa that would make a 4-wheel drive a necessity. However make sure you confirm this issue if booking into Mozambiquan places.

CAR HIRE
Make sure that you have considered the amount of daily mileage your car hire company gives you. 100km or even 200km a day is virtually nothing and the final cost can be far higher than you estimated. Try and work out roughly what distances you will be covering and ask for the correct daily allowance. There is usually a surcharge for taking your car across the border from SA into Mozambique.

MOBILE/CELL PHONES
Airports all have shops that provide mobile phones. They are invaluable and we recommend that you get one. You can buy a cheap handset or just rent one for the duration of your stay and then pay for calls as you go with recharge cards.

TELEPHONE NUMBERS
To call South Africa from the UK dial 0027 then drop the 0 from the local code.
To call the UK from South Africa dial 0944 then drop the 0 from the local code.
The numbers printed in this book are all from within South Africa.
To call Mozambique from the UK dial 0058 then drop the 0 from the local code.

TORTOISES
Look out for tortoises. They are slow, but seem to spend a lot of time, completely against the tide of advice put forward for their benefit, crossing roads.

TIPPING
* In restaurants we tend to give 15%.

* At a petrol station my policy is to give no tip for just filling up, 3 rand for cleaning the windows, and 5 rand for cleaning the windows and checking oil and water. If you really don't want the attendant to clean your windows you need to make this a statement when you ask for the petrol… or they will often do it anyway.

* At a guest-house I would typically give R15 per person staying for up to two nights. If you are staying longer than two nights then you might feel like adding more. If there is obviously one maid to whom the tip will go then give it to her direct. If there are many staff members who will be sharing the tip then give it to your host.

TIME OF YEAR
I got in a bit of a tangle in the first edition trying neatly to package up what is really quite complicated. So I will limit myself to one observation. It seems to me that most Europeans come to South Africa in January, February and March to avoid their own miserable weather and write taunting postcards home from a sunny Cape. I've been doing this myself for the last few years.

However, the very best time of year to visit the Northern Cape, Mpumalanga, Limpopo, North-West Province, KwaZulu Natal and the Karoo, i.e. the whole country except the southern Cape, is from May to October. The air is dry and warm, game viewing is at its best and there are fewer tourists keeping the prices higher. It's worth mentioning.

PAY FOR ENTRY
We could not afford to research and publish this guide in the way we do without the financial support of those we feature. Each place that we have chosen has paid an entry fee for which we make no apology. It has not influenced our decision-making about who is right or wrong for the guide and we turn down many more than we accept. The proof of this is in the proverbial pudding. Use the book and see for yourself. It is also very hard for us to write up a place that we are not enthusiastic about.

THE MAPS SECTION
The maps at the front of the book are designed to show you where in the country each place is positioned, and should not be used as a road map. There are many minor and dirt roads missing and we recommend that you buy a proper companion road atlas.

Each place is flagged with a number that corresponds to the page number below each entry.

Some have complained that it is hard to find detailed road maps of South Africa in the UK, so I suggest you buy one at the airport when you arrive in SA.

CANCELLATION

Most places have some form of cancellation charge. Do make sure that you are aware what this is if you book in advance. Owners need to protect themselves against no-shows and will often demand a deposit for advance booking.

PRICES

The prices quoted are per person sharing per night, unless specifically stated otherwise. Every now and then complications have meant we quote the full room rate. Single rates are also given.

We have usually put in a range within which the actual price will fall. This may be because of fluctuating prices at different times of year, but also we have tried to predict the anticipated rise in prices over the book's shelf life. Obviously we cannot know what will happen to the value of the rand and prices might fall outside the quoted range.

Most game lodges quote an all-in package including meals and game activities.

Although South Africa has become substantially more expensive since the first edition of this guide came out 6 years ago, it is still great value on the whole. The value-for-money increases significantly the more off-the-beaten-track you wander.

CHILDREN

We have only given the child-friendly symbol to those places that are unconditionally accepting of the little fellows. This does not necessarily mean that if there is no symbol children are barred. But it may mean chatting with your hosts about their ages, their temperaments and how suitable a time and place it will be. Most owners are concerned about how their other guests will take to kids running wild when they are trying to relax on a long-anticipated holiday… from their own children. Places that are fully child-friendly are listed in the activities index at the back of the book.

RIDING

We have only given this symbol to places with their own horses. Many places can organise riding nearby.

DISCLAIMER

We make no claims to god-like objectivity in assessing what is or is not special about the places we feature. They are there because we like them. Our opinions and tastes are mortal and ours alone. We have done our utmost to get the facts right, but apologize for any mistakes that may have slipped through the net.

Some things change which are outside our control: people sell up, prices increase, exchange rates fluctuate, unfortunate extensions are added, marriages break up and even acts of God can rain down destruction. We would be grateful to be told about any errors or changes, however great or small. We can always make these editions on the web version of this book.

DON'T TRY AND DO TOO MUCH. PLEASE.

It is the most common way to spoil your own holiday. South Africa is a huge country and you cannot expect to see too much of it on one trip. Don't over-extend yourself. Stay everywhere for at least two nights and make sure that you aren't spending your hard-earned holiday fiddling with the radio and admiring the dashboard of your hire car.

PLEASE WRITE TO US

Our email address is simon@greenwoodguides.com for all comments. Although we visit each place each edition many of the places featured here are small, personal and owner-run. This means that their enjoyability depends largely on the happiness, health and energy of the hosts. This can evaporate in double-quick time for any number of reasons and standards plummet before we have had a chance to re-evaluate the place. So we are also very grateful to travellers who keep us up to date with how things are going. We are always most concerned to hear that the hosting has been inattentive.

We also have guides to Australia, New Zealand and Canada. These books are available in bookshops or by emailing us direct or mailing us the order form at the back of this book.

It seems sad not to have any further comment to make on the Cape salmon. I have become rather fond of discussing it in these pages once a year. But I think we have now wrapped the issue up. Unless anyone can see further room for disagreement?

So that's about it for another year. My great thanks to Jamie and Ed for all their complaint-free effort. No, I'll go further… they were downright cheerful, I thought. They drove 35,000 kilometres between them for this edition, so Jamie tells me. That's two thirds of the way round the entire globe.

So I hope all of you who use the guide have a wonderful time. I hope the Greenwood Guide will be seen as the main reason why you enjoyed your holiday as much as you did.

Simon.

General Map

Approximate scale 1 : 9.2 million

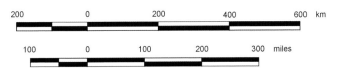

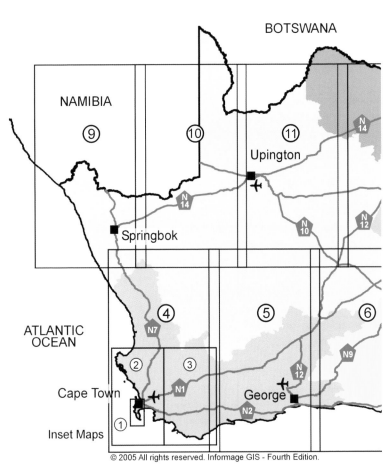

BOTSWANA

NAMIBIA

⑨   ⑩   ⑪

Upington

Springbok

ATLANTIC
OCEAN

④   ⑤   ⑥

②   ③

Cape Town

George

① Inset Maps

The size of Britain
in relation to South Africa

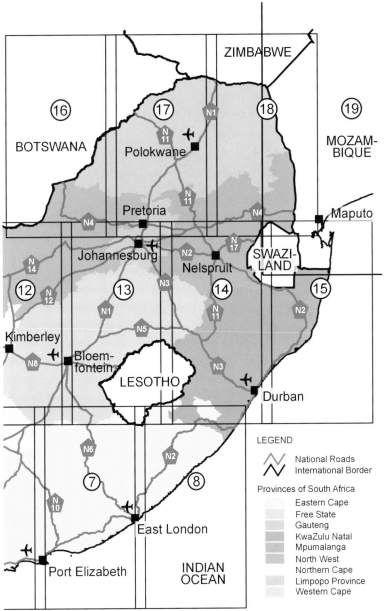

Maps by informage using ESRI's ArcGIS.

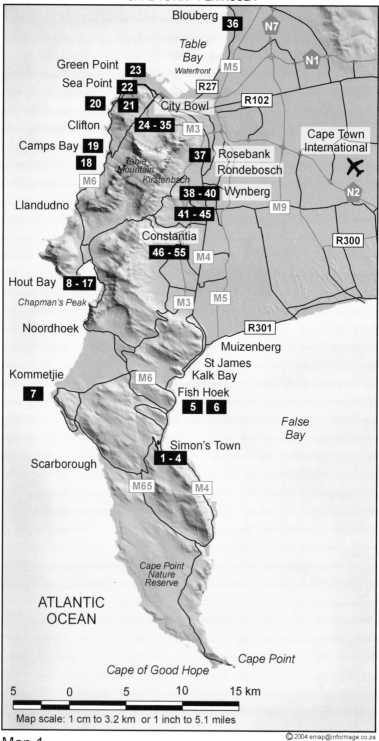

CAPE TOWN - PENINSULA

Map 1

Map scale: 1 cm to 3.2 km or 1 inch to 5.1 miles

© 2004 emap@informage.co.za

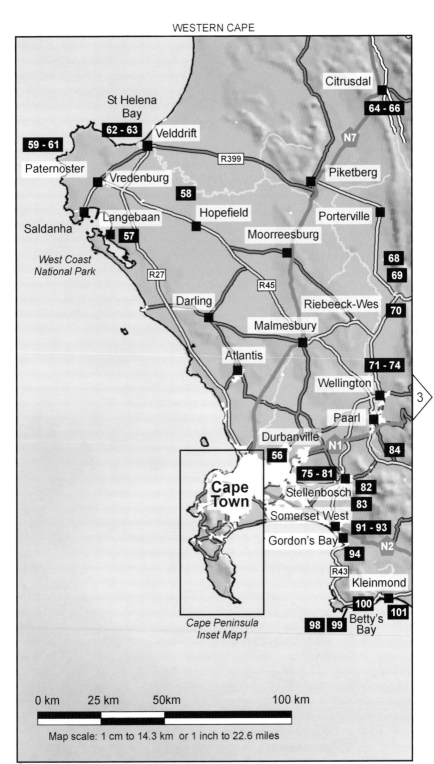

WESTERN CAPE

Map 2

Map scale: 1 cm to 14.3 km or 1 inch to 22.6 miles

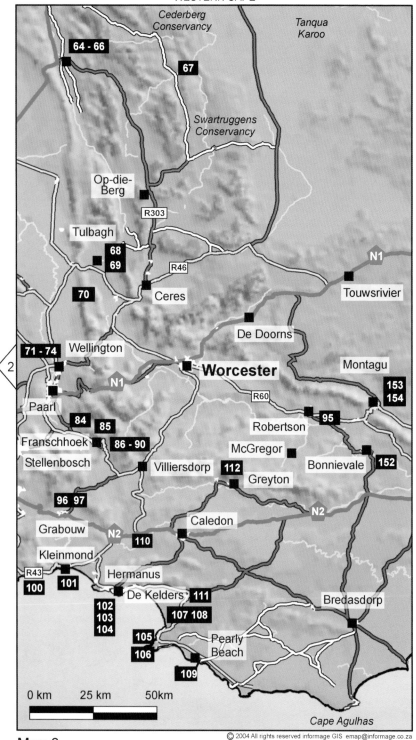

Map 3

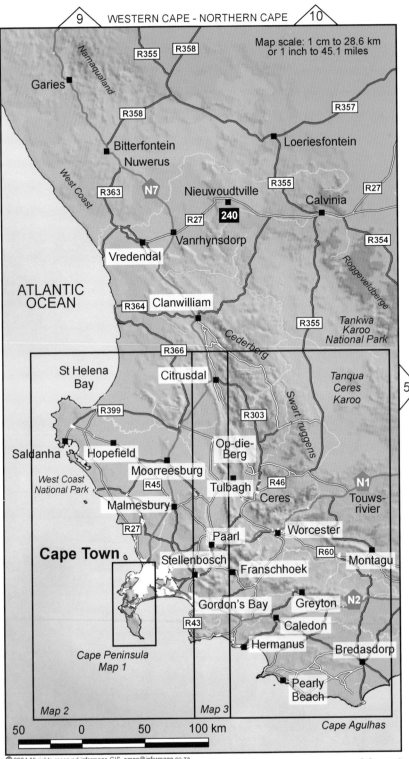

Map scale: 1 cm to 28.6 km
or 1 inch to 45.1 miles

R355   R358

Nammaqualand

Garies

R358

R357

Bitterfontein
Nuwerus

Loeriesfontein

R363   N7

Nieuwoudtville

R27   R355

Calvinia

240

Vanrhynsdorp

R354

Vredendal

Roggeveldberge

ATLANTIC
OCEAN

R364   Clanwilliam

Tankwa
Karoo
National Park

R355

Cederberg

R366

5

St Helena
Bay

Citrusdal

Tanqua
Ceres
Karoo

R399

R303

Swartruggens

Saldanha

Hopefield

Op-die-
Berg

West Coast
National Park

Moorreesburg

R45

Tulbagh

R46

Ceres

N1

Touws-
rivier

Malmesbury

R27

Paarl

Worcester

R60

Montagu

Cape Town

Stellenbosch

Franschhoek

Gordon's Bay

Greyton   N2

R43

Caledon

Hermanus

Bredasdorp

Cape Peninsula
Map 1

Pearly
Beach

Map 2

Map 3

Cape Agulhas

50   0   50   100 km

Map 4

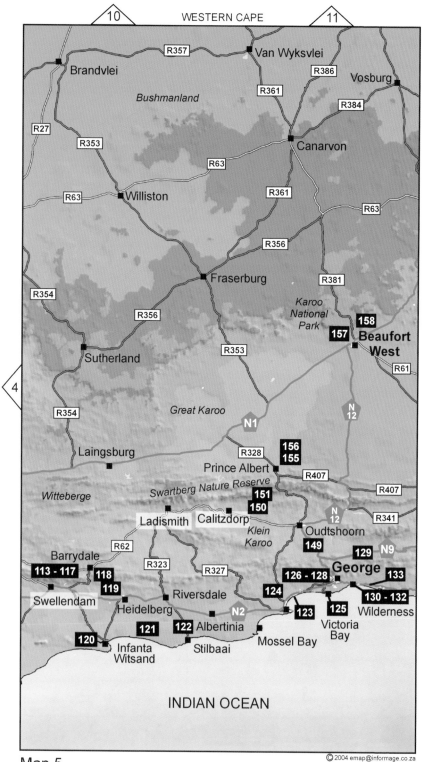

Map 5

© 2004 emap@informage.co.za

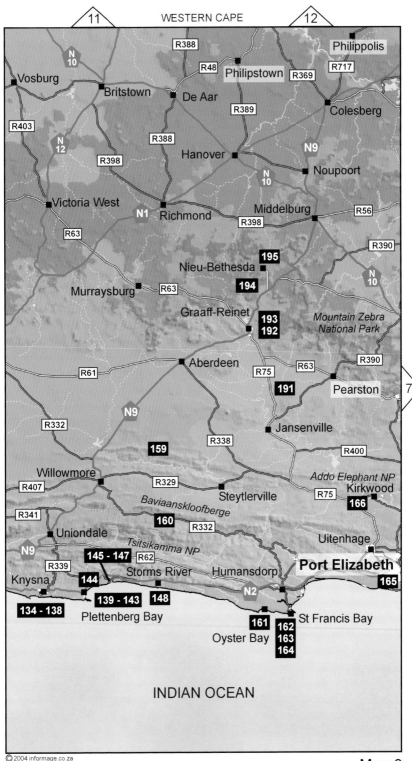

Map 6

© 2004 informage.co.za

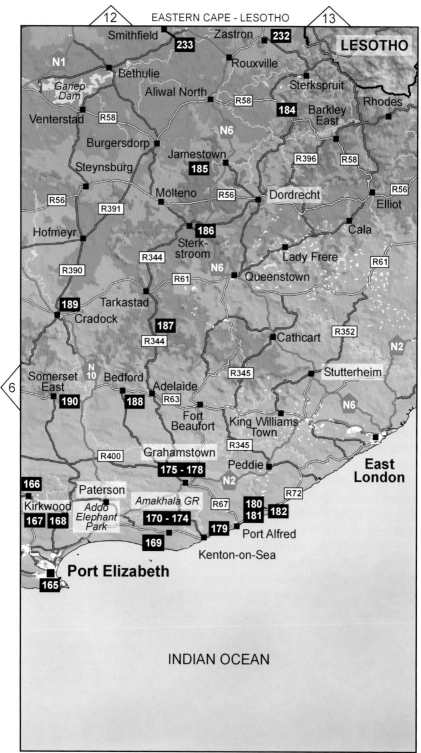

Map 7

© 2004 informage.co.za

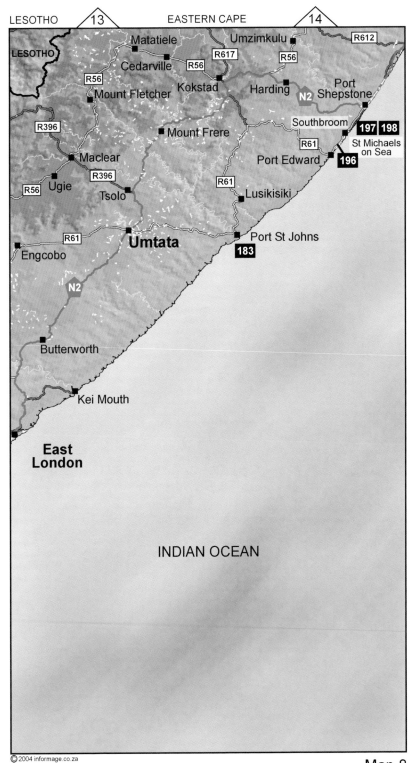

LESOTHO

Matatiele

Cedarville

Umzimkulu

R612

R56 R617 R56

Mount Fletcher

Kokstad

Harding

N2

Port Shepstone

R396

Mount Frere

Southbroom

197 198

St Michaels on Sea

Maclear

R61

196

R396

Port Edward

R56 Ugie

Tsolo

R61

Lusikisiki

R61 Engcobo

Umtata

Port St Johns

183

N2

Butterworth

Kei Mouth

East London

INDIAN OCEAN

© 2004 informage.co.za

Map 8

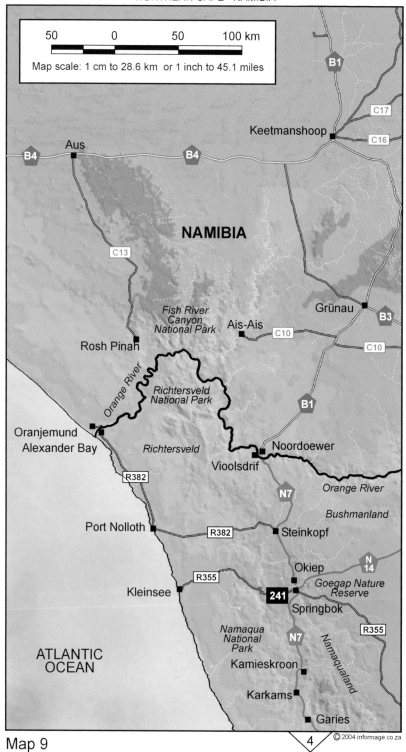

Map 9

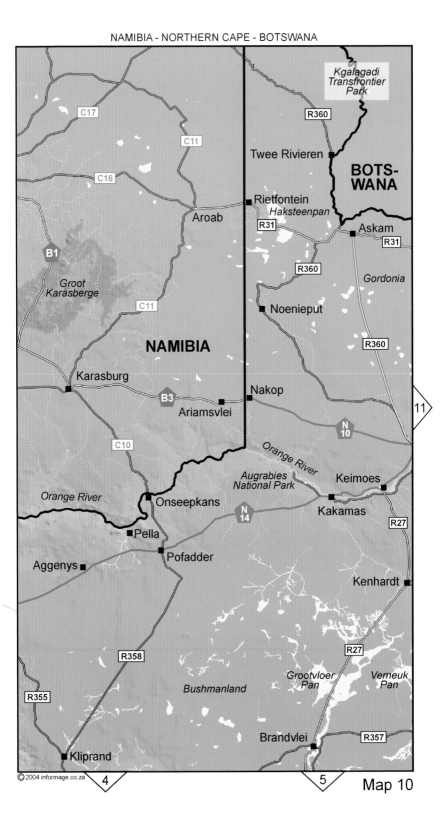

Map 10

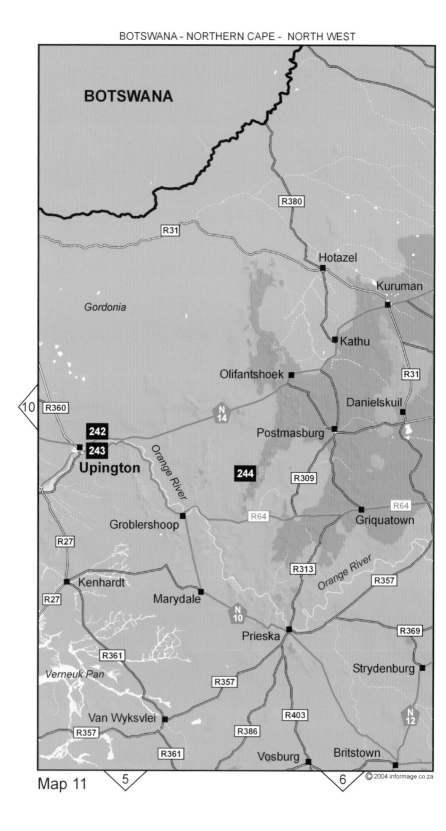

Map 11

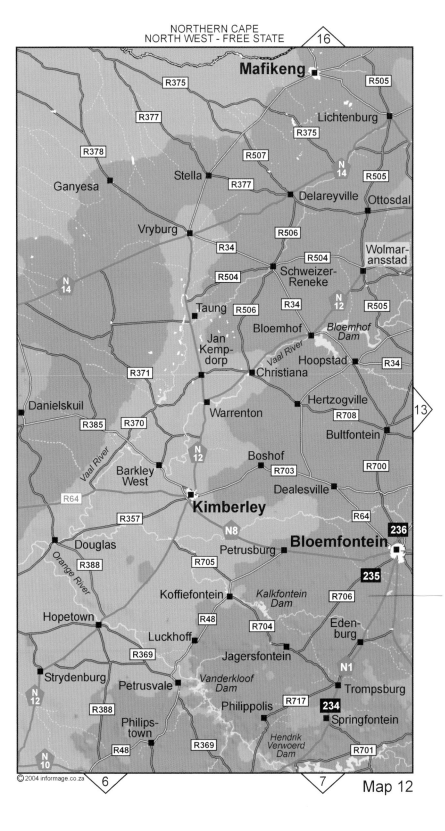

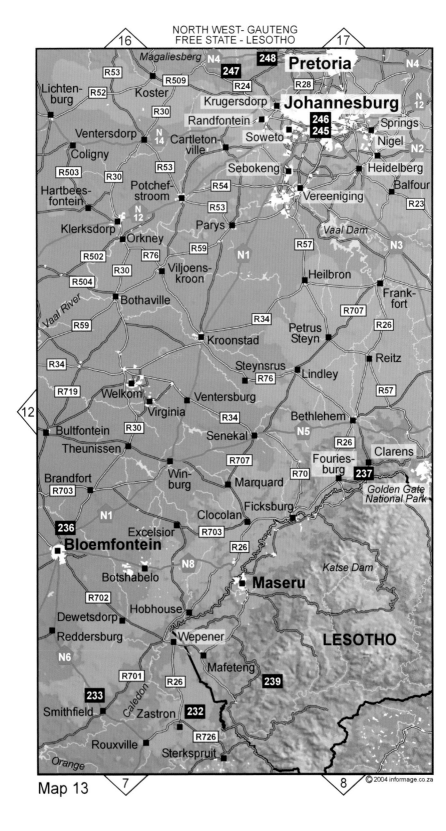

Magaliesberg   N4   **248**   **Pretoria**   N4

247

R24   R28

R53

Lichten-   R509   Koster
burg   R52

R30   Krugersdorp   **Johannesburg**   N12

Randfontein   **246**   Springs
245

Ventersdorp   Cartleton-   Soweto   Nigel   N2
ville   N14

Coligny   Sebokeng   Heidelberg

R503   R30   R53   Balfour

Hartbees-   Potchef-   R54   Vereeniging   R23
fontein   stroom

N12   R53   Vaal Dam

Klerksdorp   Parys   R57   N3

Orkney   R59   Heilbron

R502   R76   Frank-
fort

R30   Viljoens-   R707   R26
R504   kroon

Bothaville   R34

Vaal River   Kroonstad   Petrus   Reitz
Steyn

R59   Steynsrus   R57

R34   R76   Lindley

R719   Welkom   Ventersburg   Bethlehem

Virginia   R34   N5   Clarens

Bultfontein   R30   Senekal   R26
Theunissen   R707   Fouries-   **237**
burg

Brandfort   Win-   R70   Golden Gate
R703   burg   Marquard   National Park

236   N1   Ficksburg

Excelsior   Clocolan

Bloemfontein   R703   Katse Dam

R26

Botshabelo   N8   **Maseru**

R702

Dewetsdorp   Hobhouse   **LESOTHO**

Reddersburg   Wepener

N6   Mafeteng   **239**

R701   R26

233   Caledon

Smithfield   Zastron   **232**   R726

Rouxville   Sterkspruit

Orange   © 2004 informage.co.za

Map 13   7   8

12

KwaGuqa
N4
Mhluzi
Middelburg
R36
R38
Josefsdal
264
Piggs Peak
Witbank
Carolina
N12
Lochiel
Springs
Kriel
R35
N11
N17
Oshoek
Mbabane
Evander
Bethal
N17
Ermelo
N17
Manzini
Secunda
Amsterdam
SWAZI-LAND
R23
R546
R35
Standerton
Piet Retief
N2
R546
R23
R543
R33
Paul-pieters-burg
N2
N3
Vrede
Volksrust
R103
R34
N11
R34
Utrecht
Vryheid
R69
R601
Warden
Newcastle
Madadeni
R33
Dundee
R34
15
R722
238
Harrismith
N5
218
Van Reenen
217
216
215
Rorke's Drift
R66
219
Royal Natal National Park
R74
221
Ladysmith
Colenso
223
R33
Bergville
N3
220
R74
Weenen
Champagne Castle
222
Estcourt
Kranskop
Drakensberg
Giants Castle
225
224
Mooiriver
R622
Greytown
R74
LESOTHO
226
Natal Drakensberg Park
Howick
R614
Stanger
N2
Drakensberg
228
227
Pieter-maritz-burg
Tongaat
204
203
Kwa-Mashu
201
202
R617
229
Durban
Salt Rock
230
Under-berg
Queens-burgh
R603
200
199
231
R612
Amanzimtoti
R617
Franklin
Ixopo
R612
Umzinto
Matatiele
Cedarville
Umzimkulu
Umzinto
R56
N2
Harding
Hibberdene
Kokstad
8

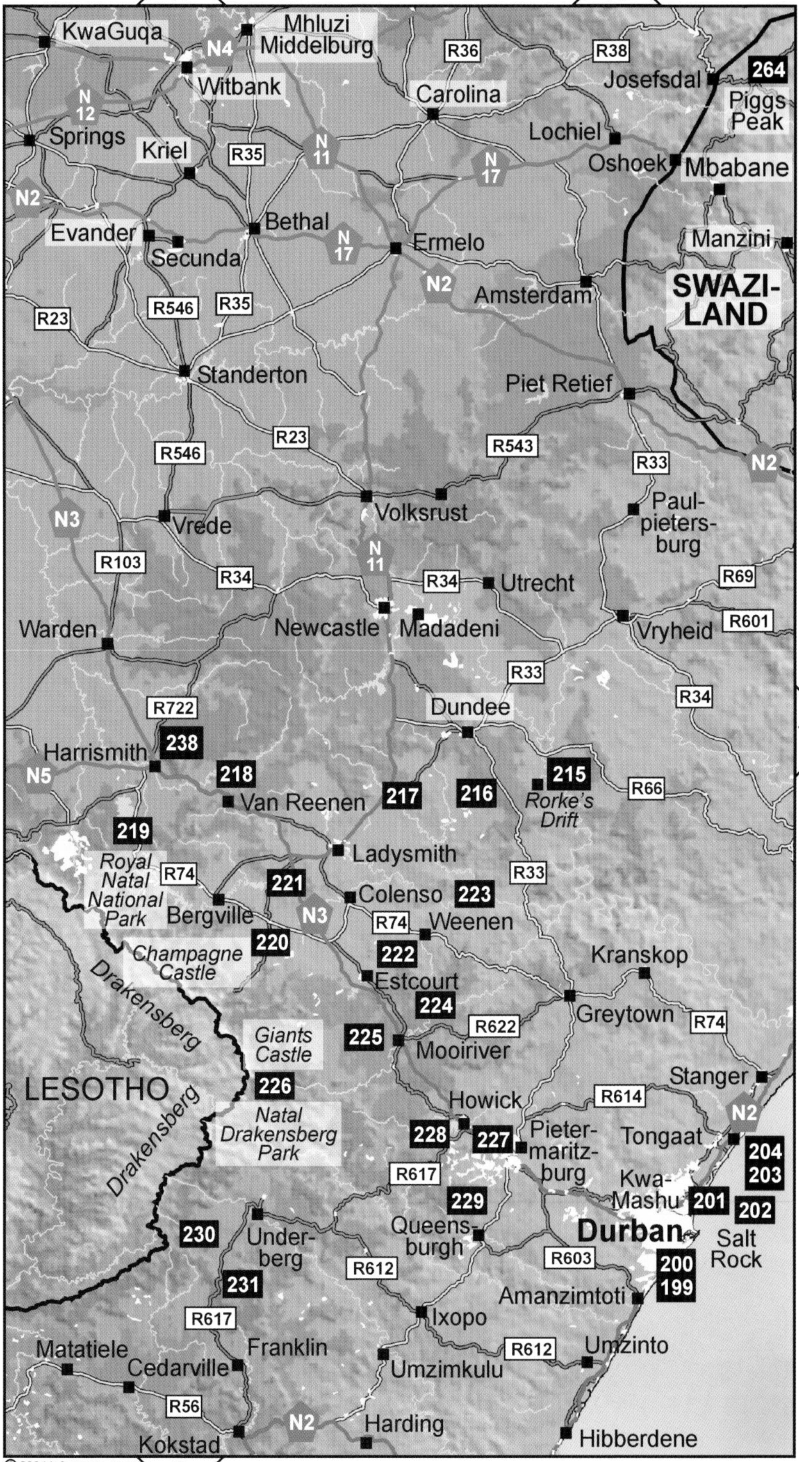

© 2004 informage.co.za

Map 14

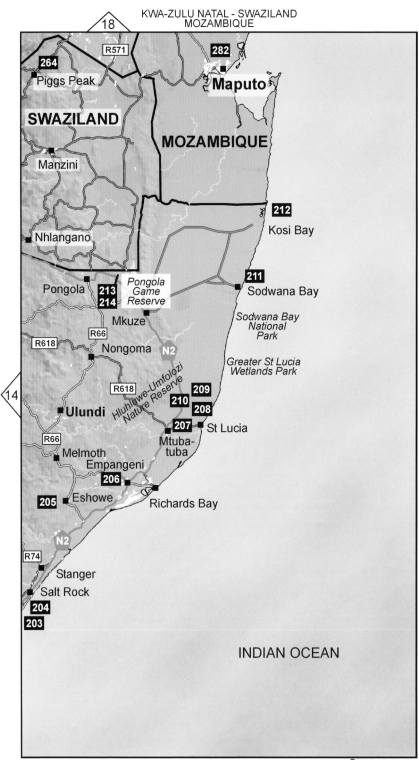

Map 15

© 2004 informage.co.za

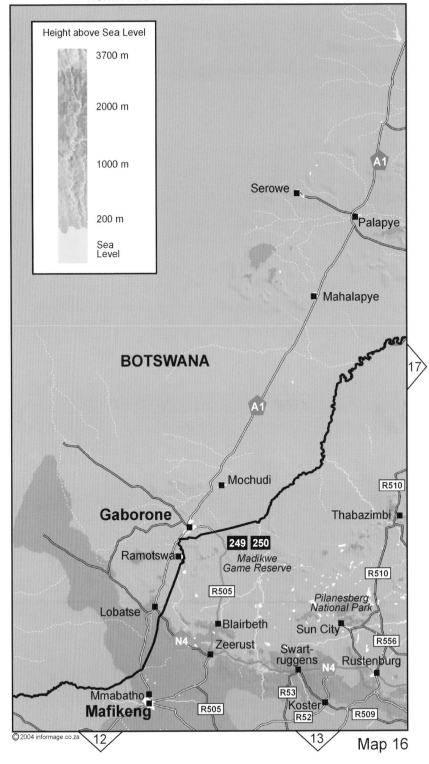

Map 16

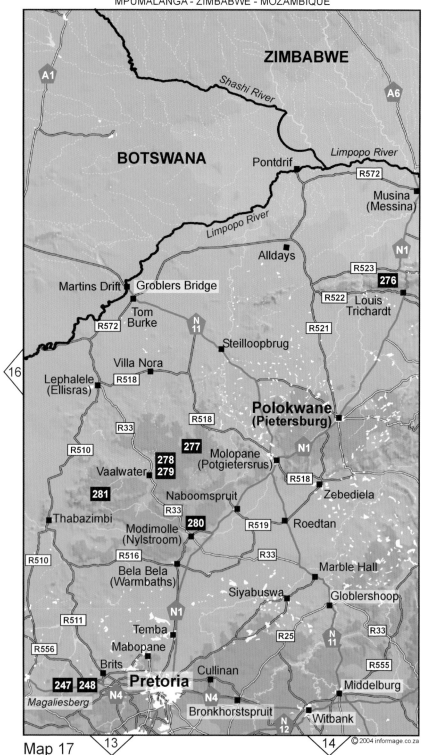

LIMPOPO PROVINCE - GAUTENG - NORTH WEST
MPUMALANGA - ZIMBABWE - MOZAMBIQUE

Map 17

© 2004 informage.co.za

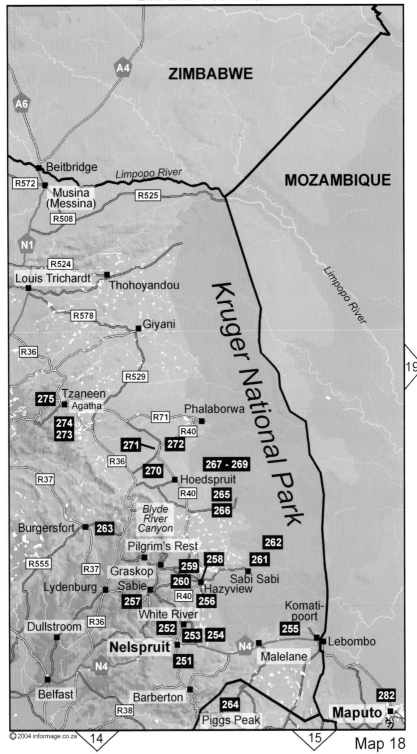

Map 18

MOZAMBIQUE

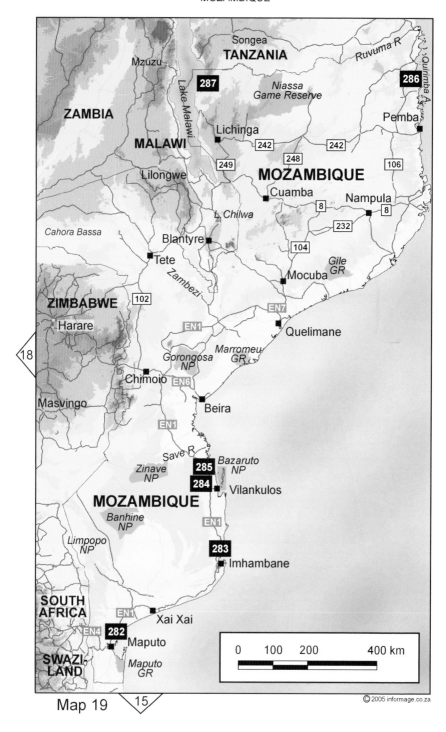

Map 19

© 2005 informage.co.za

Western Cape

Avian Leisure

Marie-Louise and Patrick Cardwell
88 Dories Drive, Simon's Town 7995
Tel: 021-786-1414 Fax: 021-786-1414
Email: avianleisure@netpoint.co.za Web: www.simonstown.com/accom/avian
Cell: 083-272-2455

The Cardwells have two smashing self-catering apartments under their Simon's Town home, but what we really liked on our pincer-movement, 2-man visit, was that they offer so very much more than that. Patrick is a naturalist and there is nothing he doesn't know about his surroundings – and that's the whole of South Africa, not just Simon's Town. Whether it's a bird-watching tour from the Zimbabwe border to the Garden Route coastline, or a detailed search for Northern Cape lizards, he's your man. But no need to go cantering off just yet, when there's so much right on your door step. High above Simon's Town proper both flats have a wonderful position, gazing out across False Bay past penguins and whales (in season) to distant Overberg mountains. Your own mountain starts just across the road. It's a two-hour walk to the top of the 678m (roughly) Swartkop peak. We didn't have time to test the theory, but Marie-Louise assures us the view from up there is even better. I don't doubt it. Both apartments are tiled throughout with massive airy bedrooms. Downstairs the glass wall slides back to give you a private wooden verandah overlooking the fynbos garden below. Upstairs, one wall of the vast lounge is taken up by a mini-library, the shelves bulging with National Geographics – one guest had his nose buried in a bird book, ticking off his sightings before the next expedition.

Rooms: 2 apartments, one with 1 twin/king and 1 twin sharing separate bath and shower, the other with twin/king and a shower.
Price: R190 – R250 pp sharing. Singles supplement on request.
Meals: Continental breakfast basket by arrangement R35 pp.
Directions: M3 from CT to Muizenberg, then Main Road through Fish Hoek to Simon's Town. Continue for 2km past golf course on L. Immediately after Oatlands Holiday Accomm turn R into Dorries Drive. House is 1km uphill on the R.

Boulders Beach Lodge

Frans Hollenbach
4 Boulders Place, Boulders
Beach, Simon's Town 7995
Tel: 021-786-1758
Fax: 021-786-1825
Email: boulders@iafrica.com
Web:
www.bouldersbeach.co.za

I screeched to a halt at the sight of three penguins sitting unperturbed on a garden wall. I excitedly snapped shots, delighted at their tame nature and vanity poses, until some passing tourists suggested that I save my film and look around the corner. Here on the beach front, with Boulders Beach Lodge on one side and the ocean on the other, was an entire colony of plumed p-p-p-penguins, some in their natural habitat on the boulders and sandy beach, and others, wherefore I know not, waddling along the streets. In the limited time I was here I ate wonderfully fresh king prawns at the in-house restaurant, sipped complimentary cream liqueur in my enormous bath and experienced the forget-everything feeling of the flotation tank (the on-site wellness centre also has a massage room). Bedrooms all have wrought-iron beds and are decorated with wooden carved sculptures of microscopic sea life. But time spent in your room will be limited by the multitude of activities on your doorstep: safe bathing from the penguin beach, kayaking in False Bay, beach walks with views of the distant Hottentots Holland mountain range, mountain hikes above Simon's Town, mountain biking, practising your golf swing at the next-door golf course, sailing at the yacht club, fishing, scuba diving and whale-watching. Phew. I suggest you stay at least three nights to take full advantage of this superb location.

Rooms: 14: 9 doubles, 2 twins, 1 triple, all with en-suite bath and shower or bath with shower overhead. 2 self-catering suites for 6, 1 double, 2 single beds and double sofa-bed.
Price: R395 pp sharing. Singles R450. Self-catering R1,000 (includes breakfast).
Meals: A choice of breakfasts is included. In-house restaurant for lunch and dinner.
Directions: Emailed or faxed.

No.6 Harbour Heights

Hamish and Alison Currie
Runciman Drive, Simon's Town
Tel: 021-794-1536 or 021-715-2498
Email: backtoafrica@iafrica.com
Cell: 082-469-2740

Hamish and Alison Currie also have this self-contained apartment in Simon's Town, whose main and not insignificant attraction is a large verandah, wide enough and protected enough to braai supper on. And what a place to while away the evening, high above the town, looking down over the boats moored in the harbour, the submarine and aquadynamic corvettes of the South African navy like action toys down there in the harbour. And then the arcing expanse of False Bay and the distant Hottentot Hollands. It is a view that will not easily be ignored. The flat itself is based on an open-plan kitchen and sitting area extending out onto the balcony, very bright and modern with the kitchen well equipped and the TV all cabled-up. The tables are wooden, the floors matting-carpeted, with tall thin animal sculptures adding a spot of vertical African appeal here and there. The two bedrooms and their bathrooms are found at the back of the flat but they too have lovely views. Hamish is a water-sports expert so if you want some advice or help organising sailing charters, fishing or diving trips then just ask. Fresh flowers and a few breakfast things to get you started are provided for your arrival. Simon's Town is a great choice, by the way. We lived round the bay a little in Kalk Bay and really enjoyed the whole area. There is also another flat higher up the hill which was too brand-new and unfurnished to comment on when I visited... but the views are great of course.

Rooms: 2 apartments: both 1 x double and 1 x twin, with bath and shower rooms.
Price: R700 – R900. R100 per day for the flat to be serviced (this is up to you).
Meals: Self-catering. Basic breakfast materials and fresh flowers for your arrival.
Directions: From Muizenberg follow main coast road to Simon's Town. Follow thro' town and turn R into Runciman Drive.

Water's Edge

Anne Browne and Patricia Martin

7 Kleintuin Rd, Simon's Town 7975
Tel: Contact David Sloan on 021-701-9343
Lodge phone number: 021-786-1958
Email: sloandaj@kingsley.co.za

If you've never lain awake and listened to the noise of whales breathing not ten metres from your very bed, then you should come to Water's Edge during the season (August to November). The Browne family retreat (and GG hot spot) is a dreamy far-away place, so relaxed and in such a beautiful location that you may have to pinch yourself as a reality check. It's not really that glam inside, think clean and comfy. There is a big proper kitchen and cavernous dormitory bedroom that can lose six kids easily. Downstairs the seaside rooms are the best. But best place of all has to be the open-fronted stoep. A table on one side and a sofa on the other channel the eyes out to sea. Locals make use of the beach during the school holidays, but always go home in the evening. Otherwise it's all yours. On both ends of the crescent of sand, huge smooth boulders are perfect for rock hopping, fishing, reading and watching for sea mammals. Adults and children alike will spend hours poking around in rock pools, barbecueing on the beach, building sand castles and watching the sun set. Kids can also go off finding fairies in the garden or making dens under up-turned dinghies.

Rooms: 5: 2 doubles and 2 twins with shared bathroom and shower room; 1 room with 5 singles and 1 double upstairs.
Price: Dec – April: R2,600 per day. May – November: R1,700 per day. Min stay 1 week. To secure booking 25% of total rent at time of booking.
Meals: Self-catering. Restaurants nearby. Catering can be organised.
Directions: Take M3 south towards Muizenberg and once in Simon's Town pass the naval base. Seaforth Rd is signed to your left. Down hill and pass the car park, turn right into Kleintuin Rd and follow brick wall to end. No. 7 beachside.

Blue Yonder

Sally and Bruce Elliott
14 Hillside Rd, Fish Hoek 7975
Tel: 021-782-0500 Fax: 021-782-0500
Email: info@blueyondercape.co.za Web: www.blueyondercape.co.za
Cell: 082-441-9589

For those of you on the self-catering trail this is a must. A three-storey house converted into flats, Blue Yonder is a luxury ocean liner of a place. When Sally opened the door to an invading GG team the sun was blasting through the wall-to-wall windows. She was keen to show me around but I spent the first ten minutes standing out on the enormous silver-railed balcony, transfixed by the view. From all three apartments here you can watch the full arc of the sun, rising over a glittering False Bay, and finally sinking behind the red-tiled roofs of the Fish Hoek bungalows below. Excellent for whale-watching. Once the trance wears off (which it won't) head inside and polish off your complimentary basket of fruit, cheese, meats and wine or make the most of the stainless steel and cream kitchens complete with all mod cons (including my personal favourite: the dishwasher). Sally grew up in this house but after a huge conversion job the Rhodesian teak floors are the only reminder of her family home. Now, gloriously indulgent queen-sized beds look out on the bay, cool, beige armchairs are just waiting to be lounged in and once you summon the energy for a dip in the ocean, your own private steps lead down to the beach, just a stone's throw away. My advice? Bring the whole family, light up a braai on the balcony and settle in for at least a month. Daily maid service available.

Rooms: 3 self-catering apartments: "Upper": 1 queen with en-suite shower & 1 twin with en-suite bath & shower; "Middle": 1 queen en-s b & sh, 2 twins en-s b & sh; "Lower": 1 queen en-s sh only.
Price: R200 – R350 pp sharing.
Meals: Self-catering, but breakfast on request R40 pp.
Directions: Head to Muizenberg from Cape Town, continue south along main road through Fish Hoek. At roundabout at the end of Fish Hoek main rd turn L towards Simon's Town. 1 km further take 1st R at traffic lights up Hillside Rd. Blue Yonder about 300m up on the R.

Dunvegan Lodge

Sylvia and Peter McLeod

106 Clovelly Rd, Clovelly, Fish Hoek 7975
Tel: 021-782-2958 Fax: 021-782-2958
Email: dunvegan@iafrica.com Web: www.dunvegan.co.za
Cell: 082-938-0380

For golf enthusiasts, Dunvegan Lodge, the McLeod highland retreat on the slopes of Clovelly Mountain, could hardly be better placed. It overlooks the Clovelly Country Club and I could see the twinge of longing in Sylvia's eye as we stood on one of the many wooden decks that enjoy bird's eye views over the 18-hole course to the white beaches that frame the peninsula. A keen fisherman, Peter was busy rounding up novices and enthusiasts alike for a crayfishing expedition in False Bay as they emerged for breakfast on the deep verandah at the top of this labrynthine house. No doubt a successful day on the ocean waves will end with a crayfish braai and heroic stories being traded in the small, tiled bar before descending the stairs to bed (it's an upside-down house). All of the rooms are different, some within the main home, each with a private patio or verandah, others hidden within the stepped, landscaped garden that borders the nature reserve. Rock steps wind their way to the different levels of the lush, overflowing garden and the pool has uninterrupted views of the Fish Hoek Valley. Venture a little further and you'll find a jacuzzi where you can watch the sun set over the Atlantic Ocean or simply rest those aching golf shoulders.

Rooms: 6: 3 suites with doubles or twins, lounge and kitchenette; 1 x 2-bedroom suite (1 double and 1 single) with lounge and kitchenette; 1 twin with kitchenette; 1 double. All bedrooms have en-suite bath and/or shower.
Price: R220 – R360 pp sharing. Singles on request. The whole lodge can be rented at R4,500 a day.
Meals: Full breakfast included. Excellent restaurants nearby. Self-catering option available.
Directions: Follow M4 through Muizenburg, St James and Kalk Bay. Turn right at traffic lights after the Kalk Bay harbour traffic lights into Clovelly Road.

The Beach House

Ingrid and Paul Righini
7 The Point, Kommetjie
Tel: 021-794-2052 Fax: 021-794-1981
Email: ruo@netactive.co.za Web: www.littleruo.co.za
Cell: 083-461-8419

If you ever flick through those glossy home and garden-type magazines looking for inspiration for your own humble abode, you've probably already seen the Beach House. When I popped round with Paul, a phalanx of photographers were fiddling with props and measuring angles for the perfect shot. Not that much needs adjusting to improve the look of this photogenic gem. A red-brick path leads through a picket gate, past lavender and across a carpet of lawn towards the white-washed thatched cottage. Once inside, I made a beeline for the floor-to-ceiling folding doors and greedily sucked in the view. Which is spectacular from just about every corner of the house: from the tiled open-plan lounge, dining room and all mod-cons kitchen; from the wrap-around timber deck with the long pool; from the galleried first floor; even from the shower. Sadly the whales had made their way further along the coast by the time I visited. The fabulous white sands of Noordhoek beach stretch towards Chapman's Peak with Hout Bay beyond and Lion's Head in the far distance… oh, and the rolling South Atlantic is just 20 metres away. It's little wonder the Beach House has fast become the darling of the glossies! White walls, deep white sofas, white-stained textured wooden coffee-table and wicker dining chairs (around a white table), fresh, stylish, modern: just the kind of thing to make you green with envy.

Rooms: 1 self-catering cottage with 4 doubles and 4 bathrooms; 2 rooms have shower only, 1 has bath only and 1 has full bathroom.
Price: R3,000 per day October to April and R2,000 end April to beginning of October.
Meals: Self-catering.
Directions: Can be emailed or faxed on booking.

The Hout Bay Hideaway

Niels van Reenen
37 Skaife St, Hout Bay 7806
Tel: 021-790-8040 Fax: 021-790-8114
Email: info@houtbay-hideaway.com Web: www.houtbay-hideaway.com
Cell: 082-332-7853

Greenwood Guides appraisal forms, while brilliantly designed, do not easily cater for the varied delights of houses such as The Hout Bay Hideaway. By the time I left Niels's magical kingdom I was all but writing on my trousers in an effort to record everything I had seen and heard. Art Deco furniture – lights, *chaise longue*, Bakelite ashtrays, armchairs et al – is the defining motif, but competes for attention with the stunning garden, bay views, fireplaces, paintings and Niels, one of Holland's finest. There are three suites and two apartments all abounding in character. Honeymooners will love the double-headed shower of the Garden Apartment, while older-school romantics can fight over the views of the mountains from the aptly-named Skylight Suite. My favourite was the Deco Apartment, with furniture from the Amsterdam school, Zambian sculptures, jacuzzi and a discreet outdoor shower where you can munch grapes hanging off the trellis. The house melts into its surroundings because its colour, which attracts strangers in off the street, derives from the garden's eucalyptus tree. Niels does not do things by halves! Want to cool off outside? Choose between pool and fully-plumbed Victorian bath. Need a drink? Enjoy the open bar in its 230-year old cupboard. Fancy a drive? Then hire one of the vintage Jaguars. I could go on for hours. *House can be hired in its entirety, children 12+ welcome. Individual safes and free ADSL internet connection in every room.*

Rooms: 5: 2 x 2-room apartments (sleeping up to 3); 3 suites sleeping 2. Or this can be converted to a "penthouse" sleeping 6. Or take the entire villa: sleeps 10 – 12.
Price: Suites and apartments: R295 – R695 pp sharing. Singles and kids on request. If you take the entire villa (sleeps 10-12) it costs from R3,450 per day.
Meals: Breakfast included and served in rooms for individual bookings. Other meals by arrangement, but excellent restaurants in Hout Bay.
Directions: Emailed or faxed on booking. Car rental company can pick up from and deliver to the airport or Niels will fetch you in one of the vintage Jags.

Map Number: 1   Entry Number: 8

The King's Place

Kim and Ian King

Valley Rd, Hout Bay 7806
Tel: 021-790-4000 Fax: 021-790-4000
Email: kim@plant-people.co.za Web: www.thekingsplace.com
Cell: 082-773-8831

Even as I trundled down the drive I could see that Kim and Ian, with a helping hand from Mother Nature, have crafted a truly special place. It's dripping with greenery and whether you're knocking up on the floodlit tennis court, somersaulting skywards on the trampoline, or simply playing dead by the pool, the views over Hout Bay and the Constantiaberg remain imperturbably lovely. An ever-smiling Kim greeted me in wellies and a bodywarmer, fresh from tending to the animals (I counted dogs, horses, chickens and Chinese geese, but I'm sure plenty more are lurking within the eight acres). Strolling through the landscaped garden (Ian is a horticulturalist) we came to the expansive, single-storey 'Valley House': light, airy and well able to sleep Von Trapp-sized families if required. It's in the open-plan kitchen, dining and living area that the heart of the King's Place beats. The maple and granite kitchen has chopping space for a whole troupe of cooks, and they'll all fit around the huge dining table too, strategically placed in front of the full-length, full-view windows. If you've exhausted all the activities on offer or have simply exhausted yourself, the lounge provides a sanctuary of cushioned, wicker armchairs that face a warming hearth in winter, or look out through glass doors to the pool terrace in summer. They can sleep 2 – 20 people.

Rooms: 2 self-contained units: 1st: 4 x double & 1 x 4-bed (2 with en-s bath/sh, 2 separate bath & sh rooms); 2nd: 1 double with en-s b/sh & 1 twin with sep' bath/sh. Units can be connected.
Price: R150 – R350 pp per day.
Meals: Self-catering, Continental breakfast available at R20 – R40 pp.
Directions: Main Road into Hout Bay from Constantia. Right into Disa River Road. Left into Valley Road. Go past World of Birds on the right and The King's Place is 150m on the left.

Paddington's at Jongamanzi

Di and Don Lilford

3 Lindevista Lane, Hout Bay 7800
Tel: 021-790-8703
Fax: 021-790-8703
Email: dlilford@new.co.za
Web: www.paddington.co.za
Cell: 083-259-6025

Standing in Di's garden, I sighed with relaxed satisfaction, gazing across a valley and beach bathed in late-afternoon sunshine. Well away from the hustle and bustle of Cape Town proper, Hout Bay runs at a pace of its own, and Paddington's and the Lilfords are right in step. After years on their valley-floor farm, they have moved up onto the hillside accompanied by a gaggle of visiting guinea fowl (impatiently tapping on the French doors for their tea when I arrived), Rollo the dog and their steady stream of guests. There's a relaxed feel of country living here and while the building itself may be new and square, it's full of old prints, family furniture and well-trodden rugs. Visitors have the run of the tiled ground floor, with both bedrooms just two yawns and a stagger from breakfast, tacked onto the drawing room and kitchen. One room gets the morning sun, the other the afternoon rays and both are blessed with gigantic beds. If you feel up to it, Don and Di will point you in the direction of the best golf courses and the beach, while for the lethargic loungers among you there's pétanque on the gravel patch or a book on the verandah. And a swimming pool is on its way. Oh choices, choices….

Rooms: 2 king/twins, 1 with bath, 1 with shower.
Price: R250 pp. Singles R350.
Meals: Full breakfast included.
Directions: Faxed or emailed on request.

Map Number: 1

Entry Number: 10

Thandekayo Guest House

Kiki and Erwin van der Weerd
14 Luisa Way, Hout Bay 7806
Tel: 021-791-0020 Fax: 021-791-0022
Email: info@thandekayo.co.za Web: www.thandekayo.co.za
Cell: 072-447-8293

Erwin's thirst for light, open space and modernity saw him knocking through walls and creating the sunshine-permeable, multi-squared windows and glass doors that now lead out onto the Thandekayo balcony. The sea view from here stretches from Chapman's Peak to the Twelve Apostles. I could see the valley channelling the Disa River into Hout Bay, the studs on the stud farm and, more immediately, the all-important braai area in the trim garden below. Open-plan is also the theme for the bedrooms, where doors do not divide sleeping and washing zones. In the first room, with Mediterranean orange walls, a large oval bath made of crushed and re-set marble faces the bed, slightly Flake-advert-esque, but with a modern touch. Each bathroom has an innovative layout, but all require you to be totally at ease with your room partner. The baths are family-sized, the rooms are individually designed (Erwin, I forgot to mention, is an architect) and the house displays a modest collection of contemporary art, including some of Erwin's mother's paintings. Stencils of elephants accompany you up the stairs and crayons are used for guest book entries. Thandekayo means 'warm welcome in our home', and Erwin and Kiki share with their guests all the enthusiasm they have for South Africa, happy to help with day plans and bookings.

Rooms: 5: 2 queens, 1 king, 2 twins. 1 twin has en-suite shower, others have en-suite bath and shower.
Price: R275 – R475 pp sharing. Singles +50%.
Meals: Full breakfast included.
Directions: Emailed or faxed.

Makuti Lodge

Doreen and Peter Wright
Farriers Way, Tarragona Estate, Hout Bay 7806
Tel: 021-790-1414 Fax: 021-790-1414
Email: doreen@makutilodge.co.za Web: www.makutilodge.co.za
Cell: 083-457-5231

Forget Kirstenbosch, head for Makuti Lodge! (Well, almost....) Gardeners will find plenty of common ground with Peter and Doreen. Even if you do exhaust the riches of their stunning garden (you'll have to stay quite a while to achieve this), then you can just walk out of the driveway and find yourself at the foot of Myburg Peak. It's not that the grounds of Makuti Lodge are especially large; but they are just so full. From the patios, the lawns, the flower beds and the 'forest' area, to the hidden bark paths that twist between the cottages, you could spend hours wandering around contemplating life (or joining in a game of pétanque, if you've the stomach for it). Play your cards right and you may be invited to a wine-tasting session in the stone depths of the cellar among the animal carvings and hanging swords. Here you can sample vinous treats from all over the southern hemisphere under the guidance of Peter and Doreen, who modestly admit to amateur enthusiast status only. The cottages themselves are quaint (Peter is responsible for construction, Doreen for the finishing touches) with local art on the walls and wood-burning fires whose black iron flumes rise up through the bedrooms upstairs, providing heating for them too. And I haven't even mentioned the dogs, the pool, the hot tub or the breakfasts.

Rooms: 5 cottages: 2 x 1-bed cottages; 2 x 2-bed with 2 bathrooms; 1 x 3-bed with 2 bathrooms.
Price: R250 – R350.
Meals: Self-catering. Full or Continental breakfast an extra R40 – R50 pp.
Directions: M63 to Hout Bay. Turn R at Disa River Rd, L at end. First R into Garron Ave. Then R into Connemara Drive. The L into Hunter's Way. R into Farrier's Way. Makuti on R.

Frogg's Leap

Jôke Glauser
15 Baviaanskloof Rd, Hout Bay 7806
Tel: 021-790-2590 Fax: 021-790-2590
Email: info@froggsleap.co.za Web: www.froggsleap.co.za
Cell: 082-493-4403

The huge Frogg's Leap verandah, with its impressive views of the Hout Bay mountains and sea seems to be the focal point of life here. At breakfast the house springs to life with Jôke (pronounced *yokie*) and Stewart engaging in easy banter with all who emerge, and chiding guests for sitting at the long wooden table inside when the parasol-shaded tables outside are so enticing. Then in the evening, with the sea breeze swinging the hammocks and a sundowner in your hand, it is not hard to get to grips with being lazy and on holiday. I can't remember a place where guests made themselves so at home. Jôke and Stewart used to run charter boats in the West Indies and Frogg's Leap has a breezy Caribbean feel with many open French doors and windows. Bedrooms are cool ensembles of natural materials: painted floors, seagrass matting, palms, natural stone in bathrooms, lazy wicker chairs, reed ceilings, thick cotton percale linen and old wooden furniture. Hout Bay itself is a fishing harbour enclosed by mountains and is within minutes of beaches and hiking trails. Jôke and Stewart keep a 26-ft catamaran there and, when the spirit moves them and weather permits, will take guests cray-fishing, or whale-watching when whales are in town. This is a place that has been consistently recommended both before and since the first edition and it is a continued pleasure to recommend it myself. *Guest telephone 021-790-6260.*

Rooms: 6: 5 doubles/twins and 1 double, all with en-suite bathrooms; 3 with shower, 3 with bath and shower. Plus extra single room.
Price: R275 – R375 pp sharing. Singles on request.
Meals: Full breakfast included and served until 10am. There are 20 restaurants nearby for other meals.
Directions: A map will be faxed to you on confirmation of booking.

Amblewood Guest House

June and Trevor Kruger

43 Skaife St, Hout Bay 7806
Tel: 021-790-1570 Fax: 021-790-1571
Email: info@amblewood.co.za Web: www.amblewood.co.za
Cell: 082-881-5430

After negotiating the Amblewoood driveway, I was rewarded by Trevor who fixed me a G&T, and amidst heavy beams and family antiques we chatted away until the rains came (which I'm afraid they do on occasion, even in the Cape). Guests wearing borrowed woollies and waterproofs returned, and Trevor raced out with a brolly for June. This softly-spoken duo love doing what they do. They share an eye for detail and an enthusiasm that will have you feeling right at home. I browsed the library and admired the beach, bay and mountains from my balcony, which I shared with two turtle doves. Friday is braai day, but tonight we headed to a steakhouse, where everybody knew the Krugers. At breakfast, a humble, hair-netted Trevor claimed that guests' plates were left spotless because the dog had been at them. I'm not so sure – I for one licked mine clean and blamed Doc. I enjoyed myself so much that I think they wondered whether I was doing a job at all. But I wasn't alone – as I left, wise-looking guests were extending their stay. For those on a return visit there are two new rooms to try, including a self-contained suite with a bedroom looking out onto the surrounding hills.

Rooms: 6: 2 doubles, 1 with en-suite shower, 1 with en-suite shower and bath; 2 twins with en/s shower and bath.
Price: R240 – R450 pp sharing. Singles rate R360 – R525.
Meals: Full cooked breakfast included.
Directions: Faxed or emailed on booking.

Buchan Estate

Fiona and Pieter van Aswegen
Welbevind Way, Hout Bay 7806
Tel: 021-791-2100 Fax: 021-791-2101
Email: info@buchanestate.com Web: www.buchanestate.com
Cell: 082-560-8165

Rolling down the drive under towering cedars, past the whitewashed stables and a football-friendly paddock I had a finger-tingling feeling that this was just the place for us. Fiona and Pieter were wrestling with renovations when my GG predecessors first visited. Twelve months down the track, construction is complete (bar the kids' jungle gym – a source of endless headaches) and their riverside farm is bubbling with life. "A Gentleman's Equestrian Estate" was how it was advertised when they moved in, but these days it's a family home complete with daughter (a chattering baby Mara), dogs (the soppiest doberman I've ever met) and tortoise (as yet unnamed). Fiona is a Scot and these two 30-somethings gave up the corporate life and the vile weather of Edinburgh to head south – about 6,500 miles south – in a Land Rover. Their three cottages have a classic African feel, "but not over the top," shivers Pieter. Roofs are thatched, beams dark and ceilings surprisingly high. Romantics will love the four-poster bed and enormous oval bath. Self-catering is the general idea, but Fiona is happy to supply a hamper stuffed with breakfast goodies to your cottage door in the morning. And if you really are loth to fend for yourself, she can rustle up a Cape-Malay curry or some local fish to whack in the oven for supper. What more can you ask?

Rooms: 3 cottages: 1 king with bath and shower; 1 queen with bath and shower; 1 two-bedroom cottage with king and king/twin beds and a shared shower.
Price: R295 – R495 pp sharing.
Meals: Breakfast on request for R35. Dinner can also be provided.
Directions: From Cape Town turn R off M3 onto Rhodes Drive, signed to Hout Bay. Follow signs for World of Birds into Valley Rd. Opposite the bird sanctuary turn R into Welbevind Way. Buchan Estate is the last property on the left.

Intaba Lodge

Valérie and Pierre-Marie Barnabé
25 Park Ave, Hout Bay 7806
Tel: 021-790-6364 Fax: 021-790-6365
Email: barnabe@telkomsa.net Web: www.intaba-lodge.com
Cell: 082-775-0718

Ah, la vie est belle! Exactly what Valérie and Pierre-Marie thought when they settled here two years ago. Exactly what I thought when I settled in for the afternoon – nowhere near long enough to unearth all the hidden treasures of colonial-style Intaba. As we meandered down the winding gravel and bark paths, past gum and lime trees, a lily pond alive with koi and boulders scattered willy-nilly around this birder's paradise, even Pierre-Marie was discovering new gems. Intaba is the Xhosa word for mountain, and whether you're relaxing in the old conservatory, now converted into a mammoth sun room, munching through breakfast as the sun rises over the never-ending verandah, or lounging lazily on the pool terrace in the heart of the indigenous garden, you can't fail to be mesmerised by the forested Constantianek rising up beyond the valley. Inside, cool, modern Mazista tiles sweep through the open-plan living area, dominated by the central chimney. Behind this, Valérie and Pierre-Marie are usually to be found beavering away in the all-mod-cons kitchen, preparing mouth-watering French dishes (but if *canard* isn't your *pain au chocolat*, Hout Bay and the surrounding areas are awash with eateries to suit all tastes). Intaba retains a distinct African ambience but, well-travelled couple that they are, the Barnabés have mixed in Japanese pictures, Indian wooden elephants and other *objects d'art* from around the world.

Rooms: 4: all doubles, twins on request; all with en-suite bath and/or shower, 1 with open-plan kitchen.
Price: R280 – R495 pp sharing. Singles on request.
Meals: Full breakfast included. Dinner on request, approx R100. Drinks extra.
Directions: Emailed or faxed on request.

Hattons Hout Bay

Liz Davis
2 Harold Close, Oakhurst Estate, Hout Bay 7806
Tel: 021-790-0848 Fax: 021-790-3050
Email: liz@hattons.co.za Web: www.hattons.co.za
Cell: 082-760-2624

Nature has run its course at Hattons since the last edition: the vine arbour has gone, leaving Liz an uninterrupted mountain view, and her son Connor is a wee bairn no more. The approach, however, remains perfectly unassuming. Only once you're inside do the building's true dimensions reveal themselves, a great surprise with breezy open spaces and a cavernous sitting room with pole beams and steepling thatched roof. Doors open on both sides, one leading to the pool, the other out to the view over the back of Table Mountain and their own garden. This is immaculately laid out with paths that wind past tropical blooms, riotous colours against white-washed walls… and where the rooms, named after plants – ivy, lavender, mimosa, kumassi – are kept. Not so much rooms as little cottages, with their own doors to the garden and fully-equipped kitchenettes. The most popular has an unusual gallery bedroom, which looks down on its own sitting room from a great height. Liz is dedicated to her guests, and she'll welcome you in with wine, OJ or coffee. Nearby, enjoy a cuppa at the local farm stall or a sunset concert at Kirstenbosch, and listen carefully when she is spilling the beans about the best spots on the coast.

Rooms: 4: 3 apartments (self-catering or B&B) with en-suite shower & bath and 1 B&B double with en-suite shower.
Price: R250 – R350 pp sharing. Singles R350 – R450. Less R40 if you don't have breakfast.
Meals: Self-catering possible. Breakfast served on the terrace or a breakfast basket can be delivered to your door.
Directions: Emailed or faxed on booking.

Cramond House

Gail Voigt

Cramond Rd, Camps Bay 8005
Tel: 083-457-1947 Fax: 083-118-457-1947
Email: gailvoigt@mweb.co.za
Cell: 083-457-1947

Easily stylish enough to keep the smart crowd calm, Cramond House is yet as walk-in-and-make-yourself-at-home as you'll find anywhere. Set high up, dandled on the knees of the Twelve Apostles, wall-to-wall windows along the ocean-facing front look down over Camps Bay's palm-fringed crescent of white sand. The glorious view is unavoidable, from the bedrooms, from the pool, from the wide sundeck. Will you get out of the house at all, I wonder! This is a dreamy place, the epitome of understated easy living, big on simplicity, space and light and small on clutter. My suite was huge and super-swish, with a cavernous walk-in wardrobe, deep spa and a sundeck… but all the rooms are special. There is a sandpit, a pool, a stunning garden, a family of tortoises…. Delicious things to eat and drink spill from the fridge, the bar and cupboards. Gail will come to settle you in, introduce you to the permanent house staff (Gerald, Jan and Beauty). Here's part of an email from her that sets the scene rather well: *My husband is a very keen hiker and would gladly take visitors on hikes… we are so close to so much in CT. Walt, my son takes folk on wine routes etc... and I am always available with my microbus for shopping expeditions, sightseeing etc. We love people and I am from the Eastern Cape originally where one's life is.... people!* Luxury at Cramond House is only half the story.

Rooms: 4: 1 queen with en-suite spa bath & sh'r; 1 twin en-s bath & sh'r; 1 double en-s sh'r & adjacent area with sleeper couch; 1 queen en-s bath & sh'r plus kitchenette. Cot, high chair etc available.
Price: For the whole house: May – July per night R2,200. Dec – Jan R4,400. All other times R3,300. Discounts for stays longer than 10 days. For all requests relating to number of guests, ask Gail.
Meals: By arrangement.
Directions: Directions will be forwarded on reservation or complimentary airport transfers can be arranged with hired vehicles delivered to Cramond House.

Ocean View House

Katrin Plotz
33 Victoria Rd, Bakoven 8005
Tel: 021-438-1982 Fax: 021-438-2287
Email: oceanv@mweb.co.za Web: www.oceanview-house.com

There's no end to Ocean View's eccentric delights with its Russian marble and award-winning gardens. Everyone has either a balcony or a terrace with fabulous views of both the sea and the garden. It is a hotel I suppose, but such a personal one. The unobtrusive style endures, so too the humour noted in our last edition. The zebra room is kitsch-but-fun, though sadly the two-ton wooden elephant that wallowed in the water fantasia garden, amongst 200-year-old milkwood trees, got worms and was removed. Of course there's a great pool and how many hotels run an honesty bar? To cap it all, Ocean View has its own nature reserve, a tropical garden that ushers an idyllic river from the mountains to the sea. They have placed tables and sun-loungers on the grassy river banks, a sort of exotic *Wind in the Willows* scenario with rocks, ferns, trees, tropical birds and butterflies. If you ever feel like leaving Ocean View, Camps Bay beach is a stroll away with its string of outdoor restaurants and zesty atmosphere. It's a good place to watch trendy Capetonians-at-play. Tired out long before they were, I walked back to the hotel. The nightwatchman was expecting me and escorted me to my room, which was also expecting me, tomorrow's weather report by my bed.

Rooms: 14: 1 Presidential Suite, 1 Milkwood Suite, 4 Royal Suites, 7 Luxury Rooms (all sea-facing). 13 have showers, 1 with bath & sh. 1 self-catering villa for families.
Price: R400 – R800 pp sharing. Singles rate available off-season. 3-bed villa R4,000 – R6,000 per day. Prices may change from Oct '05.
Meals: Full breakfast is included and served until 10.00 am.
Directions: On the coast road a mile out of Camps Bay towards Hout Bay.

Stonehurst Guest House

Jan Ludik

3 Frere Road, Sea Point 8005
Tel: 021-434-9670
Fax: 021-439-8131
Email:
stonehurst@absamail.co.za
Web: www.stonehurst.co.za

From the outside I had no idea that Stonehurst would turn out to be a near-perfect example of Victorian-era living. Built in 1893, it is one of the oldest guest-houses in Cape Town and very little has changed since it first opened. I was faintly disappointed to find they had electricity! Jan is clearly a fan of all things antique, from the Morris Minor parked outside with a GB sticker prominently displayed, to the original marble fireplaces and busts of important-looking men. The heavy oak furniture and Oregon-pine flooring dominate many of the bedrooms, with free-standing, claw-footed baths. The most unusual room was the suite at the front of the house. Negotiating my way down some tricky wooden stairs from a private sitting room (Victorian style, of course) I emerged into an underground, cell-like bedroom with unplastered, whitewashed walls and a tiled floor, ideal during a hot, sticky summer (but perhaps not suited to colder weather). Stonehurst boasts a beautiful central courtyard with potted plants, a tiled floor and a bougainvillea tree twisting its way up past the spiral metal staircase that leads to the self-contained flat – the only modernised part of the house. This is something a bit different and will intrigue anyone with a hankering for historic integrity.

Rooms: 15: 12 doubles, 10 with en-suite shower, 2 with en-suite bath; 3 singles not en-suite. Self-contained 2 bedroom flat also available.
Price: R250 – R350 pp sharing. Single rates R250.
Meals: Continental breakfast included. Self-catering in shared kitchen. Restaurants nearby.
Directions: Provided on booking.

Huijs Haerlem

Johan du Preez and Kees Burgers
25 Main Drive, Sea Point 8005
Tel: 021-434-6434 Fax: 021-439-2506
Email: haerlem@iafrica.com Web: www.huijshaerlem.co.za

Don't even try and pronounce it! Imagine, it used to be called 't Huijs Haerlem, so small thanks for small mercies! But what a great place: a secret garden, perched high on the hill above Sea Point, enclosed behind walls and gates, abloom with tropical flowers in beds and earthenware pots, with suntrap lawns, a pool (salt-water, solar-heated) and views over Table Bay. The verandah frame is snaked about with vine and small trees provide the shade. Johan and Kees have a lovely, caring approach to their guests and look after you royally. There's no formal reception area, the bar is based on honesty, all their fine Dutch and South African antiques are not hidden away for fear of breakage. In fact both of them suffer from magpie-itis and walls and surfaces teem with eye-arresting objects: a tailor's mannequin, cabinet-making tools, old linen presses. Of course breakfast is enormous with fresh breads, rolls and croissants, fruits, cheeses, cold meats and the full cooked bonanza. This is Johan's domain, a chance for him to banter with guests and make a few suggestions. All the bedrooms are different, but all have their advantage, some with private terraces, some great views, one a four-poster. Whichever room you are in you will feel part of the whole.

Rooms: 8: 5 twins and 3 doubles; all en-suite, 2 with separate bath and shower, the rest with shower over bath.
Price: R390 – R600 pp sharing. Singles plus 25%.
Meals: Full breakfast included.
Directions: Faxed or emailed on booking.

Entry Number: 21   Map Number: 1

Cheviot Place Guest House

James and Brooke Irving

18 Cheviot Place, Green Point 8005
Tel: 021-439-3741 Fax: 021-439-9095
Email: cheviot@netactive.co.za Web: www.cheviotplace.co.za
Cell: 082-467-3660

Cheviot Place is something fresh for the Cape Town accommodation scene. This was apparent to me from the moment James opened the front door, dressed in Hawaiian shirt (sunny) and trainers (trendy), Jamie Cullum (jazzy) wafting out behind him. When he moved in a couple of years ago, this venerable, early 20th-century house, with its high ceilings, pillars and arches, was in desperate need of renovation. So new wooden floors, natural hemp-style rugs and black metal light fittings now set off the original marble fireplaces. Cheviot Place has been transformed into a contemporary home while retaining the best of its Victorian heritage. And, first and foremost, a home it is. There was nothing on display to suggest that James and Brooke actually run a guest house (apart from the guest bedrooms, of course) so any visitor here would feel like an old friend come to stay. James was even sure he recognised me from somewhere. The self-catering unit below the main house is surely the ultimate in 21st-century living, reminding me of the troglodyte homes carved out of the rocks deep in the Sahara. Apart from the bed there is no free-standing furniture: everything has been sculptured from the stone. Original? Yes. Cool? In both senses of the word.

Rooms: 4: 3 queens (1 with en-suite bath and shower, 1 with en-suite bath & shower-head & 1 with en-suite shower). 1 twin with en-suite shower. Self-catering suite also available with 1 queen.
Price: R250 – R400 pp sharing. R285 – R450 for singles.
Meals: Full breakfast is included. Picnics provided on request for R35 – R150. Braai on request for R55 – R100.
Directions: Ask when booking.

Cedric's Lodge

Jutta Frensch and Inge Niklaus

90 Waterkant Street and 39 Dixon Street, Green Point – "De Waterkant" 8001
Tel: 021-425-7635
Fax: 021-425-7635
Email: info@cedricslodge.com
Web: www.cedricslodge.com
Cell: 083-327-3203 or 083-326-4438

Once Cape Muslim slave-quarters, De Waterkant's brightly-coloured, cobbled hill-side streets are amongst the most cosmopolitan in Cape Town, full of fashion labels, interior design showrooms, art galleries and trendy bars. The city's heart beats fast here and Inge and her architect sister Jutta have their finger on the pulse. They metamorphosed a 17th-century slave-house into Cedric's, a washed-grey, contemporary town house. Downstairs is given over to an open-plan living space with steel-and-chrome kitchen, sleek dining table and grey suede sofas arranged around a concrete fireplace. There's glass, polished floorboards and colourful prints throughout and, upstairs, beds have dark headboards and chinoiserie fabrics. My room also had Indian chairs, slate bath and balcony, a blissful spot in the thrall of Table Mountain for this cold-blooded European to bake. Inge and Jutta will take you up there or up Signal Hill for champagne as the sun dissolves into the Atlantic. They'll just as likely drag you off to a concert or they might invite you to join them for lunch with friends in the Cape Flats. Inge edits the village rag and is an inspirational source of what's hot in the Mother City. Spend a lazy breakfast in one of the corner cafés and meander round this forward-looking historic area and you'll be hooked. As the Eagles (almost) said: "You can check out any time you like, but you can never (really) leave." *5 minutes' walk to Convention Center. Also now opened Cedric's Country Lodge in Greyton with 3 double rooms.*

Rooms: 4: all doubles with en-suite bath or shower.
Price: R800 – R1,100 per room. The whole house can be let from R3,200 – R4,400 per night.
Meals: Rate includes vouchers for breakfast at next-door cafés. Cape Town's most fashionable restaurant on the doorstep.
Directions: For directions see the Cedric's Lodge web site.

Hillcrest Manor

Gerda and Gerhard Swanepoel
18 Brownlow Rd,
Tamboerskloof 8001
Tel: 021-423-7459
Fax: 021-426-1260
Email: hilcres@mweb.co.za
Web:
www.hillcrestmanor.co.za
Cell: 082-700-5760

Step inside my fantasy world for a moment: the real politik of real estate doesn't exist and you can choose anywhere in Cape Town to build your new home. You'd probably end up precisely where I am now. Sadly, you're a hundred years too late and Gerda and Gerhard already live here. Happily, however, they've opened their home to guests and you'll be assured a warm welcome. Situated at the foot of Lion's Head in a leafy hillside suburb, their Victorian town house looms above the street and faces the most stunning view of Cape Town. From pool, balcony or bed you can see all the detail of the city and waterfront and Table Mountain's acclaimed acclivity clearly. This elegant house, its tall windows and wooden shutters set atop an elevated blue-stone foundation, is where Gerhard grew up. Nowadays the whitewashed steps lead up past a sunny lawn, patio and pool to a sitting room with original pressed-metal ceiling and a bright breakfast room, where the local artwork is for sale. Upstairs the bedrooms are designed to give respite from the long hot summer. Floors are a mix of polished timber and seagrass, beds are pine, furniture wicker. Ceiling-fans loll lazily and curtains billow in the breeze. One bedroom is pure C. S. Lewis, though here the wardrobe leads not to Narnia, but to your own claw-foot bath.

Rooms: 7: all doubles with en-suite shower, one with bath too.
Price: R260 – R400 pp sharing. Single supplement R100.
Meals: Full breakfast included. Meals for groups by prior arrangement. 3-course dinner R45, wine not included.
Directions: Faxed or emailed on booking.

Bayview B&B

Christine Matti

10 De Hoop Avenue, Tamboerskloof 8001
Tel: 021-424-2033 Fax: 021-424-2705
Email: baychris@iafrica.com Web: www.baychris.com
Cell: 082-414-2052

Christine's partner Corinne had her arm in a sling when we met. She'd torn a tendon pulling a cork out of a bottle – an unfortunate accident, but a large tick in the "commitment to the cause" category for GG candidates. These two are passionate about their wine and, well, passionate about just about everything. When not buzzing around the house, Swiss-born Christine is usually out cranking up Cape Town kilometres on her racing bike or working on her annoyingly low golf handicap. She arrived in South Africa a wide-eyed whippersnapper some twenty years ago, and has never quite got around to leaving. Her home is an airy haven of healthy living. White-washed walls, floor-to-ceiling tinted windows and tiled floors make this a perfect mountain-side retreat from the city centre's summer heat. Breakfasts are an Alpine feast of German breads, selected cheeses and cold meats and guests are encouraged to help themselves to a bottomless bowl of fresh fruit. Take a dip in the pool, head off for a massage at any number of nearby wellness centres, read a book on your decking balcony, and – once you've done all that – lie back on the sofa and gaze at a perfectly-framed Table Mountain through the sitting room skylight. My only disappointment? I didn't have time to stay the night.

Rooms: 4: 2 queens, 1 with en-suite shower and bath, 1 with en-suite shower; 1 double with en/s shower, 1 twin with en/s shower. Self-catering: 1 queen with en/s shower.
Price: R200 – R480 pp sharing.
Meals: Healthy breakfasts included. Cooked breakfast on request.
Directions: Follow signs from the city centre to the Cableway. From Kloofnek Rd turn R into St. Michael's Rd and then third L into Varsity St. At the T-juntion turn R into De Hoop Avenue and Bayview is the second on the right.

Lézard Bleu Guest House

Chris and Niki Neumann

30 Upper Orange St, Oranjezicht 8001
Tel: 021-461-4601 Fax: 021-461-4657
Email: welcome@lezardbleu.co.za Web: www.lezardbleu.co.za
Cell: 072-234-4448

It's going to be hard to book the tree house, particularly when word gets round, but you have got to try! Surely the most wonderful bedroom in Cape Town. The trunks of two giant palm trees spear through a wooden deck at vertiginous heights and a tiny balcony is in among the topmost fronds and spikes. Lézard Bleu was just about the best guest house in Cape Town anyway, so this latest extravagant addition represents one great big cherry on a mouthwatering cake. Niki is an actress and Chris is a chef, although he has hung up his hat now… no, don't even ask! They are still young and humorous and the house remains sleek and modern with solid maplewood bedframes, white pure cotton, sandy shades and tones, bright splashes of local and modern art on the walls. Breakfast is the best beanfeast in Cape Town (and that's the opinion of other guest house owners). The Blue Lizard snakes pleasingly from area to area, each room with its own doors out to a patio and to the large pool, where deck loungers take it easy on a surrounding timber deck. There are real fires in winter, an honesty bar, free ADSL internet access – mere details, but typical. Individual, creative, very comfortable, but most importantly this is somewhere really natural and friendly.

Rooms: 7: 1 family room; 5 doubles/twins; 4 with en/s bath and shower; 1 with en/s shr; 1 tree house double en/s b and shr.
Price: R400 – R630 pp sharing. Single rate +50%.
Meals: Full (enormous!) breakfast included and served till 10.30 am.
Directions: Ask for directions when booking.

Trevoyan Guest House

Philip Lamb and Max Bowyer
12 Gilmour Hill Rd, Tamboerskloof 8001
Tel: 021-424-4407 Fax: 021-423-0556
Email: trevoyan@iafrica.com Web: www.trevoyan.co.za

Max and Phil visited in 2001 and didn't even get past the brick terrace and the front step before they had decided to buy Trevoyan. Bit rash you might think? Not once you've seen it. There's something cool and sequestered about the place that cossets you from the noise and heat of the surrounding city. It faces Table Mountain and from seats set out on the long brick terrace you can see those forbidding cliffs through the branches of the massive oak that lords it over both house and garden. It's an under-canopy kingdom, complete with glamorous swimming pool, a perfect lawn bordered by leafy perimeter hedge and a recently added eight-seat jacuzzi, a spiral staircase and rooftop sun deck. The main building was built for entertaining military types visiting the Cape in the early 1900s. Rooms are indulgent now, furnished in soft pashmina tones – mint, cadmium yellow and sailor's blue – with many extras like big TVs, cream sofas, mini-bars and safes. The main bedroom is the most indulgent of all, with its enormous double shower, and state-o'-art entertainment system. Take breakfast on the back arched terrace in summer or the sunny dining room in winter. Max and Phil share a warm sense of humour and are natural hosts.

Rooms: 7: 2 kings and 2 queens all with en-suite bath and shower. 1 king with twin showers only. 2 twins with en/s bath and shower.
Price: R650 – R800 double occupancy. Singles R450 – R600. Garden Suites R750 – R1,000.
Meals: Full breakfast included. Restaurants 5 minutes' walk.
Directions: From city centre take Buitengracht Rd towards Table Mountain until it becomes Kloof Nek Rd. Take 2nd right into Gilmour Hill Rd. 100 metres, on right before stop sign.

An African Villa

Jimmy van Tonder and Louis Nel

19 Carstens St, Tamboerskloof 8001
Tel: 021-423-2162 Fax: 021-423-2274
Email: villa@capetowncity.co.za Web: www.capetowncity.co.za/villa
Cell: 082-920-5508

Louis ditched the interior design world to focus his full creative zeal on this magnificent house – or rather houses – and when I pitched up he was hard at work, pen in mouth, bent over plans for the next step. Not content with just five fabulous rooms at nearby Liberty Lodge, he and Jimmy are converting three entire houses into a den of "African Zen". The structure may be classically Victorian, but the décor is anything but with bold, tribal colours offsetting black-painted floorboards and neutral carpets. Jimmy gave me the grand tour – trailed as ever by dachshunds Zip and Button – pointing out Louis' designer eye in every detail, from the lacquered ostrich eggs and porcupine quills (please don't pinch them, he pleads) to the hanging Zulu spears and African wedding hats. The bathrooms are compact but perfectly formed, the bedrooms are wonderfully roomy, and when you finally and reluctantly slide from between the percale cotton sheets, breakfast is a communal affair in the large airy kitchen or out on the terrace. This house is a haven, a cool retreat and while others may be sweating their way up Table Mountain just minutes away, you can be thumbing through a book in the shade of an orange tree or cooling off in the plunge pool. Go on… treat yourself. Library and Internet available to all guests.

Rooms: An African Villa: 12 king/twins: 6 deluxe, all with bath and shower; 6 luxury, 5 with shower, 1 with bath and shower. Liberty Lodge: 1 deluxe, 5 doubles, all with shower.
Price: R365 – R440 pp sharing. Singles on request.
Meals: Full breakfast included.
Directions: From central Cape Town follow signs to the Cableway. At the bottom of Kloofnek Rd double back and turn left into Carstens St. Look for the second block on the left with a yellowwood tree outside.

Redbourne Hilldrop

Jonny and Sharon Levin
12 Roseberry Avenue, Oranjezicht 8001
Tel: 021-461-1394 Fax: 021-465-1006
Email: info@redbourne.co.za Web: www.redbourne.co.za

One of the happiest and most humorous guest houses in Cape Town, so it always seems to me. Many of Jonny and Sharon's guests refuse to stay elsewhere and gifts arrive daily from overseas…well almost. One day you may be surprised to find yourself packing up toys for their kids. It's a small, intimate place and you are spoiled: free-standing baths, fluffy duvets, big white pillows, unflowery good taste in mirrors and wood floors, magazines, African artefacts, great showers. One room has a spiral staircase down to its bathroom. You eat breakfast at a dinner-style bar stretched along a wall of pretty windows with incredible city views. Guests are treated as far as possible as friends and each time I visit I notice the easy rapport that Jonny and Sharon have generated with their guests – probably overnight. The wall-enclosed pool has now been up and running for a couple of years, complete with a mini-waterfall spanning the length of it and Table Mountain looming above. A perfect finishing touch.

Rooms: 4: 2 doubles and 1 twin; 2 with en/s bath and shower, 1 with en/s sh. And 1 family room with sunroom (pictured above).
Price: R295 – R425 pp sharing. Singles on request.
Meals: Full breakfast included. Dinners by prior arrangement. Restaurants nearby.
Directions: Ask when booking.

Guesthouse de Tafelberg

Ann and Kris van Cappellen

68 Molteno Rd, Oranjezicht 8001
Tel: 021-424-9159 Fax: 021-424-9157
Email: info@detafelberg.com Web: www.detafelberg.com

We strolled across the marble floor and through the sunlight-infused room, our passage reflected in a wall of mirrors. Two wide French doors open out to the breakfast balcony and a beautiful view. Pool just below, skyscrapers next and the glittering ocean beyond. But if you actually want to see Cape Town, don't stay here since it's likely that you won't make it outside once you've settled in. I visited mid-morning and guests were still enjoying piles of warm croissants, fruits, organic yoghurts and scrambled eggs with bacon and tomatoes aside six-seed bread. The only thing they were going to shift for was to test the depth of the pads on the pool loungers, the jacuzzi or maybe reading the papers in the outside sitting room. Why they even came out of their rooms to eat beats me. Decorated in neutrals, reds and monochrome they vary in size and view. "Table Mountain or sea?" The main one is surely only free when Bond isn't in town. The statuesque bed is mounted on a plinth, the spa bath is surrounded with wall-to-wall mirrors… for your eyes only perhaps. You could hide a gondola in the arched double shower. Your hosts are relaxed and friendly people who exchanged vintage wines for the living delights of Cape Town and busied themselves creating a hotel/home for media types who needed a base in town.

Rooms: 8: 2 suites with en/s bath and shower; 2 queens with en/s shower; 2 queens with en/s bath and shower; 2 twins with en/s shower.
Price: R440 – R750 pp.
Meals: Full breakfast included.
Directions: Emailed and faxed on booking.

Villa Christina

Markus and Simone Brabetz

2 Rocklands Avenue,
Highlands Estate, Cape Town
8001
Tel: 021-461-9288
Fax: 021-461-9283
Email: christina@new.co.za
Web: www.villachristina.co.za
Cell: 082-335-4093

There's something of the Sound of Music about Villa Christina – a happy concert of mountains, music and family. Maybe it's the faintly alpine air. The house sits so close to Table Mountain that the tassels of the 'tablecloth' tickle its tiles. On my visit Simone, an accomplished violinist, was ushering the kids to music class, while Markus handled a steady stream of visitors with trademark courtesy (and without breaking into song!). His delight in providing for his guests is obvious, booking the must-see theatre, making that dental appointment or simply rustling up a bottle of merlot. As he says, "'n Boer maak 'n plan." Here in the heart of the rainbow nation I found a few of my favourite things – the freshest of breakfast plates (think paw-paw, passion fruit and mangoes on colourful crockery), the bloom of the morning flower market, the be-bop of the brightly-painted Bo-Kaap quarter… Villa Christina is a grand Italianate affair, daubed in yellow with large white-trimmed windows. The Crete-stone bedrooms are arranged on the ground floor, their French doors overlooking a manicured garden lined with lime trees, cacti and pines harbouring Egyptian geese. From the pool you can count the creeping cable cars and contemplate climbing every mountain. It's all "just-so", until you discover the charming quirks, like the garden trampoline, used by young and old alike. A drop of golden sun.

Rooms: 5: all doubles with en-suite showers.
Price: R300 – R350 pp sharing. Singles R450 – R550.
Meals: Full cooked breakfast included. Some of Cape Town's finest restaurants only moments away. Picnic baskets can be arranged.
Directions: Faxed or emailed on booking.

Dunkley House

Sharon Scudamore

3b Gordon St, Gardens 8001
Tel: 021-462-7650 Fax: 021-462-7649
Email: reservations@dunkleyhouse.co.za Web: www.dunkleyhouse.com

Dunkley House is so cunningly hidden in the city centre that, despite dozens of visits to Cape Town, you might never have found it without our help. So pats on backs all round. Tucked into a quiet street in central Gardens this compact boutique hotel is a mosaic-floored, chic-Spanish-villa of a place. Chic maybe, but delightfully relaxed with it. Manager Sara supplied me with home-made biscuits as we chatted on a massive, caramel leather sofa that I had to struggle out of when I stood up. This really is a place you are encouraged to feel at home in, no small feat for a hotel, however small and 'boutique'. You want to lounge under palms by the pool?… lounge; you want to help Eunice in the kitchen?… go for it. She's a fantastic cook and aside from endless breakfast delights (don't miss the fluffy omelettes), she has been known to rustle up a feast for those who want to eat in of an evening. The long dining table is neatly arranged next to a pot-bellied wood-burner for winter nights and framed by black-and-white prints of Dar es Salaam. Plus, the bedrooms are just a stagger away, bay-windowed, whitest linen on beds and flashes of colour in the cushions. For something on the quirky side, the retro mezzanine apartment upstairs – perfect for family stays – is decorated in blacks, whites and reds. This place really is a hidden gem worth digging for.

Rooms: 6: 2 kings, 3 queens, 1 with bath all others with shower only. One apartment with 1 double and 1 twin sharing shower.
Price: From R350 – R495 pp sharing. Singles R550 – R800. Apartment R1,150 per night.
Meals: Full breakfast included. Other meals by arrangement.
Directions: Faxed or emailed on booking, also on website.

Acorn House

Bernd Schlieper and Beate Lietz

1 Montrose Avenue, Oranjezicht 8001
Tel: 021-461-1782 Fax: 021-461-1768
Email: welcome@acornhouse.co.za Web: www.acornhouse.co.za

Bernd and Beate can barely contain the happiness they derive from Acorn House, and their enthusiasm rubs off quickly on all but the stoniest of their visitors. I was a pushover. The listed building, designed by busy Sir Herbert Baker in 1904, sits on the sunny, sea-facing slopes of Table Mountain with tip-top views to Table Bay. The house is typical Sir Herbert, timber colonnade, broad verandah et al, and there is an immaculate garden with black-slate swimming pool and a sun-lounging lawn, cleanly demarcated by agapanthus and lavender bushes. Breakfast, often served by the pool, is a no-holds-barred display of meats, cheeses, eggs and freshly-squeezed fruit juices; "probably the second-best breakfast in Cape Town" is Beate's carefully-worded claim! Upstairs, in your wood-floored bedroom you will find notes of welcome or farewell, chocolates and sprigs of lavender. Wine-lovers are also well served: Bernd is pazzo for the stuff, and regularly visits local vineyards to ensure that his house wines are up-to-the-moment (just for his guests' benefit, of course). Having lived in South Africa for five years now, Bernd and Beate are still awash with excitement about their surroundings. A stay in Acorn House will leave you feeling much the same.

Rooms: 8: 1 king, 3 twins and 3 doubles all with en-suite bath; 1 family suite with twin.
Price: R420 – R520 pp sharing. Singles R400 – R700. Family suite as double R840 – R1,040 + R200 for up to 2 kids.
Meals: Full breakfast included.
Directions: See web site or ask for fax.

Four Rosmead

David Shorrock
4 Rosmead Avenue, Oranjezicht 8001
Tel: 021-480-3810 Fax: 021-423-0044
Email: info@fourrosmead.com Web: www.fourrosmead.com
Cell: 082-900-3461

From "the back end of a bus" to the frontage of a French country house, Four Rosmead has undergone an impressive facelift since David got his hands on it. When I visited, the last licks of paint were drying and pictures being straightened ready for their first guests, but already I could tell it had élan and panache! It's a familiar story: David's a thoroughly affable ex-investment banker with a passion for art and all things French, who fled a hectic Jo'burg life for a change of gear in the Cape (no one ever seems to change career to go *into* the financial world!). And what a spot to pick... the house and its position are magnificent. Four Rosmead is a provincial monument, built in 1903, but restyled with a thoroughly modern feel. The rooms are all wonderfully light and airy thanks to chalky-toned walls and high, pitched ceilings. Cushions and oils add the colour (all the art in the house is South African and for sale) and from enormous windows (particularly in the showers) the views are great, whether looking through ancient oaks to Lion's Head, or peeking over rooftops to the City Bowl and ocean. But why spend your time inside when you can mooch by the pool or amble crunchily along the gravel paths of the Mediterranean garden soothed by the scent of lavender and the rustle of bay trees, oranges and olives? There is also a 'pamper room' offering massage, relexology and aromatherapy.

Rooms: 8: 1 cottage suite with 1 queen with shower over bath & outdoor shower; 3 twin/kings, 1 with bath & shower, 2 with shower only; 4 queens, 1 with bath & shower, 3 with shower only.
Price: R375 – R1,000 pp sharing. Singles +50%.
Meals: Full breakfast included. Snack lunches can be ordered in.
Directions: Faxed or emailed on booking, also available on website.

Cape Town, Western Cape

Cape Heritage Hotel

Nick Garsten
90 Bree Street, 8001
Tel: 021-424-4646 Fax: 021-424-4949
Email: info@capeheritage.co.za Web: www.capeheritage.co.za

Wham-bam in the city centre, on the fringe of Cape Town's historic Bo-Kaap area, the small, intimate and innovative Cape Heritage Hotel has a delightfully informal, sociable guest house feel. Central to the breakfast room is a communal table bordered by large grapefruit and pomegranate paintings and cocoon-like lampshades hanging over the coffee bar. Architects and archaeologists have played their roles in the reconstruction of the building which dates back to 1771. I admired the black-and-white photos and line drawings in the hallways depicting the building's history, amongst other old photos of Cape Town. Throughout the building patches of murals and exposed walls have been left untouched to showcase the original architecture and workmanship. High-beamed ceilings and burnished wooden floors line the rooms, and each of the bedrooms has been individually styled with antiques: sleigh beds or four-posters and rooms in Malay, African, Zulu and Japanese style. I particularly liked the Pakhuis (pack house) historic room. A major attraction is the choice of restaurants on your doostep and, come evening, in the courtyard there is a thriving atmosphere, even live music... and, as it happens, the oldest known living grapevine in South Africa. Heritage Square also houses a virtual museum of the oldest operational blacksmith in SA, a health club and a resident masseuse.

Rooms: 15: 2 suites, 6 luxury and 7 standard, all with en-suite bath and shower.
Price: Seasonal. Superior R470 – R600, Luxury R500 – R700, Suites R770 – R1,000 pp sharing. Single supplement + 50%.
Meals: Breakfast included.
Directions: From airport take N2, turn off at Strand St exit. At 8th set of lights turn left into Bree St. At 2nd set of lights hotel is on your right.

Aromasun Guesthouse

Charnell Timms and Denise Beumer

9 Winkle Way, Sunset Beach 7441
Tel: 021-551-1691 Fax: 021-551-1691
Email: info@aromasun.co.za Web: www.aromasun.co.za
Cell: 084-366-0046 (Charnell) 072-430-5813 (Denise)

Big ticks in every column for Charnell and Denise. Between them these two have every base covered, Charnell being a professional tour guide and photographer and Denise an aromatherapist. I made sure to jot down top tips on the nearby winelands, but, alas, had no time for hot stone therapy. The Art Deco house on a quiet street overlooking Sunset Beach couldn't be better placed. For views back towards Cape Town central, Table Mountain looming large above, I'd recommend the Aromasun roof terrace up a spiralling staircase. From here, Robben Island even looked swimmable. The pillared, open-plan living area, complete with cherry-wood honesty bar and black granite-topped kitchen surfaces, opened onto a small rocky courtyard, where two waterfalls cascade into the splash pool. Inside, I cut an ungainly figure struggling to haul myself up from the swamps of the sofa in front of the full-length windows. Upstairs, the landing is dotted with stylish sepia photos of Cape Town life (a hobby of Charnell's) and the substantial carpeted rooms all have sea views and access to a conservatory. From here you can see the sun setting over Table Bay and Robben Island and a telescope has thoughtfully been provided to while away the evenings gazing at the night sky. But Charnell and Denise are such good company, like me, you'll probably be stuck in that sofa all evening.

Rooms: 4: 3 king-size with en-suite bath and shower, 1 queen-size with en-suite bath and shower.
Price: R200 – R450 pp sharing. Singles R300 – R600.
Meals: Full breakfast included.
Directions: Emailed or faxed on request.

Medindi Manor

Geoffrey Bowman, Leshira Mosaka and Mamalena Molep
4 Thicket Road, Rosebank 7700
Tel: 021-686-3563 Fax: 021-686-3565
Email: manor@medindi.co.za Web: www.medindi.co.za
Cell: 082-480-0103

Medindi is a secluded Edwardian manor of grand dimensions, banded by ground and first-floor verandas with a garden and swimming pool tucked away behind tall hedges and bushes. Some of the rooms have their own doors out onto the stoep and the main building has been renovated with panache and a sensitive feel for the period. Although well-stocked with bar fridges, telephones, TVs etc, Medindi avoids like the plague any h(ot)ellish homogeneity in its décor and design. The Oregon pine floors, bay windows, intricate ceilings and marble fireplaces are original and there are unique, antique touches everywhere, such as Edwardian designs for stately marble and slate floors. Bathrooms have free-standing baths, Victorian "plate" showerheads, brass fittings and a small antique cabinet has been found for each. There is modernity too, in bright wall colours (yellows and blues), and splashes of modern art – from the turn of one century to the turn of the next. Music is an important ingredient for Geoffrey, Medindi's owner, and classical music and a bit of jazz wafts through reception. A freewheeling, relaxed and youthful place. Geoffrey, Leshira and Mamalema share the day-to- day management of Medindi and six new rooms have been created from a converted outbuilding – the smaller rooms are cheaper.

Rooms: 13: in the house: 4 dbles + 2 twns with en/s bathrooms, 3 with bath + shower, 3 with shower. Plus 6 more rooms in converted outbuilding. Plus 1 self-c cottage.
Price: R345 – R545 pp sharing. Singles R495 – R895.
Meals: Buffet breakfast included, cooked breakfast extra: R35.50. Dinner by prior arrangement. Restaurants nearby.
Directions: See map on web site or phone ahead.

The Studio

Eulalie Spamer
No.10 Seymour St, Wynberg 7800
Tel: 021-761-9554 Fax: 021-797-8183
Email: eulalie@eulaliespamer.com Web: www.eulaliespamer.com
Cell: 072-446-8152

'The Studio' was for 30 years the design office of an architect of international repute. I just knew it was going to be interesting, especially since Eulalie had furnished the place. Recently adapted to create a maisonette with garden, there are many intriguing design quirks. Take the main bedroom for example: the only solid wall doubles as the bed-head, while the rest of the room is contained by glass with a wrap-around balcony (with potted roof-garden), allowing sweeping views of the flat peak of Table Mountain and the Constantiaberg. These views can be enjoyed without even getting out of bed. Stylish, modern creations do not always have that all-important 'homely' feel to them: this is where Eulalie, whose various houses have graced GG editions since the very start, comes into her own. She has kept interiors simple but gorgeous with customary good taste: antique European and Asian pieces, rustic wicker chairs, marble dining table, wooden carvings, white sofas and masses of earth-tone scatter cushions on day beds. The large living room gives directly onto the pool terrace and its outdoor candlelit dining area is fringed with potted palms and topiary. And the small eat-in kitchen is well-equipped. Long lets are typical, but if you are lucky enough to find a slot you are equally welcome for a short stay.

Rooms: 1 duplex garden studio with 1 queen and 1 single in main room; 1 on internal gallery share bathroom.
Price: Self-catering only: R800 – R1,200 per day, minimum 3 nights. Sleeps maximum of 4.
Meals: First morning's breakfast provisions left for you. Restaurants nearby.
Directions: Off M3 Trovato Link pass Herschel Walk turn-off. After Herschel Walk it's the 4th road to your left.

Forest House

Patricia and Patrick Fraser

30 Orchard Heights,
Newlands 7700
Tel: 021-683-2387
Fax: 021-683-2387
Email: pfraser@iafrica.com
Cell: 083-236-7933

Budding mountaineers take note: Table Mountain doesn't get any closer than this. For a head start up to the rocky summit, Forest House is the perfect base-camp. Wedged into a steep hillside, this sun-kissed, storey-stacked villa does not waste its God-given views. From the wrap-around paved verandah, you can admire the wooded Constantiaberg to the south and distant Stellenbosch to the east. Your room is on the first floor, receiving the morning sunshine, with TV, fridge and en-suite shower, and you can enjoy the view from bed. From there it's just two more flights of stairs (or a ride in the funicular – under construction when we visited) past Patricia's art studio to the stunning drawing room. It's armed with a squadron of sofas and armchairs and there's a huge mirror over the fireplace and oils of seafaring battles reflect Patrick's passion for the water. We were rewarded at the top with coffee and a pile of hot, honey-spread, utterly delicious pancakes – or were they crumpets?… a source of some debate. Patricia is an excellent hostess and cook (so good in fact that we descended upon her again for supper four days later) and an artist whose prestigious commissions include the dizzy heights of the early editions of this guide. Come here, enjoy the mountain which you can walk straight onto from the back of the house, and treat yourself to an evening concert in next-door's garden – Kirstenbosch.

Rooms: 1 twin with en-suite shower.
Price: R250 – R350 pp sharing.
Meals: Full breakfast included. Picnic lunches on request.
Directions: From airport take N2 towards Cape Town and follow all signs to Kirstenbosch. Once in Rhodes Drive, take first right into Orchard Street, then second left into Orchard Heights.

Little Spotte

Zaria Dagnall
5 Cavendish Close, Cavendish St, Claremont 7700
Tel: 021-762-4593 Fax: c/o Mr C Dagnall 021-595-1173
Email: zaria@mweb.co.za
Cell: 082-374-3399

With all the shopping, dining, coffee-drinking and general urban whirl of Claremont excitedly clattering about it, Little Spotte is a time capsule of stillness and calm. A narrow path leads between designery shops to this delightful Victorian bungalow. There is no doubt of its Englishness once past the bird-of-paradise flowers in the front garden. The owners keep it a living space, in case they themselves want to come down from Jo'burg to use it. Thus you are blessed with antiques, yellowwood and oak furniture, and an astoundingly well-equipped kitchen. The cottage is self-catering, but Zaria is a very hands-on manager who will see you settled, make sure flowers, chocolates and a few breakfast commodities are arrayed for your arrival… and she is also a dynamic source of recommendation to lesser-known wineries, walks in Cape Town, local coffee-houses and restaurants. The cottage itself is far bigger than you might expect at the front door, with a central courtyard with table and green parasol, completely secure from the noise of the city and opened onto from the main bedroom and the dining area. Mod cons include TV/video with DSTV and a fully-equipped laundry and your local food shop is no less than Woolworths (M&S equivalent if you're a Brit and getting confused). A lovely pied-à-terre bang in the middle of one of Cape Town's most lively restaurant districts. Very central for all city sight-seeing spots.

Rooms: 1 cottage with 2 bedrooms: 1 twin with en-suite shower; 1 double with en-suite shower.
Price: Minimum stay 2 nights at maximum rate of R800: otherwise R550 in low season for the cottage. In high season R650 for 2 people, R720 for 3 and R840 for 4. Discounts for longer stays.
Meals: Fully self-catering, although Zaria will put a few things in for your first night.
Directions: Faxed or emailed when booking.

Hunter's Moon Lodge

Heather Nicholson
57 Southern Cross Drive, Constantia Upper 7806
Tel: 021-794-5001 Fax: 021-794-0184
Email: enquiries@huntersmoonlodge.co.za Web:
www.huntersmoonlodge.co.za (or .com) Cell: 084-722-4469

Hunter's Moon is truly a splendid Tuscan Villa, even compared to the other glitterati temples and ambassadorial homes of Southern Cross Drive, one of Cape Town's most desirable addresses. Even compared to real Tuscan villas! This impressive mansion is surrounded by terraced Italian gardens with lavender walks, rose-clad arches, citrus and olive trees, all planted around fountains and pools. Outside and inside it's a place that will open the eye a little wider. Sturdy oak doors open onto a beautiful two-story glass-roofed atrium complete with koi pond and courtyard. There are three dining rooms; one seats twelve and you'll find another, more intimate, by the pool for just four. The pale marble staircase sweeps like the train of a dress up to a colonnaded balcony walk that overlooks the lower courtyard directly below… where there are antiques and modern art and day beds deep in cushions and light which pours in from the glazed roof. The bedrooms owe much to Versace, one decorated in yellow and black, and all have hand-painted *trompe-l'oeils* on the walls. The villa is set on a terraced hillside with long long views over the vineyards of Constantia to the Muizenberg mountains and as far as Gordon's Bay and the Cape of Good Hope. Heather will do B&B or you can rent the whole house per day. *Children over 12 welcome.*

Rooms: 6: 1 large single, 2 double/twins and 3 suites, all with en-suite bath and shower.
Price: R365 – R1,375. Singles R465 – R1,110. Whole house rentals: low season, R9,000 a day; peak season, R15,000 a day.
Meals: Full organic breakfast included. Catering can be arranged. Several award-winning restaurants nearby.
Directions: Take M3 from Cape Town towards Constantia. Follow Kirstenbosch signs. Take Rhodes Drive on the right towards Hout Bay and follow for 3km. Southern Cross Drive is on left and No.57 is half way down on the right.

Montrose Palms

Jenny and Leon Jacobs

7 Montrose Terrace, Bishopscourt-Constantia
Tel: 021-762-3608 Fax: 021-762-3864
Email: jenny@mbanet.co.za Web: www.montrosepalms.co.za
Cell: 083-448-4545

The electric gates at Montrose Palms do more than merely let you in and out. They transport you to somewhere palm-fringed and water-bound in the South Pacific... somewhere serene and luxurious... somewhere like Bali. The lofty position, plummeting hillside and giant (transplanted!) date palms encouraged me to peer down into the foliage expecting to see rice terraces stepping down the mountain. In fact, wearing the Constantiaberg as a stiff high collar, Montrose Palms gazes long, high and handsome out to False Bay and the Muizenberg Mountains. Naturally, all the rooms have private terraces, which get their fair share. This house is frankly spoilt and has its every whim indulged! Smooth surfaces, satisfyingly solid fittings, sleek taps and handles, underfloor heating, and floor-to-ceiling glass doors that lead out onto the fabulous terraces; percale linen, TVs, drinks cabinet, great bathrooms, of course, and so much space. The house is surrounded by refreshing rectangles of water. Mottled-orange koi carp swim – as if they know why – in stone pools that run beneath the house itself; and the long decking-encased swimming pool with its little bridge of sighs (under which you can swim laps) and Balinese lanterns is irresistible at the other end of the house. Here you will no doubt find a day or two of your holiday plans slipping by unrealised.

Rooms: 8: 2 suites (kings) and 6 standard rooms (queens); 6 have en-suite bath and separate shower; 2 have shower only.
Price: R365 – R1,000. Single rates in low and mid-season only. Full room rates for the rest of the year.
Meals: Self-catering possible with frozen meals on request (typically R40 a meal). Full-blown dinners by prior arrangement: up to R200 p.p.
Directions: From CT take M3 towards Muizenberg, turn R at Hout Bay/Kirstenbosch turning on to M63. Follow for 1 km past Kirstenbosch. At T-jct turn R into Rhodes Drive. 1st L into Klaassens Rd. Then 2nd R into Montrose Ave. Then R into Montrose Terrace.

Map Number: 1

The Bishops' Court

Paul and Bernadette Le Roux
18 Hillwood Avenue, Bishopscourt 7708
Tel: 021-797-6710 Fax: 021-797-0309
Email: paul@thebishopscourt.com Web: www.thebishopscourt.com
Cell: 082-550-4533

Paul turned his back on an accounting career to become a guide and establish this fantastic place to stay and when I arrived he was briefing an English family who had taken over the whole place. "… Gigi will drive you into town for supper… yes, of course I can do a braai for 14, no problem…". Etc. He'll take you on tours galore, to the winelands, down the Cape Peninsular or on visits to housekeeper Connie's home in the township. For the moment this lot were going nowhere. The boys were hurling themselves into the pool and hunting for tennis racquets to test out a tree-shaded court at the foot of the long sloping garden. Their parents sat on a shaded terrace, soaking up *the best* Table Mountain view I have yet to stumble across. From this spot, a green carpet of tree canopy unrolls directly from two-storey house to hillside, with Kirstenbosch botanical gardens planted somewhere in the middle. The rooms (each one roughly the size of my entire flat) all have that view and my favourite had a mosaicked outdoor jacuzzi and shower. Wood-panelled ceilings and book-shelves give the dining/living room a relaxed beachy feel and, though there's no sand, bare feet at breakfast are more than welcome. "Barefoot luxury" – a perfect two-word description of The Bishops' Court.

Rooms: 5 king/twins, 3 with en-suite bath, 2 with en-suite shower.
Price: R500 – R1,250 pp sharing (depending on the season). Singles plus 50%.
Meals: Full breakfast and all drinks included. Dinners on request.
Directions: From airport take N2 towards Cape Town then M3 towards Muizenberg. On M3 go through 4 traffic lights then turn R to Bishopscourt on Upper Torquay Ave. Turn L at end then first R into Hillwood Ave. Property is about 200m down on R.

Dendron

Shaun and Jill McMahon

21 Ou Wingerd Pad, Upper Constantia 7806
Tel: 021-794-6010 Fax: 021-794-2532
Email: stay@dendron.co.za Web: www.dendron.co.za
Cell: 082-4911-647 or 082-296-0691

(Quite) A few years ago, Shaun bought a Land Rover in Taunton (UK) and drove it here. Hardly odd when you see the place, now replete with relaxed family atmosphere, collie dogs and cricket pegs (or whatever they're called) on the front lawn. You get all the benefits of living the South African good life by default here. Green-fingered Jill genuinely loves having guests and her enthusiasm for life is evident in everything. The cottages are private in leafy, jasmine-scented gardens and have a kitchenette stocked with basics, a braai and views to the mountains on the right and False Bay in the distance. Two cottages have terracotta-tiled or wooden floors and beds with Indian cotton throws – perfect for families. The other two are newly-renovated cottages with kilims, safari prints and plump sofas. All are fully serviced. Evening pool-side views at sunset and moonrise, helped along by wine from over-the-hedge Groot Constantia vineyard, will make you want to throw away the car keys and stay (which is exactly what Shaun did when he first clapped eyes on the place). When you are hungry, Jill will send you off there through the back gate and across the vineyards to the Jonkershuys restaurant for dinner. Return by torch- and moon-light. Dendron (GK = tree) is a small slice of heaven. Don't stay too long, jealousy will take root!

Rooms: 4 in total: 2 cottages with 1 double and 1 twin both with bath and shower; 2 cottages with twin, 1 with bath & shower, 1 with shower only.
Price: Four in one cottage R250 pp. Two sharing R325 pp. Single on request.
Meals: Essentially self-catering, but breakfast for first morning provided and afterwards if requested at R30 pp.
Directions: Fax on request.

Andros Country House

Trevor and Britta Miles
Cnr Newlands Rd & Phyllis Rd, Upper Claremont 7708
Tel: 021-797-9777 Fax: 021-797-0300
Email: info@andros.co.za Web: www.andros.co.za

A country house? In the heart of Claremont? Well… yes, actually. After a very 'urban' journey fighting through the nearby Cavendish Square shopping hub in rush hour, I was impressed by the contrast once ensconced at the Andros. Cocooned from the hustle and bustle of the city by a wall of trees, this period Cape Dutch house is in a different (and much grander) world. Deep arched doorways pilot you into the wood-floored lounge, where a roaring fire in an open hearth awaits you on wintry evenings. Persian rugs, painted beam ceilings, deep sofas and heavy wooden coffee tables are interspersed by African wood sculptures. It's here that new owners Britta and Trevor serve evening drinks before ushering guests into the next-door dining room, where chef serves a five-course extravaganza, ranging from traditional South African fare to curry. Early morning sunlight streams in through glass-panelled doors, which open onto a red-brick terrace overlooking swaying palms and a crystalline pool. All the rooms in the main homestead are quite in keeping with the general high style, but for extra luxury there is the honeymoon suite with its black-and-white tiled bathroom. Through an archway off the bedroom is the pièce de résistance, a sunken spa bath with a window looking out into dense foliage. So you don't have to go miles to treat yourself to the serenity of the countryside. Just go to the Miles'.

Rooms: 10: 9 doubles with en-suite bath and shower, 1 with shower only. Twins on request.
Price: R510 – R1,110 pp sharing. Singles R575 – R1,200.
Meals: Full breakfast included. Dinner from R150 for 5 courses. Light lunches on request.
Directions: Can be emailed or faxed on request.

At Villa Fig

Bruno and Lindsay Rolando
6 Glendyrr Walk, Constantia 7806
Tel: 021-794-7049 Fax: 021-794-1378
Email: villafig@mweb.co.za

Airbrush together your ideal of a top-notch hotel and a relaxed home for a notion of how Bruno and Lindsay host at Villa Fig. Both artists, they took four years to salvage the Burmese teak for the frame of the structure, two years to restore the timber and that was before they started building! It's made for hot summers with tall ceilings and wide doors to let in both breeze and view. Acres of grey marble soften the reflection of sunlight pouring through the skylight above the Escher-esque staircase and metre-high cymbidium orchids, which flower joyously out of giant oriental pots. There are no interior walls downstairs, just four black, cast-iron columns, which accentuate the sense of space. And what about the art! Lindsay's (Roy) Lichtenstein-inspired canvases, bronze sculptures, Persian rugs…. One bedroom has a balustraded balcony shaded by an ancient pecan tree and through elephantine doors the main bedroom reveals 50 square metres of pure shimmering luxury. Tired after swimming or tennis? Then the upper deck, complete with pergola, has been positioned with precision for you to watch the sunset behind Table Mountain whilst you loll like Cleopatra on deep cushions and a mosaicked-by-Bruno chaise-longue.

Rooms: 5: 2 suites of 1 queen and 1 twin with en-suite bath and shower; 2 kings with en/s bath and shower; 1 king with en-suite shower. 1 self-catering 2-bedroomed suite.
Price: R300 – R450 pp sharing. Singles on request.
Meals: Full breakfast included.
Directions: Emailed or faxed on booking.

Cape Witogie

Rosemary and Bob Childs

9 Van Zyl Rd, Kreupelbosch, Constantia 7945
Tel: 021-712-9935 Fax: 021-712-9935
Email: capewitogie@netactive.co.za Web: www.capestay.co.za/capewitogie
Cell: 082-537-6059

Billy, a desperately friendly Staffordshire bull terrier, is public relations officer at Cape Witogie and this is probably the only B&B with a dog that gets his own mail. His owners Rosemary and Bob are equally friendly and when I visited Rosemary was frantically shifting beds post-renovations. The latest addition to their red-bricked home is an airy conservatory/sitting room, which now adjoins one of the two bedrooms. Both rooms are whitewashed, tile-floored self-catering units that open on to a compact garden full of ferns and firs, lavender pots, lemon trees and citrus-smelling verbena. Hot-plates, a small oven and microwaves give ample scope for knocking up your own meals, though Rosemary enjoys making occasional breakfasts and bakes bread for those who'd rather not bake their own. I'd recommend coming with some pals and taking both rooms as a base from which to explore the Cape Town area. From the city bowl and beaches to Table Mountain, the botanical gardens and nearby winelands there is just so much to do in the Cape that a full week with Bob and Rosemary flies by in the blink of an eye. These are great people (with great dogs), running a great value get-away.

Rooms: 2 twins with showers.
Price: R190 – R220 pp sharing. Single supplement R50.
Meals: Breakfast R60.
Directions: Faxed or emailed on booking.

Constantia Stables

Lola and Rick Bartlett

8 Chantecler Lane, off Willow Rd, Constantia 7806
Tel: 021-794-3653 Fax: 021-794-3653
Email: tstables@mweb.co.za
Cell: 082-569-4135

I loved The Constantia Stables and would be as happy as a pig in clover to be among Lola and Rick's regular visitors. Not only is it a stunning spot of shaded indigenous gardens and beautifully renovated stable buildings (ask for the hayloft room!), but there's a genuine family feel to the place that is immediately relaxing. The Bartlett children are actors and their photos are plastered across the drawing room and bar. This is the heart of the Stables, a congenial snug of heavy armchairs, low beams and earth-red walls where guests are encouraged to tap into a well-stocked bar. I liked the breakfast room too with its red brick fireplace. As Lola reeled off the gargantuan menu I wondered why anyone would want to self-cater; fresh fruit salad with home-grown guava, quince and peaches, hams, salamis, a giant cheese board, yoghurts, cereals and croissants and that's before you even think about cooked delights. She and Rick have done a fantastic job converting the original stables into bedrooms with old, olive green stable doors opening onto an ivy-fringed courtyard. The garden suite overlooks the pool and, like the self-catering Lily's cottage, seamlessly blends into the mass of plants that spread out beneath two enormous plane trees. And once you're suitably chilled there's a whole bunch of vineyards and restaurants to explore just next door. The Bartletts also own two large, but very friendly dogs, called Wry and Miss Molly.

Rooms: 5: 1 king with bath, 1 queen with bath and shower, 1 queen with shower, 1 twin with shower; also 1 self-catering cottage with 1 queen, 1 twin and 2 showers.
Price: From R325 pp sharing. Singles on request.
Meals: Full breakfast included.
Directions: Follow M3 towards Muizenberg. Take Ladies Mile off-ramp. Turn L at traffic lights onto Ladies Mile and L at next lights onto Spaanschemat River Rd. Keep L at fork then turn L into Willow Rd and L into Chantecler Lane. The Stables is at the end on L.

Kaapse Draai

Annelie Posthumus
19 Glen Avenue, Constantia 7806
Tel: 021-794-6291 Fax: 021-794-6291
Email: info@kaapsedraaibb.co.za Web: www.kaapsedraaibb.co.za
Cell: 082-923-9869

Annelie has been charming Greenwood Guide travellers since the very first edition and should be in the running for some sort of award for B&B brilliance. Relaxed, simple and beautiful seems to be the rule here. Her daughter is an interior designer and their talents combine to make the house a peaceful temple to uncluttered Cape Cod-style living. Neutral furnishings and white cottons are frisked up with pretty floral bolsters and country checks. Sunny window-seats are perfect for reading guide-books on the area and there are posies of fresh flowers in each room. I was lucky enough to stay with Annelie and once installed in my room, she invited me down for a soup later. She is a prolific gardener and you can walk (perhaps with Annelie's dogs) from the tropical greenery of Kaapse Draai with its mountain stream, huge ferns and palms into lovely Bel-Ombre meadow and the forest next door. From there it is a three-hour walk to the Table Mountain cable station. Porcupines come into the garden at night from the mountain (they love arum lilies apparently) and there are many birds too, including the noisy (and palindromic) hadedah. A grand old willow tree is what you'll park your car under. Delicious breakfasts are taken outside in the sunshine whenever possible. All I can say is – do. *Wine estates and Constantia shopping village nearby.*

Rooms: 3: 1 double and 2 twins with en-suite shower.
Price: R295 pp sharing. Singles R350.
Meals: Full breakfast included. Annelie sometimes cooks if the mood is upon her. But do not expect this....
Directions: Ask for fax or email when booking.

Klein Bosheuwel

Nicki and Tim Scarborough
51a Klaassens Rd, Constantia 7800
Tel: 021-762-2323 Fax: 021-762-2323
Email: kleinbosheuwel@iafrica.com Web: www.kleinbosheuwel.co.za

Who needs Kirstenbosch? Nicki has manipulated the paths and lawns of her own garden (which is pretty well an extension of the Botanical Gardens anyway – less than a minute's walk away) so that the views are not dished out in one vulgar dollop! Instead you are subtly led into them, with glimpses through mature trees (flowering gums, yellowwoods and camellias) and lush flower beds. And finally your stroll leads you down to umbrellas on a ridge with Table Mountain and the Constantiaberg laid out magnificently before you and the sea distantly below. "Keep it plain" is Nicki's motto, so the upstairs bedrooms are simply white and all naturally endowed with garden views. The salt-water swimming pool is hidden deep in the garden and Klein Bosheuwel is the sort of place where you could just hang out for a few days. I was introduced to one English guest who had clearly no intention of going anywhere that day – the cat that got the cream you might have thought! *Ask when booking about children. Tim and Nicki also own Southdown next door.*

Rooms: 4: 1 twin en/s bath; 2 queens with en/s bath and shower; 1 queen en/s large bath.
Price: R375 – R412 pp sharing. Singles R580.
Meals: Full breakfast included. Can organise other meals on request.
Directions: Fax or web site.

Little Ruo

Paul and Ingrid Righini

11 Willow Rd, Constantia 7800
Tel: 021-794-2052 Fax: 021-794-1981
Email: ruo@netactive.co.za Web: www.littleruo.co.za
Cell: 083-461-8419

The Ruo, I gather, is a river that flows somewhere in Africa. The Little Ruo I can be more sure of. It bisects Paul and Ingrid's garden in the heart of the Constantia Valley and quenches the thirst of the great Persian willows that offer the red-brick cobbled driveway some welcome shade. Across the rickety wooden bridge I found clues of the old fruit farm: a lemon and a plum tree, both bursting with juicy treasure; and the old farm buildings, now converted into stylish, modern guest rooms. French doors open from the leafy brick terrace into a wood-floored lounge with whitewashed walls, soft white sofas and glass-topped dining tables. Bedrooms backing onto an enclosed lawn boast hemp-style carpets, hefty, upholstered bed heads and sunken spotlights. And to add to the style and comfort of the rooms, Paul and Ingrid are just the kind of natural hosts we pound the roads to find. They've been in the game for thirteen years but are certainly not resting on any laurels. Ingrid is constantly working on the rooms to keep them fresh and contemporary and they'll be able to point you in the direction of local eateries. A rather rotund pair of pets can be found waddling round the gardens, completing a very homely scene that you will join on the lush banks of the Little Ruo.

Rooms: 5 suites, all with en-suite bath and shower.
Price: R375 pp sharing. Singles R600.
Meals: Self-catering.
Directions: Take the M3 from Cape Town towards Muizenburg. Take the Ladies Mile exit and turn left from the off-ramp. At the traffic-lights turn left onto the M42. Continue until Willow Road on the left. 350m on left.

Long Acre

Hamish and Alison Currie
Soetvlei Aveue, Constantia 7806
Tel: 021-715-2498 Fax: 021-794-1172
Email: backtoafrica@iafrica.com
Cell: 082-469-2740

A squadron of rotund jack russels rushed out to greet me when I rolled up at Long Acre. Alison had been laying waste to the garden and pushed sacks of winter clippings aside to welcome me in with lunch-time offers of a G&T by a crackling log fire (declined of course). I sank into a fabulously springy hearth-side armchair, deposing one disgruntled dog, and, with the mantlepiece clock stopped at 11:15, happily forgot about any afternoon appointments. Officially this is self-catering (a cosy garden cottage with a private entrance and French windows on to the lawn, pool and garden), though you'll soon realise that the experience is anything but. Alison's Irish heritage means hospitality is in the blood and here the old cliché of a one-of-the-family welcome really does ring true. What a pity for them I became the in-law you just can't get rid of. Two days later I was back for supper (well, we all were actually…), devouring a huge plate of roast springbok sprinkled with home-grown rosemary, followed by steaming malva (sticky toffee) pudding. Over a nightcap, Hamish told me animatedly about his game reintroduction project and the joys of long-haul flights with air-sick antelope. He's also a vet, and a passionate fisherman and can organise all sorts of water-borne outings for the adventurous. Personally, nestled in that armchair and full of grub, I rather doubted I would make it any further than the drinks cabinet.

Rooms: 1 garden cottage with 1 king bedroom, shower, bath, kitchen, sitting room and verandah.
Price: R300. Singles R400.
Meals: Full breakfast included. Dinners by arrangement. Price depends!
Directions: From CT take M3, turn off signed Constantia. L towards Constantia at end of slip road, then L onto R42 into Spaanschemat River Rd. Follow past Peddlers on the Bend, then L into Firgrove Way, then 1st R into Soetvlei. House just before American International School.

Lusthof

Judy Badenhorst
Rose Way, Constantia 7848
Tel: 021-794-6598 Fax: 021-794-8602
Email: lusthof@mweb.co.za Web: www.lusthof.co.za
Cell: 083-412-3455

Everyone in the world seems to know Judy, whether through the Old Cape Farm Stall, from Buitenverwachting wine estate, from the Spaanschemat River Café… or in our case through obscure family links in Britain. You probably know her yourself. All her projects seem to be touched by magic and become social temples for the Constantia faithful. We spent our first two weeks in South Africa staying in her guest cottage in the garden and it was a terrible moment when we finally had to leave the nest and look after ourselves. The cottage, with cable TV, heaters for winter and kitchenette, has doors onto its own patio, where you can lie on sunloungers and admire the flower garden or wallow in the newly-installed swimming pool. Judy is truly a maestro in the kitchen and literally anything that is made by her will be worth camping overnight for. If she doesn't have time to make breakfast herself, then it will be equally good at the River Café. You shouldn't choose Lusthof if you are after a fully-catered guest house with 24-hour service. But if you like to feel part of the furniture, and among friends, then this is the place for you. Mention must finally be made of Chebe, Judy's huge, shaggy, good-natured, lemon-loving bouvier (somewhere between a Scotty and a gorilla) – an integral part of the set-up. Chebe is a dog by the way. *Airport pick-up and car rental can be organised.*

Rooms: 1 twin cottage with shower and separate bath and kitchenette.
Price: R250 – R350 pp sharing.
Meals: The cottage is self-catering and has a fully stocked kitchenette. Or Judy will provide dinner, breakfast and picnics on request.
Directions: Ask when booking for a full map.

Plough Hill Cottage

Claudia and Vivian Bickford-Smith
25 Urmarah Close, Constantia 7806
Tel: 021-794-7894 Fax: 021-794-7894
Email: mwplough@mweb.co.za Web: www.ploughhill.co.za
Cell: 083-615-3509

Vivian's a history machine – tour guide, teacher and author supreme. Claudia's a publisher, so will no doubt be appalled by my poetic flourish. Anyway they are a wonderfully welcoming couple and we were quickly talking history dons (my uni subject) and friends in common over coffee on the shaded verandah. Table Mountain and a garden overflowing with roses, lavender and jacaranda politely lined up to form the perfect backdrop on a blissful summer morning. I cast a covetous eye over an enormous mountain-facing swimming pool and imagined how blissful it would be to plunge in after a vigorous yomp in those same mountains. The cottage itself occupies a sheltered spot under a plum tree sagging with succulent fruit. French doors flood the sitting room with sunshine, picking out the old maps and prints that hang on the walls. A dark, wooden, Indian sea chest with a ship carved intricately into the top has settled under the window and I spied hardback copies of some of Vivian's published works strewn casually on the coffee table. The double bedroom also has French doors and looks onto a small courtyard and a herb garden. The Bickford-Smiths are delightfully 'hands-on' hosts, joining guests for a drink and pointing them in the direction of everything that's worth seeing. Mod cons in the cottage include satellite TV, phone, email and fax is available on request.

Rooms: 1 cottage comprising of double room with en-suite shower, lounge area and kitchenette.
Price: R350 – R500 for cottage per night. Reduced rates for longer stays. Bookings available from 15th January 2006.
Meals: Self-catering, but continental breakfast on request. Fridge stocked with eggs and bacon.
Directions: Faxed or emailed on request.

Southdown

Nicki and Tim Scarborough
51a Klaassens Rd, Constantia 7800
Tel: 021-762-2323 Fax: 021-762-2323
Email: kleinbosheuwel@iafrica.com Web: www.kleinbosheuwel.co.za

This is the second of Nicki and Tim's brilliantissimo B&Bs. They should give lectures on the art of hosting. Southdown was bought in March in a state of near-dereliction and has already been whipped into heavenly shape. With a small-scale Lost Gardens of Heligan on her hands, Nicki peeled back the jungle to find pathways, walls and, best of all, enormous stone-paved circles just in the right spot between the house and pool. Table Mountain towers behind. It is well known that people with fine gardens have fine houses and this is a leader amongst them. The house is a colonial Georgian pile orientated towards the exquisite view. Breakfast is taken in a spectacular dining room with a glass wall looking to sea in the distance. The eggs may be poached, but the mounted animal heads definitely aren't – one of Nicki's sons works in nature conservation. The house is filled with beastly surprises: zebra skins, porcupine-quill lamps, onyx lamp stands, a whole stuffed eagle, a wildebeest's head, a piano, deep carpets and couches, marble bathrooms and terraces off most rooms. Tim and Nicki do not live in-situ, but magically appear (like the shopkeeper) when needed. They are nonetheless full-on hosts, oozing vigour and enthusiasm and have a habit of adopting their guests as friends. I for one am going there for Christmas! A fabulous place. *Kirstenbosch gardens and restaurant 2 minutes' walk.*

Rooms: 3: 1 queen, 1 twin and 1 king, all with en-suite bath and shower.
Price: Double occ. from R395 – R450 pp. Singles R630.
Meals: Full breakfast included.
Directions: Emailed or faxed on booking. Also on web site.

Entry Number: 55

Map Number: 1

Vygeboom Manor

Callie & Luli Hamman
14 Valmar Rd, Valmary Park, Durbanville 7550
Tel: 021-975-6020 Fax: 021-976-5029
Email: vygeboom@gtrade.co.za Web: www.vygeboom.co.za
Cell: 083-270-4021

Vygeboom is a destination in itself. Callie is a prosthodontist and microlight pilot, Luli an artist and these disparate talents merge seamlessly to create a fantastic guest house experience in Cape Town's northern suburbs. Durbanville is an ideal location for visitors, with easy access to the bright lights and beaches of Cape Town, but also on established wine routes (including the ruling triumvirate of Paarl, Stellenbosch and Franschhoek). Prisoners of the game of golf will also find themselves embarrassed for choice. But this assumes, of course, that you feel like going anywhere. Luli has based the themes of each amazing room on her own gigantic and wonderful murals, doffing the cap to Rubens, Matisse, Manet etc. Comfort, however, does not play second fiddle to artistic whimsy – beds are huge, bathrooms luxurious. Add to this charming hosts (Callie does his dentistry next door), spectacular views to the distant wall of the Hottentots Holland Mountains, a vast sitting room with a three-quarter size snooker table and a large pool in the garden. At the same price as last year, Vygeboom remains outstanding value. *Callie can organize microlight trips for guests – an exciting way to go whale-spotting in season. Free access to health club/gym.*

Rooms: 5: 1 double, 4 twins; 3 with en-suite bath, 2 with en-suite shower.
Price: R300 – R400 pp sharing. Ask about specials for families and groups.
Meals: Full breakfast included and barbeque dinners by arrangement.
Directions: Junction 23 N1, R302 north for 5km. Turn right into Valmar Rd.

Langebaan Beach House

Claire Green
44 Beach Road, Entrance in Jacoba St, Langebaan 7357
Tel: 022-772-2625 Fax: 022-772-1432
Email: lbh@intekom.co.za Web: www.langebaanbeachhouse.com

This very popular, friendly B&B was once Claire's family's seaside retreat in the days when Langebaan was a small fishing village. It has grown since then, but still has a nice holiday feel. The house is Claire's home, complete with two typically upbeat labradors (and two cats), and set right on the lagoon. The garden goes directly down to sand and water. The original part is over 100 years old, while the rest has gradually been added as the family expanded – most of it is now for guests. Two of the bright bedrooms are 'suites', with their own sitting rooms and views to the water. There is a big communal sitting area where Claire's collection of model boats lives and the garden has a plunge pool and sun-loungers. Breakfast is served in the glass-enclosed verandah, looking down to the beach. The sea is safe and swimmable, if a little chilly, and all water sports are allowed – swimming, motor- and wind-powered vessels, fishing and water-skiing (the Cape Sports Centre hires out water sports gear just up the beach). 250,000 migrating birds, including flamingos, live at the wilderness end of the lagoon and there are five restaurants within walking distance from the house. Claire herself is relaxed, warm-spirited and extremely knowledgeable about what's going on in her neck of the woods. Which is a lot.

Rooms: 4: 2 suites, each with sitting room; 1 double and 1 twin. All rooms have en-suite shower.
Price: Suites from R350 – R500 pp sharing. Other rooms from R200 – R350 pp. Singles on request.
Meals: Full breakfast included. For other meals there are lots of great restaurants in Langebaan – 5 within walking distance.
Directions: Directions will be faxed or emailed when you book.

Kersefontein

Julian Melck

between Hopefield and Velddrif, Hopefield 7355
Tel: 022-783-9900 or 022-783-0850 Fax: 022-783-0850
Email: info@kersefontein.co.za Web: www.kersefontein.co.za
Cell: 083-454-1025

Nothing has changed at Kersefontein since the last edition. Julian's convivial dinner parties are still a reason to book in on their own. And Julian himself remains a Renaissance man, described on his business card as 'Farmer, Pig-killer, Aviator and Advocate of the High Court of S.A.' He farms cows, sheep and horses on the surrounding fields, and wild boar appear deliciously at dinner. He also hires and pilots a six-seater plane and a flight round the Cape or along the coast is a must. He modestly leaves out his virtuosity as a pianist and organist and some of us trooped off one Sunday morning, braving a 40-minute sermon in Afrikaans, to hear toccatas by Bach, Giguot and Widor at the local church. When not eating, riding or flying, guests lounge on the pontoon, swim in the river or read books from Kersefontein's many libraries. Or they use the house as a base to visit the coast or the Swartland wineries, which are really taking off. The homestead is seventh generation and the rooms either Victorian or African in temperament, with antiques handed down by previous Melcks. You are fed like a king, but treated as a friend and I am always recommending people to go there.

Rooms: 6: 3 doubles and 3 twins; 1 with shower, 2 with bath and 3 with bath and shower.
Price: R350 – R450 pp sharing. No single supplements. Aircraft hire prices depend on the trip. Julian will also do fly/picnic trips out to various destinations.
Meals: Full breakfast is included. Dinners by arrangement: R120 – R150 excluding wine.
Directions: From Cape Town take N7 off N1. Bypass Malmesbury, 5km later turn left towards Hopefield. After 50km bypass Hopefield, turn right signed Velddrif. After 16km farm signed on right just before grain silos. Cross bridge and gates on the left.

The Oystercatcher's Haven at Paternoster

Sandy Attrill
48 Sonkwasweg, Paternoster 7381
Tel: 022-752-2193 Fax: 022-752-2192
Email: honihiki@global.co.za Web: www.oystercatchershaven.com
Cell: 082-414-6705 or 083-267-7051

Sandy and Wayne, ex film and advertising people, do things in style and their guest house is a knock-out! The Cape Dutch house sits on the fringes of the Cape Columbine Nature Reserve, a spectacular, fynbos-covered, hand-shaped headland, bearing its lighthouse aloft like a nine-million-watt jewel. All along the coast and a mere 40 metres in front of the house knobbly fingers of grey and black granite merge into the sea and around the rocks there are secret white sandy coves where the dolphins come throughout the year. It is quite simply beautiful and I can assure you that the Oystercatcher is a haven by anyone's standards. Heave yourself out of that plunge-pool, off the rocks and away from the view (available from your bed) and head inside the house. The interior, with its white walls, untreated timbers and reed-and-pole ceilings, is intentionally blank-yet-rustic to showcase some exquisite pieces, such as a four-foot-high Angolan drum, some Malinese sinaba paintings (you'll have to come and see them if you don't know what they are), Persian rugs, art-deco couches, courtyards…. Just about everything is a hook for an eager eye. Beds and bedrooms too are bliss – trust me, I'm a professional.

Rooms: 3: 1 queen with en-suite bath and shower; 1 queen and 1 twin, both with en-suite showers. All rooms have private entrances.
Price: From R375 – R540 pp sharing.
Meals: Full breakfast included. Meals by arrangement and you can eat on the beach if the weather permits. Picnics from R60.
Directions: From Cape Town take the N1 and then the R27 north following signs to Vredenburg. Follow signs straight through Vredenburg to Paternoster (15km). At crossroads turn left and travel a full 1km towards the Columbine Reserve. Turn right into Sonkwas Rd, it is No. 48.

Blue Dolphin

George Koning
12 Warrelklip St, Paternoster
7381
Tel: 022-752-2001
Fax: 0866-714-5109
Email:
bluedolphin@mweb.co.za
Web: www.bluedolphin.co.za

The Blue Dolphin concept is simple, natural and refreshing. Four very comfortable rooms, with views of the sea, a verandah with a day-bed for lying on and listening to the surf, a sandy beach that stretches from the house… and two great restaurants up the road for lunch and dinner. The house is open, wooden, breezy, with whites and blues dominating in tune with the beach and sea. All you have to do is lazily watch out for dolphins (and whales in season), kick sand along the strand, eat your breakfast, chat with George, read a book… chill those nerves, untie those muscles. Book early for the flower season (end of August/beginning of September). The dune fynbos blooms impressively and a rash of tiny brightly-coloured flowers emerge like magic from the very sand itself. George has kept the number of rooms down to just four so that he always has plenty of time for everyone. The bedrooms are well kitted-out with heated towel rails, satellite TV, mohair blankets, great beds and linen. Next door is the new Baby Dolphin, a self-catering option, but you can have breakfast at the Blue Dolphin. It has a giant fireplace, a wide, sea-facing verandah and a track straight out to the beach. *Columbine Nature Reserve and the Fossil Museum are nearby.*

Rooms: 4: all doubles with en-suite shower.
Price: R250 pp sharing. Singles R350.
Meals: Full breakfast included. Excellent meals at Voorstrand and Ahoy Galley restaurants in Paternoster.
Directions: Take the N1 from Cape Town towards Paarl. Take the R27 leading to the West Coast and follow this road until the turn-off to Vredenburg. Follow signs straight thro' Vredenburg. Carry over the 4-way stop in Paternoster and follow signs to Blue Dolphin.

Hoekie

Volker and Ingrid Wessolowski
38 Strandloperweg, Paternoster 7381
Tel: 022-752-2077 Fax: 022-752-2077
Email: info@paternoster-guesthouse.co.za
Web: www.paternoster-guesthouse.co.za Cell: 082-660-6660

Volker was a boat designer and engineer before he crafted this cracking beach house. Neatly stowed in a little corner – or Afrikaans "hoekie" – of Paternoster, it's an ideal spot to bask in West Coast sunshine and Ingrid's impeccable hospitality, while guiltlessly gorging yourself on Cape crustacean and fresh fish. She's a tour guide and chef who wouldn't let me leave without sampling a bowl of her lobster bisque with home-made bread (both second to none). Steadily digesting I took a stroll around this compact house, full, it seems, of 'hoekies', each hiding a new surprise and a lick of kudu-leather, percale-cotton or exotic-wood luxury. There's the prow of a boat mounted on the wall and an exquisite miniature schooner in the sitting room, a high open-plan space that connects to a swish kitchen and a glass-roofed dining room. Upstairs (up hand-made wooden stairs, in fact) a roof terrace overlooks a small pool and connects two gabled bedrooms, deliciously dressed with distressed, wooden furniture and blessed by Ingrid's eye for detail. Beds-wise, there's also a lovingly renovated fisherman's cottage nearby for those after a little more privacy. This place just breathes seaside freshness and I would happily have whiled away my afternoon, gazing from the front verandah across a whiter-than-white beach to the bay, a whale-watching hotspot. Hoekie had me hooked. The beaches of Cape Columbine nearby can be explored in the Hoekie 4WD.

Rooms: 3: 1 queen with bath/shower in room, sep toilet; 2 twins both with en-suite with bath/shower.
Price: R250 – R550 pp sharing. Singles from R450.
Meals: Full breakfast included. Meals can be arranged. Self-catering optional.
Directions: R27 from Cape Town to Vredenburg. Drive through Vredenburg15km to Paternoster. At stop sign follow signs to Hoekie Guesthouse.

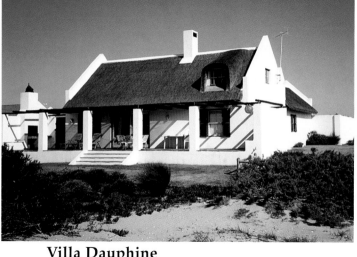

Villa Dauphine

David and Ann Dixon
166 Sandpiper Close, Golden Mile Bvd, Britannia Bay 7382
Tel: 022-742-1926 Fax: 022-742-1926
Email: dadixon@mweb.co.za Web: www.villadauphine.com
Cell: 083-409-3195

Cosseted within its own walls, Villa Dauphine shuns the harsh sandveld of the interior and focuses instead on the bay whose broad crescent passes not twenty yards from the stoep. Here you sit and peacefully beat out the rhythm of the waves. Two finned backs breached some 30 metres from shore, my first ever sighting of wild dolphins. David and Anne were unimpressed. The day before great schools of them had been leaping, frolicking, doing crosswords and playing chess right in front of the house. You can take boat rides out to cement the friendship and navigate the Berg River for bird-watching. The house is country cottage pretty, thatched and beamed with solid furniture, pots of fresh flowers, terracotta tiles, lots of whites and woods. Two atticky bedrooms are found up wooden steps, which lead from a flowery, sun-trapping, wind-breaking courtyard. The other is in the house itself. David used to be a vet and he and Anne are real bird enthusiasts. If you are too, they'll point you off to the Berg River (above 190 bird species) but everyone must visit the beautiful West Coast National Park nearby (250,000 migratory birds and a stunning turquoise lagoon). Golf courses and excellent restaurants nearby. Come here in spring and the countryside is carpeted in flowers. They appear out of nowhere and grow right down to the water line.

Rooms: 2 'units': 1 suite with 2 double bedrooms with a shared bathroom (bath & shower); 1 twin with en-suite bath and shower.
Price: From R225 – R300 pp sharing. Singles on request.
Meals: Full breakfast included.
Directions: From Cape Town take R27 to Vredenburg turn-off. Turn left to Vredenburg. At first lights, turn right to St Helena Bay. 10km to Stompneusbaai sign. Turn left. 17km turn left to Britannia Bay. 2km. Turn right at White Entrance to Golden Mile. Turn right and after 2nd speed bump turn left.

Map Number: 2

Oystercatcher Lodge

Luc and Sue Christen

1st Avenue, Shelley Point St, St Helena Bay
Tel: 022-742-1202 Fax: 022-742-1201
Email: info@oystercatcherlodge.co.za Web: www.oystercatcherlodge.co.za
Cell: 082-903-9668

You can't miss Oystercatcher Lodge. If you do, you'll end up in the sea. It's set right on the tip of Shelley Point, overlooking the full curve of Britannia Bay with its flocks of cormorants, pods of passing dolphins and wallowing whales (in season). Luc (smiley and Swiss) and Sue (home-grown, but equally smiley) are both from the hotel trade. After years doing a great job for other people deep in the Mpumalanga bushveld, they decided to work for themselves and made the move. Quite a change. Here on the West Coast the sea air has a salty freshness unlike anywhere else, the sun shines brilliantly on arcing white beaches and the crunching waves are a bottomless blue. A special spot indeed where the Christens' newly-built house juts out towards the ocean like the prow of a ship, a large pointy pool in its bows. Each of the six rooms, painted in calming sandy colours, looks across grassy dunes and beach to the sea. All have extra-large bathrooms. Breakfast feasts are served in the bar, but for other meals you can head next-door to the family restaurant. It's seafood-oriented and the local speciality is fish tongue, "deep-fried like calamari and soft like a mushroom," Luc tells me. It sounds exciting!

Rooms: 6: 4 kings, 2 with bath and shower, 2 with shower only, 2 twins with shower only.
Price: R350 – R450 per person.
Meals: Full breakfast included. Other meals available at the Christens' restaurant next door.
Directions: From R27 heading north turn L to Vredenburg. At lights turn R to St. Helena Bay. Turn L 10km on to Stompneusbaai. 17km on turn L to Britannia Bay. 2km on turn R into white Golden Mile entrance. Turn R continue right through to Shelley Point. Oystercatcher is at the far end.

Petersfield Farm Cottages

Hedley Peter
Petersfield Guest Farm,Citrusdal 7340
Tel: 022-921-3316 Fax: 022-921-3316
Email: info@petersfieldfarm.co.za Web: www.petersfieldfarm.co.za
Cell: 083-626-5145

Hedley is an instantly likable and funny host and Petersfield his family farm (citrus and rooibos tea), the property ranging over the back of the mountain behind the main house, forming a huge private wilderness reserve. De Kom, an idyllic, simple-but-stylish stone cottage perched high in sandstone mountains will appeal to your inner romantic. This charming electricity-free cottage is lit by hurricane lamps and flares with gas for the stove, fridge and hot water. A private plunge pool with river stones at the bottom overlooks this secret valley with the Olifants River and purpling Cederberg peaks as a backdrop. And what a setting, guarded to the front by a citrus orchard, to the rear by craggy sandstone and looking deep and far from the stoep down the mountain. There is a secluded farm dam nearby (300 metres) to swim in or picnic by while watching nesting eagles. Or, 2km away, there is (electrified) Dassieklip cottage, a sweet wooden mountain cabin secreted in its own kloof and reached down an avenue of oaks. It too has a plunge pool to cool off in and other mod cons such as fridge, air-conditioning, TV and CD player. Bring your own food for both cottages, although breakfast materials for you to cook can be provided. *Wood is provided at no extra charge and pets are also welcome.*

Rooms: 2 cottages with 2 bedrooms each.
Price: Week-nights: R400 for 2 people, R480 for 3, R550 for 4, R600 for 5/6. Weekends, public holidays, flower season (15 Aug-15 Sept): R450 for 2, R550 for 3, R650 for 4, R750 for 5/6. Prices are per night and for whole cottage.
Meals: Self-catering, but breakfast materials provided in the fridge by prior arrangement.
Directions: From Cape Town 4km after Citrusdal on your left on the N7 travelling towards Clanwilliam.

Boschkloof and Oude Boord Cottages

Mariet and Doempie Smit
Boschkloof, Citrusdal 7340
Tel: 022-921-3533 Fax: 022-921-3533
Email: boschkloof@kingsley.co.za Web: www.citrusdal.info/boschkloof
Cell: 082-734-9467

We bumped along six or so sandy kilometres, past orchards of citrus trees and stumbled upon some sort of prelapsarian idyll! A private valley, cocooned in the Sneeuberg Conservancy, in the Cederberg foothills, flanked by sandstone mountains, its orange groves watered by a natural stream, the rocks and plants etched in hyper-real clarity by a setting sun. There are Bushman rock art sites, natural pools in the river to cool off in and hiking on mountain trails to be done from the house in the early morning and evening. We parked under an oak tree and were met by Mariet, her two small daughters and two large dogs. On return from a dip in the river we met Doempie and a glass of wine and were soon being treated to crayfish kebabs from the braai, seated under the oak with views up the kloof and a sensational tone to the air. The Smits live in one of the original farmhouses here, their guests next door in another or in a new-built, old-feel cottage, Oude Boord, hidden across the stream and under the orange trees with klipspringers for early morning company. Although it is a self-catering arrangement, you are in such comparative proximity out here that you might as well be at a B&B, except with far more space and privacy. And the beds and baths? No time for detail – just trust me, they're spot on!

Rooms: 2 cottages sleeping 6 with 1 double, 1 twin and double sofa-bed, all bedrooms have en/s bathrooms.
Price: R400 – R500 for 2 people. R100 for each extra person.
Meals: Fully-equipped kitchen – these are self-catering cottages. Mariet can provide breakfast materials for you by prior arrangement.
Directions: N7 to Citrusdal – turn into village, go left into Voortrekker Rd and right into Muller St. Carry straight on, it becomes a dirt road, follow it for 7km.

Rockwood Cottage

Pam and Noel Mills

Rockwood Farm, PO Box 131, Citrusdal 7340
Tel: 022-921-3517 Fax: 022-921-2653
Email: amills@new.co.za Web: www.citrusdal.info/rockwood
Cell: 072-222-3344

Rockwood is an extremely beautiful protea farm in the Cederberg highlands 800 metres above sea level. Both the main house where Pam and Noel live and their large and lovely guest cottage (self-catering) have front stoeps that overlook a succession of dams, the hinterland channelled away for miles and miles by rugged sandstone mountains. The highest peaks of the Sneeuberg Conservancy are often covered with snow in winter. The guest cottage is cradled among giant rocks with the eponymous rockwood trees growing from beneath. And to the front a story-book stream burbles past the stoep and oak trees there. A wide expanse of lawn leads to more treasure. Noel has created a natural rock swimming pool that is filled all year round by a river with fresh, drinkable water that cascades gently over the rocks. A sundowner either in the pool or in the jacuzzi just above allows you time to digest the magnificent view and feel properly smug. Behind this there is a deep gorge and waterfall, an idyllic world of water and rock, full of wild flowers in season with two bush trails cut through natural gardens. Pam and Noel will happily show their guests all there is to do on the property and in the region, still so unspoiled by tourism. *Children over twelve permitted.*

Rooms: 1 cottage with 2 bedrooms; 1 double and 1 twin sharing 1 bath with shower above. Plus an outside bedroom with twin beds and en-suite shower.
Price: R550 per night for two people, R100 for each additional person. Also R100 per day for use of the jacuzzi (electricity doesn't come cheap in the hills!).
Meals: The cottage is self-catering. Noel and Pam will point you towards local restaurants which are 5 minutes away.
Directions: From N7 into Citrusdal. At four-way intersection in centre of village straight over and up mountain for 7km. 2nd white gates on your left.

Map Number: 2 & 3

Entry Number: 66

Mount Ceder

André and Jaen Marais

Grootrivier Farm, Cederberg, Koue Bokkeveld 6836
Tel: 023-317-0113 Fax: 023-317-0543
Email: mountceder@lando.co.za Web: www.mountceder.co.za

Do not lose confidence as you rumble along the dirt roads that lead through the Koue Bokkeveld nature conservancy to this secluded valley – it's always a couple more turns. Finally you will arrive in the very heart of the Cederberg, dry sandstone mountains rising all around you in impressive dimensions. You will be given the key to your new home and drive off along half a kilometre of sand track to one of three fantastic rustic stone cottages. The river flows past the reeds and rock right by the cottages, clear, deep and wide all year round. You can swim and lie around drying on flat rocks. Birds love it here too. I imagine sitting out on that stoep, on those wooden chairs, looking at that view, beer or wine in hand… a piece of heaven as they say. You can either self-cater or you can eat at André and Jaen's restaurant back at the lodge. There are a few other cottages nearer the lodge, which are fine, but you must ask for the stone cottages, which are in a league of their own. A pristine slice of unspoiled nature, cherished by a very knowledgeable Marais family who will help with Bushman rock art, horse-riding and fauna and flora. Do not reach for your red pen by the way… that *is* how you spell ceder (in Afrikaans) and that is how you spell Jaen!

Rooms: 3 river cottages with 3 bedrooms each.
Price: R800 – R1,350 per cottage per night self-catering (cottage sleeps 6).
Meals: Meals on request, breakfast R40, dinner R85 (extra for wine).
Directions: From Ceres follow signs to Prince Alfred's Hamlet/Op-die-Berg, up Gydo Pass past Op-die-Berg. First right signed Cederberge – follow tar for 17km then straight on on dirt road for another 34km into a green valley.

Villa Tarentaal

Christine and Mike Hunter
Tulbagh 6820
Tel: 023-230-0868 Fax: 023-230-0101
Email: mhunter@intekom.co.za

Known locally as 'Man of the Mountain', Mike's knowledge of the walking routes around the sleepy town of Tulbagh is surely unsurpassed. But his pride and joy, and the defining feature of Villa Tarentaal, is his garden. He has created lawns that would make the green-keepers of Augusta, well... green with envy, and a stroll around this sanctuary with the Man of the Mountain is a horticultural and ornithological education. Spidering their way up the mustard-coloured house are wisteria and grape vines, adding to the orgy of colour provided by the roses. As we sauntered past the tulbaghia, the liquid ambers and the strelitzias, Mike suddenly stopped in his tracks and pointed skyward: with its distinctive cry, a fish eagle swooped over our heads and soared off towards the Winterhoek Mountains that provide the backdrop to Villa Tarentaal. The terrace overlooks the pool and I sat sipping tea, as Mike and Christine plastered over some of the gaping holes in my knowledge about the natural world surrounding me. They claim to cater for the quiet traveller and where better to unwind than in a snug, well-equipped cottage overlooking garden, vineyard and mountain? Christine also offers therapeutic massages and aromatherapy.

Rooms: 2 cottages: one with 1 twin and 1 double and separate bath/shower room; one with 1 double (with extra single on request) and sofa-bed in lounge, separate bath/shower room.
Price: R210 – R250 pp sharing.
Meals: Full breakfast included.
Directions: N1 from Cape Town to exit 47 Wellington/Franschhoek/Klapmuts turn-off, left onto R44 via Wellington. Follow for approx. 1 hour to Tulbagh. Straight through town, 1.2km on left.

Tulbagh Country House

Ginny Clark
24 Church St, Tulbagh 6820
Tel: 023-230-1171 Fax: 023-230-0721
Email: tulbaghguesthse@mweb.co.za Web: www.tulbaghguesthouse.co.za
Cell: 082-416-6576

This 200-year-old B&B in the heart of the historic village of Tulbagh looked too inviting to drive past without taking a peek. Built in 1809 and still retaining many of its original features, the house is the epitome of classic Cape Dutch living and has been beautifully restored to its former glory by Ginny. Antiques and original artwork catch the eye at every glance and guests are free to roam and admire. Seated on her twin gargantuan couches, or around her dining table, Ginny will happily impart her extensive knowledge of Church Street's history, thereby completing the picture of the historic charm of the Witzenberg Valley. She treats her guests as friends and they naturally treat her likewise. In her guest book, Ginny has appraisals galore, markedly for her breakfasts, a table spread with antique crockery, silver cutlery and the feast itself: 'For those who follow, beware Ginny's breakfasts – they are wonderful' and such like. We crossed the road, escorted by a peacock, to find the self-catering cottage. Simple and charming, this cottage, which was formerly a wagon shed, is kitted out with board games, reference books and a large French-cricket-sized garden that stretches to the river. The authenticity of Ginny's hospitality makes a stay here a real treat. *Ask about children. A few minutes' walk to very good restaurants. DSTV now available by request in bedrooms.*

Rooms: 3: 1 king en/s bath with shower above, 1 suite with 1 double + 1 twin, en/s bath. Self-catering cottage with 2 doubles & 1 twin, 1 bath with shower + sep toilet.
Price: From R250 pp sharing. Singles R300. Self-catering cottage: R175 pp sharing, R100 pp for 6+ people, R200 for a single person.
Meals: Full breakfast included for the rooms. Breakfast at the main house an optional R40 for self-catering cottage.
Directions: From Cape Town take N1 to exit 47 Wellington/Franschhoek/Klapmuts turn-off, left onto R44 via Wellington. Follow R44 to Tulbagh. In village centre take a left to be parallel to main road.

Entry Number: 69   Map Number: 2 & 3

Bartholomeus Klip Farmhouse

Lesley Gillett
Elandsberg Farm, Hermon 7308
Tel: 022-448-1820 Fax: 022-448-1829
Email: bartholomeus@icon.co.za Web: www.parksgroup.co.za
Cell: 082-829-4131

Heavenly scenery cossets this Victorian homestead in its lush gardens and stands of oak and olive. The wall of the Elandsberg Mountains rises up from the game reserve, reflected in the dammed lake by the house. Here guests can have breakfast on the balcony of the boathouse before heading out for an excursion onto the wheat and sheep farm. You are also taken on late-afternoon game drives to see the zebra, a variety of Cape antelope, buffalo, quaggas (a fascinating experiment to reintroduce an extinct variety of zebra), eagles, flocks of blue crane... and the largest world population of the tiny, endangered geometric tortoises. But just to be out in such nature! The spring flowers are spectacular and there are more than 850 species of plant recorded on the property. Back at the homestead you can cool down in the curious, round, raised reservoir pool, sit in chairs on the stoep; or, if you have more energy, bike off into the reserve or go on guided walks in the mountains. Staff are very friendly, food is exceptional and a reason to stay on its own (and all included in the price). I recommend splashing out on at least two nights. A great place indeed and very popular so book ahead of yourself if possible. *Closed June – July and Christmas.*

Rooms: 5: 2 doubles and 3 twins, 5 with bath and shower. New self-catering cottage that sleeps 8 with 3 doubles and bunk beds.
Price: R850 – R1,050 (winter), R1,175 – R1,375 (summer) pp sharing. Singles on application. Includes meals & game drives. R530 – R700 pp for self-c cottage, 0-3 free, 3-15 half-price in cottage.
Meals: Coffee & rusks, brunch, high tea, snacks & sundowners & 4-course dinner included in price.
Directions: From CT take N1 towards Paarl. Exit 47, left at Stop. Follow Agter-Paarl Rd over 4-ways. L signed Ceres. Follow 30km, past Malmesbury sign to L. Go next R signed Bo-Hermon. Gravel road for 2km. Bartholomeus Klip signed to L – 5km.

Map Number: 2 & 3

Entry Number: 70

Oude Wellington Estate

Rolf and Vanessa Schumacher
Bainskloof Pass Rd, Wellington 7654
Tel: 021-873-2262 Fax: 021-873-4639
Email: info@kapwein.com Web: www.kapwein.com

There seems to be so much to catch the eye even as you rumble along the 800 metre paved and cobbled road to Oude Wellington: vineyards on both sides, ostentatious peacocks, geese and hadedas, pet ostriches peering over a fence. And that afternoon four pregnant alpacas that had just arrived all the way from Australia were to be added to the menagerie. Rolf and Vanessa are clearly the hospitable types (how else could ostriches find a home on a winery?). It took them two years to restore the whole estate to its former glory as a wine-grape farm. Four rustic double rooms are in the original farmhouse (built in 1790) with high, thatched ceilings, low pole beams, whitewashed walls and yet underfloor heating and air con; the other two are in the more modern main building (well, 1836!), along with the beautiful farm kitchen with old-fashioned pots, pans and irons, billiard room and bar, and a terrace overlooking the vineyards, where breakfast is served in the summer. There is a partly-shaded pool off to the side of the main house, a brandy still in the barn, and handily on the premises is a restaurant popular with the locals (always a good sign). Guests are also invited to watch wine-making taking place at the right time of year. "We farm and dine and love company," say Rolf and Vanessa in their brochure!

Rooms: 6: all doubles with en-suite Victorian baths.
Price: R250 pp sharing. R350 single.
Meals: Full breakfast included. Restaurant on premises.
Directions: Turn into Church Street (Kerkstraat) in Wellington which becomes the Bainskloof Rd (R301/3). 2.5km out of Wellington on right-hand side follow brown signs to Oude Wellington.

Kleinfontein

Tim and Caroline Holdcroft
PO Box 578, Wellington 7654
Tel: 021-864-1202 Fax: 021-864-1202
Email: kleinfon@iafrica.com Web: www.kleinfontein.com
Cell: 072-108-5895

An evening leg-stretch with Tim proved the perfect antidote to a long and stressful day on the road. Guided by a labrador, an almost-labrador and a hairy, mobile sausage, we strolled past Jersey cows, through a shaded stream and between rows of sunlit vines. Kleinfontein is just an hour from Cape Town at the foot of the Bainskloof Pass and the Holdcrofts are delightful hosts. They'll eat with you, show you their farm and even have you out there clipping the vines or feeding the horses if you show willing (and riding them too if you're saddle-hardened). In fact there's enough to keep you busy here for days, from hiking in surrounding mountains and cellar tours galore, to the leisurely delights of a good book beneath magnificent oak trees, or a wallow in the pool in Caroline's fabulous garden. She is of Kenyan stock and Tim's British, but they spent years in Botswana and over a superb supper we washed down tales of Africa with home-grown cabernet sauvignon. Like me you'll stay in a roomy, restored wing of the thatched Cape Dutch farmhouse with poplar beams and reed ceilings. Like me you'll sleep like a baby. And, like me, you'll wake to breakfast on the verandah with fresh butter and milk, newly-laid eggs and honey straight from the beehive. Sound idyllic? Well, it is. *Closed June and July.*

Rooms: 2 suites, both with sitting room. 1 with en-suite bath and shower, 1 with en-suite bath with shower overhead.
Price: R900 – 1,150 pp sharing. Single supplement + 20%. Includes all meals, drinks and laundry.
Meals: Breakfast, tea/coffee tray, picnic lunch and 4-course dinner included in the price.
Directions: Directions are down dirt roads so map can be emailed or faxed.

Belair

Janet Plumbly
Suid Agter-Paarl Rd, Paarl 7624
Tel: 021-863-1504
Fax: 021-863-1602
Email: info@belair.co.za
Web: www.belair.co.za
Cell: 082-572-7062

A straight 300-metre drive up two narrow strips of weathered red brick, past roaming gangs of guinea-fowl and rows of vines, takes you up to Belair, a beautiful guest house on its own farm beneath the round dome of Paarl Mountain. The view from the doorstep (and the garden and pool) across the valley towards Franschhoek and the Groot Drakenstein is spectacular… and it is rather lovely inside too. Steps lead up from a large threshing-circle style driveway into the hallway and open sitting room, which mixes antique furniture with comfy sofas and bookshelves bursting with swashbucklers. Behind is the bright breakfast conservatory, which looks onto a rose-filled garden. There are definitely green fingers at work here. Janet's light but stylish touch is in evidence everywhere at Belair, from the terraced gardens to the bedrooms themselves, each with its own distinct character. My favourite was the 'red' toile room at the end. From the house, it's a short walk up to the dam where bird life abounds among the reeds (look out for buzzards when it all goes quiet), a great spot for a sundowner. For the more energetic, Paarl Mountain Nature Reserve is further up the hill, and there are lots of golf courses nearby. *Cape Town Waterfront is also only 35 minutes away and there are great restaurants in and about Paarl. Closed June – August 2005.*

Rooms: 4 doubles with en-suite bathrooms. 2 are twins joined together.
Price: R250 – R350 pp sharing. Single supplements not specified.
Meals: Full breakfast included.
Directions: On Suid-Agter Paarl Rd off R101 (next to Fairview Wine Estate).

Roggeland Country House

Gordon Minkley

Roggeland Rd, Dal Josaphat Valley, Paarl 7623
Tel: 021-868-2501 Fax: 021-868-2113
Email: rog@iafrica.com Web: www.roggeland.co.za

The highlight of a stay at Roggeland must be the food! All reports glow with praise: 8-12 different wines to taste pre-dinner, an opportunity to chat to other guests and Gordon himself; then four mouth-watering courses each with a different wine specially chosen to accompany it. Vegetarians will be particularly happy and meals and wines are never repeated during your stay. The house is an 18th-century Cape Dutch homestead with large, thick-walled rooms – sometimes huge – with a variety of original features: beam and reed ceilings, thatch, antique furniture. The dining room, for example, is in an old kitchen with its original grate and cooking implements. Some bedrooms are in the main house and some are separate from it, but none let the side down. Character abounds; floors slope, beams curve and attractive bright-coloured walls are often uneven with age; and there are always fresh flowers and home-made soaps in the rooms. Roggeland is family-run and the atmosphere is friendly and caring as a result. Farmland and mountains surround the property and the Minkleys will organise evening rides on horseback into the foothills. Great hospitality and very good value too. *Children by arrangement. Mountain biking and fishing.*

Rooms: 11: 6 twins, 4 doubles, 1 single. All with en/s bathrooms, 7 with baths and showers, 4 with baths and showers overhead.
Price: Seasonal R520 – R970 pp sharing. Single supplement in high season + 50%.
Meals: The highlight is a 4-course dinner with a different wine at each course and wine-tasting, all included in price. Full breakfast too. Lunches on request.
Directions: Approximately 60km from Cape Town, take exit 59 onto R301 towards Wellington. After 8km on R301 turn right at Roggeland sign. Follow sign onto gravel road for 1km.

Map Number: 2 & 3

Auberge Rozendal

Tanya Louw-Ammann

Jonkershoek Valley, Omega Road, Stellenbosch 7599
Tel: 021-809-2600 Fax: 021-809-2640
Email: rozendal@mweb.co.za Web: www.rozendal.co.za

Kurt, Tanya's father, swears by his home-made vinegar apéritif. This concoction of ten-year-old matured vinegar infused with lavender, coco, carrob, wild olives, seaweed and chillies is said to aid digestion and blood circulation. Apparently some guests love it, although I confess that I winced when swallowing. But then Tanya started to laugh when my stomach rumbled afterwards – the digestive catalyst obviously does the trick! Here on the organic bio-dynamic wine farm their philosophy is health and well-being and the proof is in the eating. With a focus on organic food, delicacies such as abalone, crayfish and free-range duck breast are not to be missed. Meals are served either on the verandah under the vines or in the dining room with its gallery of canvases by world-famous local artists such as Paul Emsley (Tate exhibitor), Cecil Skotnes and Larry Scully. From their 26 hectares, the Ammann family harvest fruits and vegetables, collect eggs from the chickens and milk from their Jersey cows and guests can even participate in the trampling of the grapes in February/March. Separated from the main house, the purpose-built rooms fronted with olive trees and rose bushes have terraces with magnificent views that stretch over vineyards to either Table Mountain or the Botmaskop mountains. If the fresh air and natural environment do not provide you with enough feel-good endorphins, there is a massage therapist who visits on request. *Restaurant closed June – September.*

Rooms: 16: 9 queens, 7 twins, all with en-suite bath with shower overhead.
Price: R430 pp sharing. Singles R575.
Meals: R50 for breakfast. 4-course evening menu R150, 3 courses for R130. Lunch also available.
Directions: From Cape Town take N2, then take exit 33 to Stellenbosch on R310. Turn R at T-jct. After station turn left onto Adam Tas Rd. At second traffic light turn R onto Merriman Rd. At roundabout look out for L'Auberge Rozendal sign. After 2km turn left into Omega St. "A.Rozendal" signposted at top of Omega St.

Cape Winelands, Western Cape

Glenconner

Emma Finnemore
Jonkershoek Valley, PO Box 6124, Stellenbosch 7612
Tel: 021-886-5120   Fax: 021-886-5120
Email: glenconner@icon.co.za   Web: www.winelands.co.za/glenconner
Cell: 082-354-3510

Looking up at the imposing mountains, which rise on both sides of the property, and surrounded by lush vegetation – including all that wild strelitzia and agapanthus – it's almost impossible to believe that you're just four kilometres from Stellenbosch. Such a spectacular location. Sit with a glass of wine on whichever stoep belongs to you for the night and watch the lowering sun paint the mountains a deep pink. You don't need to do any more than this to leaven the spirits by many notches. There are two private-terraced, light-filled, simple country-furnished sleeping locations to choose from: the homestead room with its four-poster bed and English country feel; The Studio, a separate cottage with open-plan bedroom, quaint stripy sitting areas, and second bedroom. A round, spring-water-fed swimming pool sits directly in front of the homestead and a tan-coloured river is a little further away for paddling, picnics and otter-sighting. And horses graze peacefully on the luminous green grass in the paddocks. If all this is not enough for you, the Jonkershoek Nature Reserve is just down the road with some of the best hiking in SA, from two-hour to two-day trails.

Rooms: 3: 2 self-catering B&B cottages (The studio, double, twin & bathroom; Rose Cottage, twin, bathroom & alfresco shower); 1 double room in The Homestead.
Price: R300 – R375 pp sharing B&B; R275 pp sharing self-catering. Discounts for extended stays.
Meals: Continental breakfasts included in B&B or R50 for self-caterers. 5 minutes drive into Stellenbosch with restaurants aplenty.
Directions: From CT, N2 to Stellenbosch, follow signs to Jonkershoek Nature Reserve. 4km from Stellenbosch turn right and cross over bridge on right just after entrance to Neil Ellis vineyard.

Map Number: 2

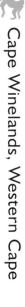

River Manor Country House & Spa

Johan and Leigh Swanepoel
No.6 The Avenue, Stellenbosch 7600
Tel: 021-887-9944 Fax: 021-887-9940
Email: rivermanor@adept.co.za Web: www.rivermanor.co.za

Since the first edition of this guide, River Manor has annexed the listed building next door, and it is fair to say that Johan and Leigh have gone from strength to strength as a result. A central Stellenbosch historical house has become two, and thanks to unwavering Swanepoel enthusiasm and attention to detail, both with their guests and with the decor – the African colonial theme has been successfully carried over to the second, older house – the experience remains a rich one. The new rooms are as large as those in the original house and also furnished with antiques. Beds and bedding are fit for a king and there are many added comforts such as soft towelling bathrobes and port and sherry trays. Old maps on walls, restored leather suitcases and travellers' trunks complete the effect. With the second house also came another garden, where you will find an intimate health and beauty spa (massage, steam room and spa) overlooking a second pool, ideal for pampering the weary or the self-indulgent. Breakfast is served at the poolside or in the large conservatory, another new addition to the original building. Guests have plenty of different spaces in which to relax between exploratory walks around town. *Closed for the month of June.*

Rooms: 16: from Petit (small) to Classic (very nice indeed) to Superior (yet nicer).
Price: Seasonal from R295 – R952 pp sharing. Singles from R550 – R1,600.
Meals: Full breakfast included. Restaurants nearby.
Directions: From CT take the N2 turning to Somerset West. Follow signs to Baden Powell Drive and then to Stellenbosch. On entering Stellenbosch, turn right at 2nd set of traffic lights into Dorp St, follow the road all the way to the top, round to the right and take first left which is The Avenue.

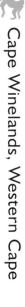
Cape Winelands, Western Cape

Summerwood Guest House

Christian and Ann Baret

28 Jonkershoek Rd, Stellenbosch 7600
Tel: 021-887-4112 Fax: 021-887-4239
Email: summerwood@mweb.co.za Web: www.summerwood.co.za
Cell: 072-633-9341

You notice the huge stinkwood tree first, then the swimming pool (a proper one for swimming in). The smooth, well-tended lawns of the garden seem to beckon the guests, who convene round tables on the terrace in the evening or take a few hours out from wine and history to brave the sun by day. The house itself was built in 1904 by an Italian architect – light and airy, with pretty 'Italian' windows. All the bedrooms are furnished with a summery feel (lots of yellows) and uncluttered, allowing for much clean wall and floor space. The 'room at the top' has panoramic views of garden and mountain. Having seen Ann in action, it is clear that she revels in the relaxed and friendly atmosphere at Summerwood, a far cry from her old life in bustling Johannesburg. She takes the greatest care that all guests are properly orientated by suggesting local excursions and booking you into the best restaurants in town. Some of the best are a short walk away, as is the Jonkershoek Nature Reserve and its mountain trails. And obviously Summerwood is an ideal base for the Stellenbosch wineries. *Stellenbosch is only twenty minutes from Cape Town International Airport. Closed in June.*

Rooms: 9: 5 king-size doubles, 4 twins. All have en-suite bathrooms with baths and showers.
Price: R440 – R725 pp sharing. Singles R650 – R1,000.
Meals: Full breakfast included and served until 9.30 am. Restaurants nearby.
Directions: Exit 33 from N2, L to Stellenbosch R310. At T-jct turn R for 2.5km. 2nd lights turn R up Dorp St to pancake roundabout. L into Meul St, next roundabout R into Plein St, becomes v. Riebeeck St. Keep L at fork, house on R.

Malans Guest House

Laetitia Malan
4 Keerom St, Stellenbosch 7600
Tel: 021-887-8859
Fax: 021-887-9909
Email: malansgh@hotmail.com
Web: www.malansgh.de
Cell: 083-664-1517

Laetitia has uniquely and beautifully decorated each of her guest rooms with antique furniture, kilims on beds, fresh flowers and even proper home-found shower caps in the bathrooms! (Ladies with long hair will know what I'm taking about.) She also collects Voortrekker wedding dresses that date back to the 1860s, while her other lace collections are displayed under glass-covered breakfast tables. And what a breakfast room!, antique Chinese vases and vessels, exotic orchids, furniture inlaid with mother-of-pearl, 'grandparent' clocks, newly-painted frescoes and a flower-imprinted Chinese screen. Laetitia admitted that she may have lived in China in a previous life. She also collects porridges (!) after a fashion: try Matabela porridge (a traditional black-corn variety), maize or oatmeal at breakfast. And if you're not a porridge fan (no reason why you should be), there are plenty of mueslis, fresh fruits, bacon, eggs and all. Laetitia and her daughter treated me to their home-made chocolate cake and my first-ever rooibos tea, and sitting on the verandah in the sunshine I felt serene. A rare quote from one of our other hosts in this book: "I have stayed there myself and I often send guests on to her. Incredible value for money and an experience in its own right. A very interesting owner, with staff who know the art of hospitality and the most beautiful antiques." This all turns out to be pretty exact. *Nearby: cycling, horse-riding, golfing, fly-fishing and wine-tasting.*

Rooms: 5: 1 queen and 1 double with en-suite showers; 3 twins with en/s bath and shower.
Price: R275 – R350 pp sharing. Singles R350 – R450.
Meals: Full breakfast included. Restaurants aplenty nearby.
Directions: From Cape Town take N2, then R310 to Stellenbosch. Drive into town, at railway turn right into Dorp St. After right-hand bend turn left up The Avenue, first left to Neethling St and first left again into Keerom St.

Natte Valleij

Charlene and Charles Milner

R44 betw' Stellenbosch and Paarl, Klapmuts 7625
Tel: 021-875-5171 Fax: 021-875-5475
Email: milner@intekom.co.za Web: www.nattevalleij.co.za

Come and lose yourself in the depths of this wild and fecund garden – or do I mean jungle? Ancient trees such as the rare gingco (the oldest in South Africa, once thought extinct), several 200-year-old oaks and a wealth of growth besides keep the pool, 'moon gate' and old brandy stills secreted in their midst. Guests stay in the simple B&B room next to the main house, its verandah festooned with grandiflora, and eat a breakfast in this most lovely of Cape Dutch homesteads (pictured above), built in 1775. If the weather's fine then you eat out on the patio under its cooling roof of vine. Or you can take one of the cottages lost down garden paths. Vineyard Cottage (pictured below), with direct access to the swimming pool, is the oldest building on the property, its original 1714 reed ceilings still intact. While Cellar Cottage is the most recent addition at 'Nutty Valley', small, cute, rustic, perfect for couples. Come for great charm, rather than luxury, from house and hosts alike. Walks are in all directions up mountains and into surrounding vineyards. *Local bird-watching tours with Charles are a speciality. Well positioned on the Stellenbosch and Paarl wine routes. Self-catering available in the cottages. Horse-riding from the farm.*

Rooms: 3: 1 B&B room, double with en/s bath; 2 cottages (self-catering or B&B): Cellar Cottage sleeps 2 (plus 2 kids' beds); Vineyard Cottage sleeps 6.
Price: B&B R220 – R260 pp sharing. Rates for the whole cottage per night depending on number of people and length of stay: Vineyard R450 – R850; Cellar R420 – R470.
Meals: Full breakfast included in B&B and an optional extra in cottages.
Directions: From Cape Town take N1 exit 47. Turn right onto R44. Farm 4km on left.

The Beautiful South Guest House

Lars and Emily Feldscher
4 Hospital St, Stellenbosch 7600
Tel: 021-883-8171
Email: enjoy@thebeautifulsouth.de Web: www.thebeautifulsouth.de
Cell: 072-545-3072

The genial answer-phone message informs you that Lars and Emily are 'probably out buying lovely things for your breakfast'. They probably are too! This is a special meal at The Beautiful South, with a promise of something different every morning, always home-baked bread, muffins, scones, tomato-mozzarella toast and such specials as 'Fruity Djibuti' from the buffet bar. Not wanting to miss out on their own handiwork, the Feldschers (minus the most recently-arrived family member, clues to whose existence can be spied throughout the house) join their guests at the feasting table. It is here that excursions into the winelands and the surrounding hills are plotted and restaurants are suggested for the evening. The house is quaintly thatched and whitewashed, with wooden windows and the surrounding garden with its mature trees and large pool is directly accessible from each of the bedrooms. While outside is all rustic cottage, inside the emphasis is on style, modernity and function: clean lines, natural materials, modern fittings in bathrooms and high-quality orthopedic beds. A waist-high wall is all that separates the oval, free-standing bath from the sleeping area in the Desert Rose room with its sandstone-tiled floor. While the Sunset Room, with its lime-washed floor and walls, boasts a private wooden terrace. Although new to the guesthouse game, hosting comes only too naturally to Lars and Emily.

Rooms: 4: all doubles, with twins by arrangement. 3 have en-suite bath or shower, 1 has private shower room opposite.
Price: R225 – R395 pp sharing. Singles R290 – R450.
Meals: Breakfast included with new 'special' every morning.
Directions: From N1 or N2 take turn-off marked to Stellenbosch. On entering Stellenbosch turn into Merriman Street. After white pedestrian bridge turn 2nd left into Bosman. Take 1st right into Soete Weide. Next left into Hospital Street.

Babylons Toren

Margie and David Louw

Klapmuts – Simondium Rd, Simondium 7670
Tel: 021-863-3494 Fax: 021-863-1804
Email: babylon@mweb.co.za Web: www.babylonstoren.co.za
Cell: 082-334-3340

Babylons Toren (the Tower of Babylon) is named after the koppie or rocky hill by the house, thought to resemble a ziggurat by earlier (much earlier – the house was built in about 1700) romantics with a bit of imagination. The property is all that you could hope for from a working Cape Dutch farm. There are the old gabled house, the surrounding outbuildings and vineyards, the backdrop of mountains, the sporadic sound of tractors, dogs… and Margie has opened up one of the courtyard outbuildings – these were once dairy, butchery, bakery – and created a rustic, but very stylish cottage for guests next to the old hen house that is now used for wine-tasting. The ceiling of the cottage is of pole beams and cut reeds (the width of the house was apparently dependent on the length of the wagon that carried these beams), walls are thick and whitewashed, and the main bedroom itself is of grand dimensions with high ceilings and a decorative mosquito net over twin beds. You can self-cater or indulge in Margie's healthy breakfasts, which are delivered every morning to your cottage. The large pool in the garden is as much yours as your hosts'. In fact a major reason why Margie has guests at all is to share what Babylons Toren has to offer with new people. *27-hole golf course nearby. Horse-riding easily arranged.*

Rooms: 1 cottage with 2 double rooms sharing 1 bathroom with bath. Self-catering or B&B. One-group booking only.
Price: R220 – R280 pp sharing B&B. Singles supplement. Self-catering R200 – R250 pp depending on numbers and length of stay.
Meals: Breakfast basket of local produce provided in cottage each day. For other meals self-catering or restaurants aplenty in the area.
Directions: From Cape Town take the N1 exit 47 onto R44 towards Stellenbosch. Turn left signed Simondium/Franschhoek. Follow road for 6km. Babylons Toren is on your right in vineyards.

Map Number: 2

Graceland

Susan McNaughton
Stellenrust Rd, PO Box 7066, Stellenbosch 7599
Tel: 021-881-3121 Fax: 021-881-3341
Email: graceland@iafrica.com Web: www.gracelandvineyards.com
Cell: 082-441-2680

Graceland is a small model wine farm and the ideal place from which to experience the winelands. Sue and Paul live in a thatched manor house at the end of a long driveway. Behind the house are rolling lawns, an extended garden, a large pool, tennis court, turf cricket net and a small putting green. Beyond this is the cottage, which houses one of the bedrooms, while the other is a secluded gem in the loft with antique furniture, thatched roof and pole beams. The free-standing bath, the loo and World War 1 officer's washstand are screened off from the sleeping area. The lawn gradually gives way to the vines and cellars beyond. Wine tastings are a must... usually at 6 in the evening. Guests are free to roam the property with walks up through the vines to the awesome Helderberg (the distinctively craggy mountain you can see from Cape Town). Every morning Sue's whim and her guests' preferences determine what you eat and even what you eat off. In fact Sue is so generous with both her energy and the space she gives you that you may experience a moment of distress when the time comes to leave. Suddenly it will dawn on you that all this is in fact someone else's! But you can at least take something away with you – I recommend the shiraz. The name Graceland derives from the three Graces who feature on every bottle of wine the vineyard produces (shiraz and cab sav).

Rooms: 2: 1 twin cottage with shower; 1 double with bath.
Price: R300 – R400 pp sharing. Cheaper rates for longer stays.
Meals: Full breakfast included.
Directions: Take R44 south out of Stellenbosch for 5km and Stellenrust Rd turn-off is on the left-hand side. 700m along dirt track on right. There is no right-hand turn on R44 from south.

Lekkerwijn

Wendy Pickstone

Groot Drakenstein, Franschhoek Road, near Boschendal 7680
Tel: 021-874-1122 Fax: 021-874-1465
Email: lekkerwijn@new.co.za Web: www.lekkerwijn.com

Lekkerwijn (pronounced Lekkervain) is a 1790s Cape Dutch homestead with a grand Edwardian extension designed by Sir Herbert Baker. You would probably have to pay to look round if Wendy didn't live there. It positively creaks with family history. You can tell when one family have lived in a grand house for generations – all the furniture, fittings and decoration look so at home. This is not some country house hotel nor some converted annexe. You share the house fully with Wendy, whose family have lived here since the late 19th century – unless of course you would prefer the privacy of the Coach House and Ballroom cottages. My strongest impressions are of the central courtyard with its gallery and cloister, the yellowwood floors and beams and the towering palms planted by Wendy's grandfather, the informal taste of the nursery bedroom, a wonderful breakfast... and Wendy herself, who is full of character and so caring of her guests.

Rooms: 5: 3 doubles in the house, 1 with en-suite bathroom, 2 private bath + shower; 2 cottages provide self-catering option for couples, either alone or with children.
Price: R270 (winter rates) – R520 (summer rates) pp sharing. Singles on request.
Meals: Full breakfast included for B&B. You can self-cater in the cottages and breakfast in the courtyard of the homestead is an optional extra.
Directions: On R45 at intersection with R310 from Stellenbosch (after passing Boschendal), alongside the new Meerrust entrance walls.

Map Number: 3

Entry Number: 84

Cathbert Country Inn

Ann and Robert Morley

Franschhoek Rd, Simondium, Franschhoek 7620
Tel: 021-874-1366 Fax: 021-874-3918
Email: info@cathbert.co.za Web: www.cathbert.co.za
Cell: 082-414-0604

Ann and Robert have a complete set of correct attitudes, as far as we are concerned: they have purposefully kept Cathbert's small (only eight rooms), "so we get to know our guests"; it's smart without going over the top and yet totally relaxed; and the food is a major focus. Bedrooms have views over a reservoir, farmland, vineyards, and the Simonsberg Mountains loom behind the house. Guests can walk up Kanonskop from Cathbert, a hill from which they used to signal to ships out at sea. You sleep in chalets with open-plan bed/sitting rooms and are refreshingly simple in style (and well-equipped with towelling bathrobes and other welcome luxuries). Each chalet has its little front garden where you might be honoured with a haughty visit from one of the resident peacocks, whose home this really is. Ann spends her day between reception and the kitchen where she is *maestro* – (set) menus are based on what she finds freshest around her. Her food is truly delicious, beautifully presented (only to residents) – 'modern' without being outré – and a real pull for Cathbert's burgeoning fan club. Robert, meanwhile, acts as (and *is*!) the charming and knowledgeable sommelier and host.

Rooms: 8 suites: 2 standard, 4 luxury, 2 executive. All with en-suite bath and shower. All king-size/twin beds. All air-conditioned.
Price: R495 – R650 pp sharing. Single supplement +50% .
Meals: Full breakfast included. Set menu 4-course dinner (except on Sundays).
Directions: From CT take N1, take exit 47, turn right at end of ramp, over 4-way stop, left at next road towards Franschhoek. Pass Backsberg Wine Estate. At the stop just before railway crossing turn right onto private tar road. Follow for 2.5km.

Résidence Klein Oliphants Hoek

Ingrid and Camil Haas

14 Akademie St, Franschhoek 7690
Tel: 021-876-2566 Fax: 021-876-2566
Email: info@kleinoliphantshoek.com Web: www.kleinoliphantshoek.com

Sometimes it all comes together so satisfyingly! Ingrid and Camil opened their first restaurant in a Dutch windmill, at the venerable age of 23, then worked their way across Europe – Turkey, France, Belgium – before moving out to South Africa in 2000 and falling in love (at first sight) with Klein Oliphants Hoek. The building has been reincarnated many times in its hundred and some years, built by an English missionary as a chapel in 1888 and at other times a school and a theatre. I'd only been at the guest house a very brief while before I knew instinctively that no single aspect of the place was going to let the side down. The centrepiece inside is the chapel hall itself, with its high-vaulted ceiling, fireplace and original beams, now the guest sitting room; but there are the bedrooms, the scented garden, the verandah and salt-water pool, the views. The highlight, for me, are Camil's evening meals which mix I'm-at-home-and-these-are-my-friends informality, guests drifting in and out of the kitchen (try doing that in London), with the hautest of haute cuisine, created on (and in) a restored wood-burning stove. Ingrid selects wines for each course to complement the dishes and explains why she has chosen them too – like a wine lesson. All in all, a real treat. *Closed in June.*

Rooms: 8: all twins or doubles (as required), all with en-suite showers and baths; 1 is a sundeck suite with jacuzzi while 2 have private pools.
Price: R430 – R1025 pp sharing. Single supplement.
Meals: Full breakfast included. 9-course dinner extravaganza R295, excluding drinks. No evening meals on Wednesdays and Sundays.
Directions: Akademie St is parallel to the main road in Franschhoek (Huguenot St), two streets up the hill.

The Garden House

Barry and Annette Phillips

29 De Wet St, Franschhoek 7690
Tel: 021-876-3155 Fax: 021-876-4271
Email: info@thegardenhouse.co.za Web: www.thegardenhouse.co.za
Cell: 083-340-3439

As soon as I met Barry who runs the local newspaper (The Franschhoek Tatler) and Annette who rescues and re-homes cats, a small inner voice instinctively told me "Ah, this is somewhere I feel at home!" Annette and Barry have fully immersed themselves in village life since their impulsive holiday decision to leave London in '01 and buy their Cape Victorian house. Their enthusiasm is palpable. And, quite frankly, why shouldn't it be? From the restaurants and wineries we saw when we went out in Barry's "Maigret"-style 1951 Citroen, I could see why Franschhoek claims to be the food and wine capital of the Western Cape! And the Garden House, originally called Belle Vue, with views across the valley to the mountains beyond and an abundant garden, well deserves both names. Guests stay in the air-conditioned and stylishly decorated cottage with its original wood-beamed bedroom and large bathroom with underfloor heating. If the cottage is occupied, Annette and Barry invite you to share their home in their pretty guest room with its Victorian brass bed. Come morning, Barry took me on a rigorous ride on a mountain bike – he keeps two for guests – while Annette prepared a smoked trout breakfast for our return. Village folk talk and I had already heard on the other side of the valley about Annette's local trout treat. Lovely, down–to-earth people. Nearby fishing, horse-riding, hiking and tennis.

Rooms: 2: 1 queen with en-suite bath and shower; 1 standard double with en-suite bath and shower overhead.
Price: R250 – R425 pp sharing. R450 pp sharing for one night.
Meals: Breakfast included.
Directions: N1, then R45, then, as you come into Franschhoek, turn left into de Wet St just before the canon and go up the hill. The Garden House is on your right.

Akademie Street Guesthouses

Katherine and Arthur McWilliam Smith

5 Akademie Street, Franschhoek 7690
Tel: 021-876-3027 Fax: 021-876-3293
Email: katherine@aka.co.za Web: www.aka.co.za
Cell: 082-655-5308

The parade of flowers and stepping-stones through citrus trees, fig trees, rose bushes and bougainvillaea made an otherwise rather thundersome day (ooh and the gale that was blowing!) much brighter. The airy cottages, which sit detached within the flower arrangements, open out onto private stoeps, gardens and even swimming pools. Vreugde, meaning 'joy', is a garden suite for two that has a neat kitchenette in an alcove and a sofa on the terrace. Oortuiging is a restored 1860s cottage for three that retains the old Cape style with antiques throughout. And Gelatenheid is a luxurious villa with, again, a private swimming pool and a wide wrap-around balcony. At the end of the balcony, suitably screened by tree-tops, is an outdoor, repro Victorian bathtub in which you can soak while gazing out at the mountain views… then wrap up in a towel from the heated bath rail. Inside, an expansive open-plan studio is home for just two people (though there's space enough for a four-bed house), with high wooden ceilings, Venetian blinds and French doors… a decadent holiday home. As full as a full breakfast can be (including boerewors – a type of SA sausage if you really didn't know) is served under the vines at the homestead. Katherine and Arthur – he was formerly Mayor of Franschhoek and they are both sooo nice – are easy smilers and happy to help with any day-tripping tips.

Rooms: 3 cottages: Vreugde: twin or king on request, en/s bath + shower; Oortuiging: 1 single + 1 double, both en/s bath + shower; Gelatenheid: 1 king + en/s bath + shower.
Price: R275 – R1,050 pp.
Meals: Full breakfast included.
Directions: From Cape Town take N1 then R45. Akademie St is parallel to main road in Franschhoek, two streets up the hill.

Clementine Cottage

Malcolm Buchanan

L'Avenir Farm, PO Box 333, Green Valley Rd, Franschhoek 7690
Tel: 021-876-3690 Fax: 021-876-3528
Email: lavenir@iafrica.com Web: www.clementinecottage.co.za
Cell: 082-320-2179

Running late with my mobile battery dead, I was touched to find Jef waiting expectantly for me just beyond the low-lying bridge that marks the entrance to L'Avenir Farm. He kindly guided me through the orchards of plums and clementines to meet Malcolm, who has recently taken over the running of this 21-hectare, family-owned, working fruit farm. Jef, by the way, is a two-year-old boerboel, as loyal to Malcolm as Robin is to Batman. In retrospect, my timing was perfect: the sun was setting behind the mountains that frame the Franschhoek Valley and from the stoep of Clementine Cottage, looking out over the pool and the vineyard beyond, the sky was stained a deep red. The only sounds I could hear, as I enjoyed a most welcome cold beer with Malcolm and his folks, were the frogs croaking contentedly in the dam that forms the centrepiece of the farm. If you find the pool too confining, a few lengths of this dam should satisfy any Tarzanesque impulses you may harbour. Being only 3km from the village I was able to enjoy a fine meal at the legendary Topsi's, before returning to the biggest bed I've ever had the pleasure of sleeping in. Recently refurbished in the original farm cottage style, Clementine Cottage has everything you could desire from pool, braaing area and satellite TV to large, stylish en-suite bedrooms.

Rooms: I cottage: I double with en-suite bath and shower and I twin with en-suite bath and shower.
Price: R600 – R1,200 dependent on season and number of people.
Meals: Self-catering, but numerous restaurants nearby.
Directions: Emailed or faxed on booking.

Les Chambres

Bill and Sandy Stemp
3 Berg Street, Franschhoek 7690
Tel: 021-876-3136 Fax: 021-876-2798
Email: info@leschambres.co.za Web: www.leschambres.co.za
Cell: 083-263-4926

So much to take in even as I ambled up one of many garden paths towards the house: the palm tree, reputed to be the tallest tree in the village, the herb garden boiling over with basil, rocket and tomatoes – that stone bench would be the perfect spot to make some progress with a paperback, I noted. Venturing further, I found Chinese poplars, gardenias and numerous shrubs and bark-strewn flowerbeds. And finally the house, a verandah-fronted Victorian gem, with Bill, Sandy and Archie (a cat) and Frank (another cat) forming a reassuring welcoming committee. Refreshed with a cool drink, I was shown through to the breakfasting patio where goldfish waft prettily about in a stone pond and French doors provide easy access to the continental-style buffet: fresh fruits and cereals, home-made granola and bread. Cooked options might include poached eggs on English muffins, or eggs Benedict, or scrambled eggs with smoked salmon-trout. Ze bedrooms of ze title are furnished in a mix of the antique and the contemporary with mahogany dressing tables and wicker bed-heads; while the bathrooms have travertine tiles, roll-top Victorian baths and separate showers. Some rooms are carpeted, others display the original wood flooring, complemented by a fireplace and Persian rugs. Private courtyards are available to two rooms, red-tiled with whitewashed walls and an overhanging orange tree. There is much to enjoy cloistered behind these gates. Not least the heated swimming pool.

Rooms: 4: all king size doubles or 2 twins, all en-suite bath and shower.
Price: R310 – R425 pp sharing. R470 – R600 singles.
Meals: Full breakfast included.
Directions: From R45 drive through village of Franschhoek and turn left into Berg Street just before monument.

Lalapanzi Lodge

Hamish and Annie Anderson

Sir Lowry's Pass, Somerset West
Tel: 021-858-1982 Fax: 021-858-1983
Email: info@lalapanzilodge.co.za Web: www.lalapanzilodge.co.za
Cell: 082-221-3812

With a lot of world outside their door and glorious adventures to be had, Hamish and Annie upped sticks and bought a round-the-world ticket. Luckily for us, they never made it past their first stop, and I can't blame them for discarding their plans in favour of Lalapanzi. Winding my way up the steep, red-brick road, through pine and gum trees, I already knew this was going to be a corker. The ski chalet-esque, stilted log cabins make the most of the awe-inspiring views of the Hottentots Holland Mountains (a botanist's haven) and across False Bay where, in the misty distance, my youthful eyes caught a glimpse of the flashing Cape Point lighthouse. 147 species of bird flutter about in the greenery that disappears down the steep slopes beneath the cabins, and with buck roaming the many miles of walking trails, make sure the binos are handy as you watch the sun set over the bay from your stoep. The rooms in the main homestead (another snug log cabin) open directly onto the lawn with their own private patio. Creaking wooden stairs lead up to the deep verandah, where a breakfast of freshly-baked muffins is taken in the morning sun. A brick path meanders through the pine trees to the lapa overlooking the pool, and beyond… well, it's more fun if you discover this 'place of tranquillity' for yourself.

Rooms: 6: 2 doubles, 2 twins and 2 self-catering cottages with 2 bedrooms and 3 bedrooms. All rooms have en-suite bath and/or shower.
Price: R350 – R380 pp sharing B&B. Cottages R805 – R1,020 for 2 people per day, R220 for each additional person.
Meals: Full breakfast included for non-self-caterers, R40 pp for self-caterers. Dinners on request.
Directions: From Cape Town, take N2 thro' Somerset West. Turn L at Sir Lowry's Pass Village. Through village & over railway, then R at T-jct. Take first L onto redbrick road, signed Knorhoek. Turn L just before Knorhoek Estate, go thro' Wedderwill gate house (or ring #3). Lodge 1.2km on L.

Longfield

Pieter and Nini Bairnsfather Cloete

Eikendal Rd, off R44, Somerset West 7130
Tel: 021-855-4224 Fax: 021-855-4224
Email: ninicloete@longfield.co.za Web: www.longfield.co.za

Longfield occupies a sensational vantage, gazing out like an Inca from the dramatic Helderberg across the panorama of the Winelands and all the way to Cape Point. The luxurious new cottage, adjoined to the homestead, is decorated in a relaxed country-house style: tables and chairs, as in the cottage up the hill, are rare early Cape family heirlooms; the bedroom, through folding double doors, has French antique beds; the pictures are an eclectic mix of style and artist. Glass doors and arched windows with inside shutters frame the sweep of vineyards below to Table Mountain. Both cottages are light and airy, with fresh flowers, up-to-date mags, coffee table books on SA wine, flora and fauna etc, pretty china and touches of Africa in the objets d'art. Comfy beds are made up with finest quality hand-embroidered linen and there are spoiling lotions in the pretty bathrooms. Sit out on the terrace of one or in the private garden of the other, with a glass of chilled white wine from the surrounding vineyards, to savour the sun setting behind Table Mountain. At night the lights of Cape Town make a spectacular display. The cottage up the hill has a fully-equipped kitchen, the new cottage a well-equipped kitchenette; fridges and cupboards are restocked each day with breakfast materials for you to help yourself to. It's self-catering but you'll enjoy chatting with Nini and Pieter who live up on the mountain with you. Restaurants and golf courses within easy striking distance; exclusive garden and wine tours by arrangement.

Rooms: 2 cottages: both twin beds with bath and separate shower.
Price: R250 – R400 pp sharing. Single supplement by arrangement.
Meals: Breakfast included.
Directions: From CT take N2 past the airport, take exit 43 Broadway Bvd. Left at lights. From the next lights 6.3km exactly, then right into Eikendal Rd. Follow up gravel road, jink left onto tarmac and follow to top and Longfield House.

Helderview Homestead Suites

Carl and Sibylle Linkmann (owners) & Gesa Cooper (front office)

16 Prunus St, Somerset West 7130
Tel: 021-855-1297 Fax: 021-855-1297
Email: linkmann@mweb.co.za Web: www.linkmann.com Cell: 072-424-1360

As nice timing would have it, I rolled through the gates of Helderview just as an impressive tea was being unleashed on the terrace. I enjoyed many biscuits and much cake, whilst gazing down to False Bay and the Hottentots Holland Mountains… and getting caught up in Carl's enthusiasm for this dramatic 19th-century house. A self-confessed anglophile, he has collected together period furniture on what must have been several grand tours around the Commonwealth: dressing tables, hefty drinks cabinets, throne-like armchairs around an open fire in the cigar lounge (where Carl holds court), swallow-you-whole brown leather sofas in each of the enormous suites. The three largest are 90 square metres! Commonwealth is a suggestion not an order and there's plenty from elsewhere too, such as the Italian polished granite tiles that lead to the Buffalo suite, and a heavy-looking wooden sculpture from Malawi that guards the bar. Helderview may be lavishly furnished, but these are not laurels upon which Carl has rested. This is a place where you will be pampered. Fancy watching the latest DVD? It's waiting for you in your room. Want to catch up on the news from home? Carl will find your newspaper of choice. Carl's quest for a home fit for a connoisseur naturally includes a sophisticated wine list. Even if you have no idea what you are looking at, or what you're drinking, I think you will find a way to settle in.

Rooms: 7 suites: 5 with 1 bedroom and 1 shower room; 1 with 2 bedrooms and 1 bathroom and 1 shower room; 1 with 2 bedrooms and 1 shower room.
Price: R500 – R1,200 pp sharing (minimum of 4 nights). Single supplement + 50%.
Meals: Full breakfast included. Weekly braai available on request at a small cost.
Directions: Airport transfer included and can arrange car hire. For those not coming from Cape Town International, directions can be emailed or faxed.

Manor on the Bay

Hanél and Schalk van Reenen

117 Beach Rd, Gordon's Bay 7140
Tel: 021-856-3260 Fax: 021-856-3261
Email: manorotb@mweb.co.za Web: www.manoronthebay.co.za
Cell: 082-896-5790

Hanél and Schalk van Reenen are a young couple, and their enthusiasm for the job is palpable. They have poured great vats of time and energy into restoring their property, moving an impressive tonnage of earth to create a raised garden at the front, below a long terrace. This is a great place for watching sunsets over False Bay or even whales in spring, and the view is conveniently framed by two large palms. A brace of Old English sheepdogs complete the very friendly reception committee. Beach Road, you won't need telling, is just next to the sea, and a hop, skip and a dive takes you across the road and into the water. If you don't fancy the walk, however, there's also a pool out the back. Of the six rooms, four are sea-facing and open onto the terrace, but the other three are just as enticing and luxurious, and look out over a large garden that climbs up the Gordon's Bay hillside. Breakfast is either healthy (in Hanél's case eaten after an early run on the beach – you don't have to join her, so don't worry) or hearty, and is served in the bright dining room or on the terrace outside.

Rooms: 6: 3 doubles, 3 twins; all with en-suite bathrooms, 4 with sea view, 2 looking on to the garden court.
Price: R350 – R600 pp sharing. Singles + R200.
Meals: Full breakfast included.
Directions: From Strand on the R44, take Beach Rd turning just before BP garage. From N2 take Sir Lowry's Pass to Gordon's Bay and cross over on to van der Bijl St, down to Beach Rd and L.

Cape Winelands, Western Cape

Fraai Uitzicht 1798

Axel Spanholtz and Mario Motti

Historic Wine and Guest Farm
with Restaurant, Klaas Voogds
East (Oos), Between
Robertson and Montagu on
Route 62 6705
Tel: 023-626-6156
Fax: 023-626-6156
Email: info@fraaiuitzicht.com
Web: www.fraaiuitzicht.com

'Fraai Uitzicht' means 'beautiful view' in Dutch – no idle promise as it turns out. The 17th-century wine and guest farm is four kilometres up a gravel road in a cul-de-sac valley ringed by vertiginous mountains. People come from far and wide for the well-known restaurant and the seven-course *dégustation* menu is basically irresistible. Matched with local wine, it features trout salad, springbok carpaccio, beef fillet with brandy sauce and decadent Dream of Africa chocolate cake. Shall we just say I left with more than one spare tyre in the car. You could also be entertained by a Xhosa choir who give performances every other Wednesday night. Where to sleep is not an easy decision as you are spoilt for choice. A few cottages take it easy in the garden, each comfortable and pretty with impressionistic oils and views of the mountains, while others offer you masses of character with metre-thick walls and timber interiors; my favourite was the loft bedroom in the eaves. Or opt for one of the garden suites with their own entrances and balconies. Make sure you take a peek at the wine cellar – guests have first option on the (uniquely) hand-made merlot. I can't count the number of recommendations we had pointing us to Axel and Mario's door. *Restaurant closed June & July. Limited menu available for guests.*

Rooms: 8: 4 cottages, 2 with 2 bedrooms (1 x queen & 1 x twin), 2 with 1 bedroom (queen & extra sleeper couch); 4 suites, 2 with king, 2 with queen, all en/s shower.
Price: Cottages are R660 pp. Suites are R400 pp.
Meals: Continental breakfast included. R30 extra for English. Lunch and dinner available on premises.
Directions: On R60 between Robertson & Ashton. Approximately 5km from Ashton and 12km from Robertson, Klaas Voogds East turn-off, 4km on gravel road, turn-off to left.

Wildekrans Country House

Alison Green and Barry Gould
Houw Hoek Valley, Elgin 7180
Tel: 028-284-9827 Fax: 028-284-9624
Email: wildekrans@kingsley.co.za Web: www.wildekrans.co.za

From the tufts of moss poking out between the old flagstones of the front path I knew that this was my sort of place. The 1811 homestead is raised above its garden and looks down on lawns, abundant roses, pear orchards, the large swimming pool and old oak trees. The scene is magnificent with the 'wild cliffs' ('wildekrans') of the berg setting the property's limits, rising from a meadow at the back of the garden. Take a stroll beside landscaped watercourses and lily ponds that neighbour the orchards, and you will encounter wonderful, some might think surreal, sculptures that have been positioned with much thought, and I think argument, where they now stand. They add a touch of the unexpected to this magical garden. Finally a rickety bridge – that inspires little in the way of confidence, but is quite safe – crosses a stream and you find yourself at the foot of the steep, forested mountain. A path leads straight up or you can cross a neighbour's land in search of gentler gradients. The bedrooms are charming, each with a four-poster bed, originally parental gifts to Alison and her many sisters, and views out to the garden. There is a large pool, a contemporary art collection and the Wildekrans winery nearby.

Rooms: 4: 3 four-poster doubles in the homestead with en-suite bath (one has a shower too); and 1 self-catering cottage.
Price: B&B R280 – R330 pp sharing. Singles R360. Self-catering R195 – R295 pp sharing.
Meals: Full breakfast included. Dinners from one-course simple supper R75 to three courses R120. All meals are self-served.
Directions: On N2 from Cape Town for 1 hour approx., past Grabouw and 12km further turn left signed Houw Hoek Inn. Through Houw Hoek gate posts (no gate), follow road round to left. Farm on your right.

Map Number: 3

Paul Cluver Guest House

The Cluver Family
Grabouw 7160
Tel: 021-844-0605 Fax: 021-844-0150
Email: info@cluver.co.za Web: www.cluver.com

I trundled through vineyards and more vineyards, fruit trees (apples, pears and plums), past grazing springbok, eland, tame ostriches, horses, cows, blue crane (twelve of them), past the Reebok river, a large oak tree and finally I arrived at the Cluver family's early eighteenth-century house, mule stable and school. What an estate! All 2,000 hectares of it! And the Cluvers set their substantial – and one assumes very time-consuming – wine and fruit production to one side in order to accommodate, welcome and feed their guests. Inge, one of Dr Cluver's daughters, introduced me to part of their family history: a Grégoire on the wall depicts the house and its outbuildings from before Inge's grandmother's time and antiques passed down through generations of Cluvers are plentiful. The buildings have been totally renovated with clay-tiled floors and there are such things as electric blankets, heating and a lounge with satellite TV and videos. There are three rooms in the homestead and the other two are the converted cottages (the mule stable with its fireplace is especially popular in winter). You can have breakfast in bed; or a breakfast picnic basket is a tempting option to take on a riverside amble among the rich array of proteas and disas. *The Paul Cluver Amphitheatre season runs from October to February. Closed June.*

Rooms: 5: 3 twin rooms and 2 doubles. All en-suite showers.
Price: R240 – R400 pp sharing.
Meals: Full breakfast included. Lunch and supper on request. Gourmet cuisine available every other weekend, May – September.
Directions: From Cape Town take N2, past Somerset West, over Sir Lowry's Pass. You will see the Orchard farm store on the left and the Paul Cluver Wine Estate sign follows shortly on the left (about 20km from Somerset West).

Wild Olive Guest House

Gloria and Peter Langer
227 Hangklip and Bell Rds, Pringle Bay 7196
Tel: 028-273-8750 Fax: 028-273-8752
Email: g-langer@mweb.co.za Web: www.wild-olive.de or www.wild-olive.co.za
Cell: 082-442-5544

After restauranteering for 27 years, Peter decided to dedicate his love of cooking to his B&B guests in the white sandy-mouthed bay of Pringle. Food is certainly the *spécialité de la maison*. I couldn't believe my luck when I noticed the certificate in the kitchen declaring him a top-ten SA chef of 1999. While preparing the freshly-caught yellow-tail he informed me that in the summer, when the bay is calm, he takes guests out in his engine-powered dinghy (rubber duck to South Africans). The guests catch the crayfish and Peter cooks it for supper. The breakfasts eaten on the sundeck (with ocean view... and whale view too between July and November) boast fresh, home-baked breads, pancakes, croissants, fruit, muesli, yoghurt and the full 'English' breakfast. I almost popped. The bedrooms have private terraces and baboon-proof window locks. I scanned the mountainside for primate life in my (private and enclosed) open-air washroom. I can imagine that when it is sunny it must be so lovely to have your skin sun-kissed while showering. I had blustery weather, but still wanted to test it out (hot water – phew). There is an inside option too, of course. All the bedrooms have this novelty and the twin/king has an up-a-ladder bed for couples with a child (8+). Gloria and Peter are very attentive and professional hosts.

Rooms: 3: 2 queens, 1 with en-s bath with shower overhead & 'al-fresco' shower, 1 with en-s shower & 'al-fresco' shr & separate loo; 1 twin/king with loft, en-suite shower and 'al-fresco' shower.
Price: R225 – R325 pp sharing. Singles on request.
Meals: Full breakfast included. 3-course evening dinner prepared by Peter.
Directions: From Cape Town on N2, turn towards Gordon's Bay, follow coast road for 30km to Pringle Bay turn – follow signs.

Barnacle B&B

Jenny Berrisford

573 Anne Rd, Pringle Bay 7196
Tel: 028-273-8343 Fax: 028-273-8343
Email: barnacle@maxitec.co.za Web: www.deadduck.co.za/ads/barnacle/
Cell: 082-925-7500

Come and explore Jenny's seaside idyll. Several natural environments collide right outside her cottage. From the deck at the back – with views all the way to Cape Point – you walk down rickety (but safe!) steps to her lawny enclaves in the marsh reeds where narrow paths lead you to the river and beach. The sea is a hundred yards of the whitest, finest sand to your left; beyond the river fynbos and milkwood 'forest' climb the mountain, a nature reserve. You don't have to be a kid to love this. There are otters in the river, baboons on the mountain, estuarine and fynbos birds aplenty… and Jenny is a horticultural expert in one of the world's most amazing natural gardens. Rooms are simple, rustic and country cosy, one with a Victorian slipper bath, another with a solid brass bed and the whole place is super relaxed… a hidden gem. Jenny has canoes and paddle skis to take out on the river. This area has been proclaimed a world biosphere reserve.

Rooms: 2: 1 outside annexe double with en-suite shower and small sunroom; 1 double with en-suite 'slipper' bath and kitchenette. Annexe can be self-catering.
Price: R200 – R270 pp sharing. Singles R250 – R300. Longer stays on request.
Meals: Full breakfast included. Restaurants in Pringle Bay.
Directions: From Cape Town along N2 turn towards Gordon's Bay before Sir Lowry's Pass – follow coast road for 30km to Pringle Bay turn – follow signs down dirt roads.

Buçaco Sud

Jean Da Cruz
2609 Clarence Drive, Betty's Bay 7141
Tel: 028-272-9750 or 028-272-9628 Fax: 028-272-9750
Email: bucaco@hermanus.co.za Web: www.bucacosud.co.za
Cell: 083-514-1015

Everything in this beautiful place has been designed and built by Jean, including the house itself, which sits halfway up a mountain in South Africa's first Biosphere Reserve, a nature lover's paradise with tranquil lakes, stunning beaches, the Harold Porter Botanic Gardens and a penguin colony. Buçaco Sud was once Jean's castle in Spain (or Portugal I should say), now a flight of personal fancy come true. The upstairs sitting room has windows on both sides, and light streams through to mountain views in one direction and sea views in the other. Guest bedrooms are eye-catching, full of startling colours, flowers and eclectic 'stuff' collected by Jean or donated by friends. They all look down over the sea, except 'Shangri-La' at the back – perhaps my favourite – where you can walk straight out through French doors onto the Kogelberg mountain. Local artists' work (for sale) adds even more colour to the vibrant decor. It's not a place for TVs and mobile phones. Genuine care, a sense of humour and enthusiastic hospitality in a house where every detail is home-spun. *Arabella Gold Estate is about 18km away.*

Rooms: 5: 4 doubles and 1 twin; 4 with en-suite shower, 1 with en-suite bath.
Price: R200 – R295 pp sharing. Singles on request.
Meals: Full breakfast included. Variety of restaurants in the area.
Directions: Follow R44 from Gordon's Bay along coast for 30km, house signed to left in Betty's Bay, 1 hour from Cape Town. Directions emailed or faxed on booking.

Map Number: 2 & 3

Overberg, Western Cape

96 Beach Road

Annelie and Johan Posthumus

Kleinmond 7195
Tel: 021-794-6291 Fax: 021-794-6291
Email: info@kaapsedraaibb.co.za Web: www.kaapsedraaibb.co.za

When the family bought "the beach house" in 1954, the milk was delivered by bike. Kleinmond still feels like a sleepy little town, but it's hardly surprising that more have fled here since. The house is but a kite-tail's length from the sea, the blue Atlantic stretching forth beyond a strip of fynbos. You can choose to watch the whales passing by (from August to December) from two spots, the sea-side verandah or the upstairs bedroom. The latter runs from one side of the house to the other under a vaulted ceiling and ocean-side the walls stop and the glass starts, forming a small square sitting room jutting out towards the blue. Here there is a soft couch and a rocking chair, perfect for siestas, sunsets (and of course whale-watching). Downstairs is equally adorable. It feels a bit like a Nantucket Island house: white, light, airy and adorned with simple understated beach furnishings. Interior designers, *nota bene*! It is totally self-catering here, but walk a kilometre west and you'll find some untouristy cafés in the old harbour; a three-minute drive east will take you past a decent restaurant and miles of white, sandy, blue-flag beaches, perfect for kids, flying kites, swimming and walking. Kleinmond is near the Arabella Golf Estate, the Kogelberg Biosphere with its myriad fynbos species, the wild horses of the Bot River Estuary and Hermanus, but avoids its touristy-ness.

Rooms: 2: 1 double with en-suite shower, 1 twin with bath.
Price: Max 4 persons. Minimum R600 per night or R1,000 if 4 persons. Min 2-night stay.
Meals: Self-catering.
Directions: In Kleinmond town face east. Drive through 3 stop signs and turn towards the sea on 6th Avenue. Keep going to the sea then turn left and No 96 is the penultimate house from the corner.

Entry Number: 101

Map Number: 2 & 3

Schulphoek Seafront Guesthouse

Petro and Mannes van Zyl

44 Marine Drive, Sandbaai, Greater Hermanus 7200
Tel: 028-316-2626 Fax: 028-316-2627
Email: schulphoek@hermanus.co.za Web: www.schulphoek.co.za

Waves roll into the bay, five foot high when I visited, and crash against rocks right in front of Schulphoek Seafront Guesthouse. The sitting room has one of the most exciting sea views you could hope for and, naturally, whales steal into Schulphoek Bay during the season for private viewings. The best room, Scallop – I don't think there is any doubt, despite the extremely high standard! – is upstairs, the whole seaward wall an expanse of window with a sliding glass door and parapet. The smells of the sea are powerful. The other rooms, although without sea views, have solid, hand-crafted oak or mahogany beds and spectacular bathrooms with double sinks, double showers and spa-baths… I mean, you will not find better *anywhere*. Not many places in this area feel the need to provide in-house dinners but your hosts are not taking chances on outside eateries. Guests who want to guarantee themselves delicious food stay in (4-course *menu du jour* herbs, salad and veg picked straight from their vegetable garden) and eat at one long table, on chairs made from vintage wine vats. You can choose from an exhaustive cellar of the finest South African wines. Schulphoek is an intimate, state-of-the-art seaside lodge, but still the sort of place where guests socialise with each other, drinks are on an honesty system and meals are all eaten together. *Closed in May.*

Rooms: 8 suites: superior, luxury and standard, all with luxurious en-suite bathrooms. Family suites available.
Price: R454 – R826 pp sharing. Single supplement + 50%. Seasonal and discounted rates for longer stays. Whole guest house on request.
Meals: Professional kitchen with chef. Dinner: 4-course menu du jour. Lunch: on request. Wine cellar with 7,000 SA wines. Full breakfast included in tariff. First night dinner complimentary.
Directions: Take R43 towards Hermanus. At Engen petrol station by traffic lights (signed Sandbaai) turn R. At 2nd 'stop' turn L into 3rd St. At next stop turn L. Marked by flags – entrance off Piet Retief Crescent.

Map Number: 3

Entry Number: 102

Otters Inn

Estelle and Pieter Spaarwater
28 Marine Drive, Vermont, Greater Hermanus 7201
Tel: 028-316-3167 Fax: 028-316-3764
Email: otters@hermanus.co.za Web: www.wheretostay.co.za/ottersinn
Cell: 082-898-7724

Estelle and Pieter are hugely enthusiastic about the charms of the Overberg and love talking about its history, environment and potential. From their house (built in 1926 by the Speaker of the South African parliament) near Hermanus you can visit most of the area's 'jewels' within 30 minutes. You can also join Estelle on a twelve-kilometre beach hike to walk off the superb breakfast, which always includes a house speciality such as crêpes filled with crayfish. Those of a less active disposition can, in season, watch whales frolicking right in front of the house. The Spaarwaters can show you a tidal swimming pool, and there is a fynbos garden too with tiny orchids, a natural playground for local birds. The guest house is arranged around a central hall and an enclosed verandah, and the four wood-floored rooms have shutters, mohair rugs, silk duvets and particularly attractive beds. They are bright and fresh in feel and the Spaarwaters have brought great taste to bear. Two have their own sea-facing sitting rooms and two have bigger bathrooms with baths and showers – you choose. They have a swimming pool too and many books (on whales) to read beside it. *Excellent golf nearby. Closed end of May – mid July.*

Rooms: 4: all doubles/twins; 2 with en-suite bath and shower; 2 with en-suite shower and private sitting room.
Price: R360 – R420 pp sharing. Singles supplement 40%.
Meals: Full breakfast included and served till 9.30 a.m.
Directions: From Cape Town take N2 for 110km until signed left to Hermanus. Follow R43 until signed right to Vermont/Onrusrivier. Follow this road straight down to the sea. Left at the bottom, house on left.

Pebble Beach Guest House

Chantal and Gideon Malherbe

8 Fernkloof Drive, Hermanus Heights 7200
Tel: 028-313-2517 Fax: 028-313-2517
Email: info@pebblebeachguesthouse.com
Web: www.pebblebeachguesthouse.com Cell: 082-444-5199 or 082-444-5199

I arrived on a Sunday morning to find the entire Malherbe family hard at work, applying the finishing touches to their brand-new guest-house, in readiness for their first-ever guests later in the week. I very much doubt there was any early dissatisfaction. They designed and built the house themselves, with high vaulted ceilings and a colonial-style wrap-around balcony. Here guests congregate for evening drinks to contemplate remarkable views down the tree-lined 16th fairway of Hermanus Golf Course… and to pass derisive comment on the golf swings on show. This can be enjoyably achieved with equal smugness on colder days in the Rocky Lounge with its open fire. Others will eschew golf criticism altogether and settle down by the swimming pool among the olive trees. The house, with its Indo-African furnishings, draws on Gideon and Chantal's experience in the tropics and in Indonesia where they used to sail the Indies Explorer, a charter yacht. Natural materials have been used wherever possible, with sunset-slate flooring, stone baths, wooden mirrors, and the harmonious result is restful on both eye and spirit. For non-golfers, the front door opens onto the Hermanus Mountains, complete with nature trails through the fynbos, and both beaches and village are close by. Both Gideon and Chantal are happiest outdoors, and will guide you if time permits along the hiking trails, organise shark diving, mountain-biking, golf etc. Pebble Beach has so much to offer both the action man and the poolside potterer.

Rooms: 6: 3 twins, 2 with en-suite bath and shower, 1 with en-suite shower; 3 doubles, 1 with en-suite bath and shower, 2 with en-suite shower.
Price: R380 – R520 pp sharing. Singles + 50%. Children under 5 stay free.
Meals: Full breakfast included. Seafood barbeques and other meals on request, not included.
Directions: From N2 take R43 to Hermanus. Go all the way through village and left at Shell garage. Hug the golf course and turn first right before the school. House is 2nd after the bend.

Cliff Lodge

Gill O'Sullivan and Gideon Shapiro

6 Cliff St, De Kelders 7220
Tel: 028-384-0983 Fax: 028-384-0228
Email: stay@clifflodge.co.za Web: www.clifflodge.co.za
Cell: 082-380-1676

This is the closest land-based whale-watching you could possibly find. I could see the whites of their eyes (I was only shooting with a camera!) and the callosities on their heads. It was as though Gill and Gideon had paid them (in plankton) to put on a special show for me; blowing, breaching, spyhopping, lob-tailing. I applauded delicately from the royal box. The viewing from my room and on the breakfast conservatory-balcony was don't-turn-your-eyes-away-for-a-minute magnetic. But the fun wasn't just in the looking. As soon as I walked through the door, Gideon, formerly a dive-master, whisked me down to the ocean for a swim through the cave (bring shoes you can swim in for the rocks) and Gill kindly booked me a whale-, sea-lion- and penguin-watching boat trip for the following morning. For the 'help-danger' adrenaline rush, there is also the shark-cage diving. The guest house décor is classy and modern and there are whale-spotting terraces for those rooms on the side of the house. On the cliff edge is also a small swimming pool. Gill and Gideon are wonderfully hospitable hosts and really look after their guests. After the best breakfast you could possibly have – not only because of the food but also the panorama – indulge in an aromatherapy massage from Gill, nature reserve walks in front of the house and the nearby flower-farm. Cliff Lodge rocks.

Rooms: 3: 1 twin/king with bath and shower, 1 queen bed with bath and shower overhead, 1 twin/king with bath and shower overhead
Price: R500 – R750 pp sharing. Single supplement +50%.
Meals: Full breakfast included.
Directions: N2, then R43 through Hermanus. Past Stanford towards Gansbaai. Turn right at first De Kelders turn-off, then right into De Villiers Rd, left into Kayser Rd and right into Cliff St.

Whalesong Lodge

Stanley and Lainy Carpenter

83 Cliff St, De Kelders 7220
Tel: 028-384-1865 Fax: 028-384-1866
Email: stanley@whalesonglodge.co.za Web: www.whalesonglodge.co.za
Cell: 082-883-5793

Am I a rain god, I sometimes wonder in my less humble moments? Here was another fabulous ocean view obscured by a veil of heavy rain. There were whales out there somewhere! Stanley and Lainy used to run the Pontac Hotel in Paarl, but I suspect they always hankered after a nice small place where they could give their guests more love and attention, cook for manageable numbers… and be themselves. Whalesong Lodge, with just five rooms, is it. All the bedrooms have sea views, of course, either from a panoramic window or a small, private balcony, and under-floor-heated bathrooms are separated from the sleeping areas by shoulder-high walls. All is slick and modern. Many cookbooks and a well-ordered, well-stocked kitchen loudly trumpet Stanley's culinary expertise. So will he be cooking for his happy hordes? The eyes narrow. "Only if I'm feeling inspired," comes the reply, through a suppressed smile, "but we're quite happy to have guests cook for us". In fact it is true! You are encouraged to help with preparation if you want… much great seafood fresh from Walker Bay and delicious desserts made by Lainy. But Stanley does not want to HAVE to cook every night so ask when you book. Breakfast ("from 8 till late") is fresh and all-encompassing, with homemade preserves and jams (Lainy's), local cheeses, seasonal fresh fruit, muesli, yoghurt as well as all the eggs and bacon and stuff. Oh yes, and great coffee.

Rooms: 5: 2 twins, 3 doubles, all en-suite bath and shower.
Price: R420 – R750 pp sharing.
Meals: Full breakfast included.
Directions: From N2 take R43 through Hermanus and Stanford. Take first right signed to De Kelders and follow down to the sea. Turn right into Cliff Street. Third house on right.

Fair Hill Private Nature Reserve

Val and Tim Deverson

R43 between Stanford and Gansbay, Stanford 7210
Tel: 028-341-0230 Fax: 028-341-0230
Email: fairhill@yebo.co.za Web: www.fairhill.co.za
Cell: 082-788-2086

A gate in the middle of nowhere, then a sandy track which leads into the fynbos, arriving finally at Val and Tim's single-story guest house. I guarantee that you will be stunned by the quality of natural silence that envelops you as you step from your car. I think you can hear the fynbos growing! Just walk out in any direction and encounter the eland who, Jeeves-like, only materialise when you aren't looking. We stayed here for a weekend break from Cape Town (two hours max) and completely refilled our energy tanks. Walks are lovely down through Fair Hill's fynbos to the beach, which is hard to get to any other way and will most likely be deserted. Those with more momentum can walk all the way to Hermanus and, if she can, Val will pick you up there. Or you can sunbathe by the pool, protected from the wind in the lea of a natural cave. Big rooms are all blessed with verandahs whence to commune with the wilderness. To top it off, the Deversons themselves couldn't be nicer and delicious dinners are part of the (*incredibly* good value) package – with a choice at every course. Fair Hill is an authentic, uplifting and special experience. We recommend you stay for a minimum of two nights.

Rooms: 4 doubles with en-suite bath and shower attachment.
Price: B&B R330 – R370 pp sharing. Dinner B&B R440 – R480.
Meals: All dinners included with choice for each course.
Directions: From Hermanus follow R43 to Stanford. Continue past for 8.7km. Electric gates on right. From the Garden Route take R326 after Riviersonderend. At Stanford turn left, continue for 8.7km, electric gates on the right.

Bellavista Country Place

Georges and Sonja Schwegler
R43 between Gansbaai and Stanford, Stanford 7210
Tel: 028-341-0178 Fax: 028-341-0179
Email: bellavista@hermanus.co.za Web: www.bella.co.za

On the slopes of Middleberg Hill with panoramic views down to the Atlantic and fynbos ad infinitum (300 hectares to be precise), Georges and Sonja are blissfully ensconced in their dream South African home. So happy, in fact, that they converted the old tumbledown farm buildings, a mere stroll from the homestead, into a set of three luxurious suites for Swiss relatives and friends to come and stay. Fortunately a change of heart (and a slight miscalculation – it's a long story) expanded this idea somewhat. So now you too can enjoy basking in the rim-flow swimming pool as the wilderness of the Walker Bay Reserve stretches out below you to the coast. Unfortunately for me and my rumbling stomach, I arrived a week before the grand opening of the small restaurant. But if the food is half as good as the setting, diners will be in for a treat: the floor-to-ceiling windows allow the sun to flood over the round tables, and the glass doors slide back to reveal a pillared Romanesque stoep, where breakfast is served from the buffet table. Georges couldn't help wondering whether the two main suites were too big for a guesthouse with their large Italian-tiled bathrooms, huge sitting rooms and private patios. I don't envisage too many complaints, Georges!

Rooms: 4: 3 doubles or twins with en-suite bath and shower; 1 cottage with 2 doubles or twins, one with en-suite bath, separate shower room.
Price: R300 – R600 pp sharing. Singles on request.
Meals: Full breakfast included. Fully licensed restaurant on site.
Directions: From Hermanus follow R43 to Stanford. Continue for 8km. Follow signs to Bellavista on the left. From the Garden Route take the R326 after Riviersonderend. At Stanford turn left. Continue for 8km. Follow signs, Bellavista is on your left.

Klein Paradijs Country House

Susanne and Michael Fuchs

Pearly Beach, Gansbaai 7220
Tel: 028-381-9760 Fax: 028-381-9803
Email: kleinparadijs@lando.co.za Web: www.kleinparadijs.co.za

Paradise would be a proud boast, so perhaps Little Paradise is a more defensible claim. But you can see why the name stuck: nature on the one hand, man-made environment on the other, and all rounded off by delicious cooking and green fingers. I'll elaborate. The property stretches up a mountain covered in indigenous fynbos vegetation and nearer the house there is a reed edged dam with weaver birds, an old camphor tree in the courtyard and an amazing garden whose swimming pool acts as a moat to a tiny island of plant life. Inside, high open spaces are punctuated with lovely things: bright paintings, vases of proteas and pincushions, a stinkwood grandfather clock for example. A-shaped rooms have soaring thatched roofs, dormer windows, beams, window-seats, balconies and the curtained-off bathrooms are truly luxurious. The Fuchs are Swiss and have brought many talents with them. Susanne was a translator and speaks English, German and French, while Michael is a chef – they open a small but excellent restaurant in the evenings. *Large dam with canoe and rowboat available on the property. Whale-watching possible nearby from June – November.*

Rooms: 5: 2 twins and 3 doubles all with en-suite bathrooms; 2 with bath and shower, 3 with showers.
Price: R450 – R800 pp sharing. Single supplement +50%.
Meals: Full breakfast included. Light meals and dinner by arrangement. The restaurant is fully licensed.
Directions: From Hermanus take the R43 through Stanford and Gansbaai. Go left at Pearly Beach crossing, then 1st left again. The house is on the right.

Beaumont Wine Estate

Jayne and Raoul Beaumont
Compagnes Drift Farm, PO Box 3, Bot River 7185
Tel: 028-284-9194 (office), 028-284-9370 (home) Fax: 028-284-9733
Email: beauwine@netactive.co.za Web: www.beaumont.co.za
Cell: 082-928-2300 or 083-440-6319

Jayne's guests stay in the charming buildings of an 18th-century former mill house and wagon shed, today snug with wood-burning heaters, but left as far as comfortably possible as they were, with original fireplaces in kitchens and hand-hewn, yellowwood beamed ceilings. Outside, you can sit around an old mill stone and admire the antediluvian water wheel, while the willow-shaded jetty on the farm lake offers one of the Western Cape's prettiest settings for sundowners and wheatland views. While meandering through the flower-filled garden I realised that there is no real need to move from the farm, despite being only half an hour from Hermanus. While Jayne and her family busy themselves producing their annual 150,000-odd bottles of wine, you can swim in the informal swimming pool – being the lake – under the weeping willows where the weaver-birds make their nests or you can roam about on their land – they own half a mountain! You can even put the idea of cooking on the backburner and instead arrange to have home-cooked meals delivered to you. The Beaumonts, whose estate is in the middle of tranquil Bot River, make a pinotage for London wine merchants Berry Bros and Rudd's own label and you can wine-taste in the cellar flanked by an old wine press. To find the horses and horse-riding you only have to trot down the road. The setting is beautiful – well worth spending several nights here.

Rooms: 2 self-catering cottages. Mill House has 2 bedrooms (plus 2 extra can sleep in living room); Pepper Tree has 1 double (again 2 extras possible).
Price: R190 – R250 pp sharing. Extra people R80 pp. Call for high season rates.
Meals: Self-catering but breakfast and home-cooked meals by arrangement. All meals self-served.
Directions: From N2 take exit 92, sign-posted to Bot River. Follow signs to Bot River and Beaumont Wine Estate is signed off to the right-hand side. Map can be faxed.

Overberg, Western Cape

Blue Gum Country Lodge

Nic and Nicole Dupper
PO Box 899, Stanford 7210
Tel: 028-341-0116
Fax: 028-341-0135
Email:
reservations@bluegum.co.za
Web: www.bluegum.co.za
Cell: 082-564-5663

After a day spent rattling my bones on dirt roads, my eventual arrival at Blue Gum, bathing in the lengthening shadows of the Klein River Mountains, was an immeasurable pleasure. There is a very long list of things you can get up to here… but after such a tiring day, I'm afraid I was grateful not to have time. I had to give myself over instead to some lounging around and some terrifically good food. Blue Gum is not half good at this. Around the crackling fire in the main lounge, other guests had had the same idea, sprawled in deep sofas, chatting jovially and sipping apéritifs, waiting for their à la carte dinner, whose enticing aromas could almost be seen emanating from the kitchen. Disappointment was not on the menu: succulent steaks melted in mouths and Nic ensured our wine glasses were kept pleasingly full. Back in my Lion Room I sampled the cheese and sherry that had appeared from nowhere on my private terrace, before dismantling the mountain of pillows and collapsing into a long, satisfying sleep. As morning broke over the vines, weaver birds busied themselves by the dam and guests prepared for the day ahead, some clutching tennis racquets or mountain bikes. Others motored off to explore the majesty of the surrounding Overberg: whales, curios and art in Stanford and horse-riding, birding and fishing galore. So… good food, a beautiful setting, R&R and tons to do – not a bad definition of 'holiday'.

Rooms: 10: 5 queens, all with en-suite bath and shower. In manor house; 4 twins, 1 king, all bath and shower except one which is double shower.
Price: Seasonal. R650 – R810 pp sharing. Single supplement + 50%.
Meals: Full breakfast included. Light lunches, 4-course evening dinner (R160 – R180).
Directions: From CT take N2, then R43 turn-off to Hermanus. Drive through Hermanus on R43, following signs to Stanford. At Stanford turn left onto R326 for 6.7km, then left onto dirt track for 4km.

The Post House

David Donde

22 Main Rd, Greyton 7233
Tel: 028-254-9995 Fax: 028-254-9920
Email: info@posthouse.co.za Web: www.posthouse.co.za
Cell: 082-446-3884

David reckons he makes the best cappuccino in SA and frankly (having travelled the length and breadth of the country) I'm inclined to agree. But make no mistake; this is no fancy Italian coffee-house. Imagine instead a wholesome, English country pub of warped walls and wonky windows. The Post House started life in the 1860s as (surprise, surprise) the post house. These days though, the shop-front is a well-stocked bar (single malts are another of David's passions), bedrooms line the country garden and the old kitchen with its cavernous, inglenook fireplace, is a snug retreat of well-loved sofas, sporting prints and pub games. I had time for a beer and a natter there before dinner. The restaurant is excellent and open to all. I modestly opted for the pan-fried sole, then guiltlessly scoffed some surely-this-can't-be-good-for-me chocolate terrine, courtesy of new chef Brad (fresh from the unmissable Olympia Café in Cape Town). It's at most a two-hour drive to the Cape but with so much to get up to in and around Greyton you simply can't dash off after just one night. David will happily hook you up with some fishing (please excuse the pun) or pack you off (sorry) with expert walking guides. Sadly, I was part of the wish-I'd-stayed-longer camp and settled instead for a long soak in my vast, copper-plated bath, dreaming of what might have been.

Rooms: 12: 6 kings, 1 queen and 5 doubles. All with en-suite bath or shower.
Price: R200 – R550 pp sharing. Singles plus 50%.
Meals: Full breakfast included for house guests. Also open to the public for all meals throughout the day. High tea is served at 4 pm.
Directions: From the N2 turn left signed to Greyton. Travel for 32km. The Post House is smack in the middle of the village on the left.

Roosje van de Kaap

Nick and Ilzebet Oosthuizen
5 Drostdy St, Swellendam 6740
Tel: 028-514-3001 Fax: 028-514-3001
Email: roosje@dorea.co.za Web: www.roosjevandekaap.co.za
Cell: 082-380-4086

Nick, a lawyer, chef, dad and food-magazine editor (his dog can ride a skateboard…), wants people to come here for food, space and good living. And you'll get it, at "nearly ridiculous" prices. I mean, where else can you get mussels for R25, a bottle of exceptional Springfield Sauvignon Blanc Special for R85 and listen to a live jazz band while you enjoy them! The candlelit restaurant, named by *Eat Out* magazine as one of the ten best restaurants in the Garden Route, is charming and encourages intimacy, with guests often ending up chatting to each other across the tables. It's not open for lunch though. Some rooms at the lodge face the pool, some are bonsai Cape Dutch cottages that face the mountain and next-door's sheep. The Honeymoon suite is all about the view and has a huge four-poster. They vary in feel and size, but all are adorable with bunches of wild flowers everywhere you look. Guests can bask like reptiles in the garden or pool on those hot Swellendam summer days. Nick also has a secret track to a ravine where you can swim below a waterfall. He'll pack you a picnic.

Rooms: 9: all doubles with en-suite shower, except 1 king with bath.
Price: R220 – R300 pp sharing year round.
Meals: Full breakfast included. The restaurant is open from Tuesday till Sunday evening, but not for lunch.
Directions: From Cape Town, take the 4th exit off the N2 to Swellendam. (Count the turn-off to Swellendam industrial area as the first.) After turning off, take the first street left. From the east, after turning off the N2, it's the first street on the left.

Kliphoogte

Herman and Marita Linde
Swellendam 6740
Tel: 028-514-2534 Fax: 028-514-2680
Email: kliphoogte@telkomsa.net
Cell: 084-581-4464

Three kilometres of dusty track bring you to Kliphoogte, one of South Africa's most charming farm B&Bs. Herman, absurdly cheerful for a man who gets up at 4.30 a.m., runs a fruit and dairy farm on the banks of the Leeurivier… while his mother Marita looks after the guest house. Herman represents the fifth generation of Lindes to work the property and will take guests on walks around the farm, or leave them in the company of the boisterous weaver-birds to swim at the lake. At meal times, Marita takes charge and cooks typical South African dinners. Bread, butter and milk are all home-made, as is the lemonade and brandy cake. After dinner, Herman will probably sing to you, and then take you in his 4x4 up a nearby hill to look at the stars. The main bedroom is a sweet, blue affair with sturdy old Afrikaner furniture, family photos and rugs made by the farm workers. The other two rooms, which also share a bathroom, are more functional (though one has a four-poster bed), but this is not a place where you will want to spend long in bed; there is too much going on outside. To sit on the Kliphoogte stoep, listening to the cicadas, and look out over the small, lush valley is to know contentment indeed.

Rooms: 3: 2 doubles and 1 twin; 1 en-suite shower, 2 with shared bathroom.
Price: R300 – R350. Singles on request.
Meals: Dinner by request and will be 3 – 5 courses. Marita will ask you what you want when you book. Lunches and picnics available too. Ask about prices.
Directions: Turn off N2 onto R60 (Swellendam turn-off). After 10km, Kliphoogte (blue sign) is on your left. Then 3km more on gravel road.

Map Number: 5

Jan Harmsgat Country House

Brin and Judi Rebstein
Swellendam 6740
Tel: 023-616-3407 or 023-616-3311 Fax: 023-616-3201
Email: brinreb@iafrica.com Web: www.jhghouse.com

A true country house, Jan Harmsgat is a breath of fresh air in an often-chintzy genre. Judi (a producer in the film industry) and Brin rescued it from tumbledown oblivion in 1989. They swept out the old rotted beams, mould, even pigs, and set about pouring a cellar-full of TLC into it. It is a beautiful place. The restaurant and its increasingly famous staff are starting to catch the food-media's eye… or that your hosts are so gracious. Past resident Hermanus Steyn proclaimed the Independent Republic of Swellendam in 1795 and farmed wine here originally, but I doubt he dined on butterfish bobotie stacks with coriander. Perhaps he did! His 25-metre barn-cellar (now the dining room, complete with grand piano) today looks out of a glass wall. Guests are housed in old slave quarters whose large rooms and great comfort might make you forget the history of the place. However, sympathetic renovation means that windows in the clay walls have not been enlarged, and the wonky lintels, wooden shutters and vast beams all play their part in preserving the original character here. Mine was high up in the apex of the thatch, had a free-standing Victorian bath, gilded chairs and come morning I had a colour-me-happy moment when I opened my shutters and was drenched in a sweet citron-scented breeze gusting across from the orchard. Bliss.

Rooms: 4: 1 dbl with shr & 1 twin with en/s bath; 1 dbl & 1 twin, Victorian baths in room & en-s toilet. Self-catering cottage (1 dbl & 1 twin sharing bathroom).
Price: From R375 – R450 (winter). From R450 – R690 (summer).
Meals: Full breakfast included. Lunch by arrangement. Restaurant open for dinner to public (reservations essential). 4-course set menu R180 pp.
Directions: From Cape Town on N1 to Worcester turn R into R60 (Robertson) at Worcester. Carry on thro' Robertson & Ashton. Turn R after Ashton & stay on R60. House on L after 21km.

Bloomestate

Niels and Miranda Hillmann
276 Voortrekker Street, Swellendam 6740
Tel: 028-514-2984 Fax: 028-514-3822
Email: info@bloomestate.com Web: www.bloomestate.com

"This is simply our ideal holiday spot," Miranda told me as we wandered past the citrus orchard and lily-littered pond. Just what we like to hear, I thought. Bloomestate is overflowing with originality and enthusiasm and their builders battle to keep up with the Hillmanns' endless stream of new ideas. Niels and Miranda arrived from Holland in 2001 and, building from scratch, have already made a name for themselves among the chic boutique set, with endless press clippings singing their praises. But what really impressed me was their genuine and infectious passion for what they are up to. "We just do what feels right. What you see is what you get," says Niels. And what you get is a Mecca of modern living. The seven enormous garden rooms are identical in size and furnishings, with chunky beds looking through French windows to a bright blue pool. Each is strikingly coded by season or element, with one brightly-painted wall, matching cushions and a spray-painted canvas (Niels' handiwork). "Spring" is a vibrant green, "Summer" a sun-burnt orange and the honeymooners' "Fire" a passionate red. This is a place that naturally inspires and delights and – with a resident chef set to arrive imminently – I hereby submit my application to visit again next year.

Rooms: 7: 4 kings & 3 twins, all with bath and shower.
Price: From R375 (May-Sept) – R550 (Oct-April). Singles plus 50%.
Meals: Full breakfast included.
Directions: From CT and N2 take Swellendam West exit (R60) towards Ashton. At the crossroads turn right and Bloomestate is first on the right.

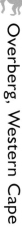

Augusta de Mist Country House

Madeleine and Rob Harrisson

3 Human St, Swellendam 6740
Tel: 028-514-2425 Fax: 028-514-2057
Email: info@augustademist.co.za Web: www.augustademist.co.za
Cell: 082-775-0834

Cool, contemporary decor meets rustic heritage architecture at Augusta de Mist, each setting the other off to great advantage. And Madeleine and Rob are grandmaster hosts at this most laid-back of guest houses. Since our last visit two new luxury garden cottages have sprouted in the garden with white-linened, king-sized beds, spa baths and walk-in showers. Under reed-and-pole ceilings you'll find fireplaces, large indigo sofas or chairs and organza curtains billowing in the breeze. The main house is a unique Cape Dutch national monument, built 50 years after the foundation of Swellendam, i.e. at the beginning of the 19th century. Rob does up old tools and farm implements in his workshop, so all round the house you'll find intriguing wagon boxes, shutters, hinges, doors and once-cherished peasant furniture that has been tailored and restored under his furnace and bellows. The rose nursery garden is a peaceful haven with red-brick paths winding up the hill through banks of lavender towards the swimming pool with its swanky canvas brolly and loungers… and then off to the right over a stream. All the indigenous trees and shrubs mean an abundance of birds. Madeleine is a big fan of modern art; and of growing food at home; and, while we're at it, of breakfast pancakes with banana, crispy bacon and syrup too!

Rooms: 8: 3 kings with bath and/or shower; 1 queen, 1 double and 2 twins with en-suite bath & shower; 1 double with adjoining single and en/s bath & shower.
Price: R280 – R575 pp sharing. Singles on request.
Meals: Full breakfast included.
Directions: From Cape Town thro' village centre, past white church on left. As road bends to R, carry on straight for 20 metres. Then L into Human Str. From Garden Route down hill, past Drostdy Museum, over bridge, take R leg of triangle, then L, then R into Human Str.

Honeywood Farm

John and Miranda Moodie

Between Swellendam and Heidelberg, Heidelberg 6665
Tel: 028-722-1823 Fax: 028-722-1823
Email: john@honeywoodfarm.co.za Web: www.honeywoodfarm.co.za
Cell: 083-270-4035

Attention all botanists, ornithologists, dendrologists, zoologists and, well, pretty much any kind of "–ist"; Honeywood is the place for you. Part conservation area, it's an open, free place, bang next-door to the bird-watching mountain paradise of the Grootvadersbosch Nature Reserve. John is a bee farmer and an expert on everything from olive-back shrikes to yellowwoods and tree frogs. He'll point out the highlights on the five-kilometre trip to the wind-swept and wistfully romantic Hunters Cottage. A truly wild spot, this little bothy tossed in a sea of green hills, is lit only by hurricane lamps and warmed by an open fire. Down in the valley, the track winds past thick forest to the Bush Camp. Incorporating parts of the original homestead site, it feels like a wooden hay-barn with a cinematic element, since a quarter of the blackwood walls slide out of sight so you can observe the scenery. It has an enormous fireplace, old couches, chunky beds and you only need to BYO sleeping-bag and sustenance. For those who prefer their creature comforts there's the more conventional farm cottage near the main house and Miranda, who trained as a cook in Italy, can provide all meals on request. This Moodie clan hasn't moved house since 1817 and, frankly, after a few days at Honeywood, you'll understand exactly why. *Children under 12 half price.*

Rooms: 7 self-contained cottages, each with 2 or 3 bedrooms, some with en/s bathrooms. Oakvale sleeps 6 – 8. 1 booking per cottage (sleeps 10).
Price: R200 – R250 pp sharing.
Meals: Full breakfast R40 pp. Lunch platters R55 for two sharing. Dinners R80 pp for 3 courses including wine. All meals must be pre-booked.
Directions: From Cape Town on N2 take the first road to Suurbraak (R324) after Swellendam and continue straight (you will pass the turn to Tradouws Pass) until you arrive at a dirt road. Carry on straight until you start seeing signs for Honeywood.

Skeiding Guest Farm

Neels and Anné-Lize Uys
Route N2, Heidelberg 6665
Tel: 028-722-1891 Fax: 028-722-2223
Email: skeiding@sdm.dorea.co.za Web: www.skeiding.co.za
Cell: 082-451-4965

Neels and Anné-Lize are fantastically energetic – you need to be to run a farm, a young family and a guest house in the same lifetime. You are welcome to become involved in the workings of the farm as far as possible. This could mean watching the 1500 ostriches being fed in the morning, but there are also indigenous beef cattle, and some sheep, two dogs called Asterix and Jessie... and a couple of young children too. The farm is on high, open, rolling terrain, but it is only a short drive into surprising, Garden Route-style forest and the beautiful Grootvadersbosch Nature Reserve for day hikes. The area is a birder's paradise too with 17 endemic species and they have counted at least 50 species on the farm itself. Alternatively, you can head down over South Africa's only working ferry to the De Hoop Nature Reserve or go to Witsand (35km) for the whales (June to November) and boat rides. It's an outdoorsy sort of place and bedrooms have all you need, their own patios, strong showers, ostrich-skin slippers and there are sitting rooms in the cottages too. Guests eat at the family dining table, wholesome farm fare like ostrich filet, bobotie, pumpkin fritters etc. A friendly family farm and an education for city slickers. *Professionally run horse rides can be arranged.*

Rooms: 4: all doubles/twins; 1 with en-suite bath and shower; 2 with en-suite shower; 1 with wheelchair-friendly en-suite shower.
Price: R250 – R350 pp sharing. No single supplement.
Meals: R70 for 2 courses pp. R100 for 3 courses pp. Price excludes wine.
Directions: From Swellendam take N2 towards Mossel Bay. 45km after Swellendam (12km before Heidelberg) farm signed to left. Follow 2km then signed left again. 3 more km then signed left again. House on hill.

Waterkloof Guesthouse

Hannes and Christine Uys

Witsand
Tel: 028-722-1811
Fax: 028-722-1811
Email:
info@waterkloofguesthouse.
co.za
Web:
www.waterkloofguesthouse.
co.za
Cell: 083-270-2348

Ever played chicken with an ostrich? Now's your chance. Admittedly I had the protection of a bull-barred pick-up truck but it was exciting stuff, rattling around the farm collecting still-warm eggs for the incubator and doing our best to avoid overly ruffling their fathers' feathers. Waterkloof is an ostrich farm through and through and there is nothing that Hannes (only the seventh generation of the Uys family to work this land!) doesn't know about these feisty fowl. They use the leather for bags, the eggs for breakfast, the eggshells for lampshades and the meat for supper. The only thing you can't do with an Uys ostrich is ride it – there are horses for that, and Hannes and Christine's daughters will happily take you out on a tour. Sunk into rolling fields of barley and wheat, this is a hard-working farm but a great place to take it easy. Cool, luxurious bedrooms open onto the garden and fountain, wild fig trees shade benches built for reading on and the pool area has its own kitchen for help-yourself Sunday lunches. And if you feel like a change of scenery (and wildlife) Witsand is the place to see migrating whales. Back at the house Hannes patiently answered my babble of questions as we sank into ostrich-leather-covered armchairs and tucked into Christine's cheesecake – no ostrich in that, I take it.

Rooms: 4: 2 doubles and 1 twin all with bath, 1 twin with shower.
Price: R200 (winter) – R400 (summer).
Meals: Full breakfast included. Dinner on request.
Directions: From the CT and the N2 turn R onto R324 after Swellendam 32 to the farm. From Mossel Bay take R322 to Witsand. At the crossroads turn R. Farm is on the L after 17 km.

River Magic

Bosky and Paul Andrew
Reservations: 35 Pear Lane Constantia, Cape Town, 7806, Physical address: Vermaaklikheid, Nr Riversdale
Tel: 021-794-6294 or 028-713-2930 Fax: 028-713-2930
Email: rivermagic@zsd.co.za Web: www.vermaaklikheid.co.za Cell: 082-732-3(

Welcome to the centre of the universe," said Paul, as our tubby little rowing boat sliced through the early morning mist, its oars stirring the clear cola-coloured water and groaning in their rollocks. We bumped gently against the jetty and hopped out onto a dew-damp riverbank, the best and, for that matter, only way to arrive at River Magic's "Glory Be". Silence. I fumbled for an appropriate superlative. What a spot… what a find. Two low, stone-built, thatched cottages, buried in the folds of brush-carpeted, ancient sand dunes and, without doubt, the most enchanting place I had yet encountered. I longed to return with a gang of pals, threading our way between the banks of Spanish reed, ferrying supplies across the river, fishing for grunter from the jetty (or canoes) and sharing beers and a braai around the enormous outdoor table. Inside, the cottages are comfortably (not extravagantly) kitted-out with wooden furniture and all kitchen essentials. There are beds for as many as you can muster, some secluded, others tucked into tents or in sociable four-man rooms. On a hot tip, I wheeled mine outside to sleep under the stars where I lay heaped in a duvet, inventing constellations, listening to the hadedahs in the blue gums and scribbling notes by torchlight. Sound alright?

Rooms: 2 cottages: 'Glory Be' sleeps 12 (3 dbles, tented garden hut & 4-bed room), shared ablution block; 'Back Track' sleeps 6 (2 twins en/s shr, 1 tented hut).
Price: From R130 – R150 pp sharing. Min R350 per cottage per night. Min R500 – R800 over long weekends & R800 – R1,000 over Christmas hols.
Meals: Self-catering, bring your own wood, towels and torches. Seafood restaurant nearby.
Directions: From CT take N2. 50km after Swellendam turn R, signed "Port B'ford; Witsand". After 6km, turn L onto dirt rd signed Vermaaklikheid. After 14km turn L at T-jct, cross river over causeway. Follow signs to V'kh'd & then to River Magic.

Otters Spring River Lodge

Sue Byrne and Craig Saxon

Waterblom Street, PO Box 676, Stilbaai 6674
Tel: 028-754-3112 Fax: 028-754-3112
Email: suebyrne@webmail.co.za Web: www.ottersspring.co.za
Cell: 082-775-5053

I heard Sue before I saw her. Her laughter is often heard echoing around the house, emblematic of a thoroughly jolly place, equally suited to family fun as to lazy, pampered getaways. Otters Spring is plugged into the hillside above the Goukou River and surrounded by 90 hectares of paddock, river bank and dam to let the kids loose on while you sink into a good book, the pool or both. Rooms, each with a basic but brightly-coloured bathroom, are hidden under the thatched roof or tucked into the hillside. A clumpy meadow mowed by podgy sheep tumbles down to the river. Sooner or later, you'll be down there too, hurling yourself in from the bobbing pontoon, or (probably not 'and') looking out for the elusive otters. You're welcome to fish too, though to date no one has ever caught anything substantial in size. Back up at the house the chickens provide the eggs, the goose chases the dog, Sue does massages and evening meals (sometimes at the same time!… not really), Craig scurries around doing maintenance when not filling guests with a scrumptious breakfast... and you? Your job is to lie back in a hammock. Water-skiing and wake-boarding are available further down-river and Stilbaii has excellent surf.

Rooms: 6: 1 twin and 3 doubles, all with bath and/or shower; 1 family suite with 2 doubles, separate toilet and shared bathroom.
Price: R250 – R400 pp sharing.
Meals: Full breakfast included. Dinners on request.
Directions: From N2 take the Stilbaii turning between Riversdale and Albertinia. Arriving in town, cross the bridge and turn immediately right into Waterbloom St. Otters Spring is 13km upriver on the right.

Riversyde

Dora Hattingh

2 Long St,Great Brak River 6525
Tel: 044-620-3387 Fax: 044-620-3552
Email: riversyd@mweb.co.za Web: www.riversyde.co.za
Cell: 082-784-5885

Slowly submerging into a hot bath, I sent up a silent thank-you to the removals men who had ferried Dora's Victorian tubs from the Free State to their new home, the impeccably elegant Riversyde, a decade ago. The steaming water and a night by the Great Brak River proved the perfect antidote to a long and dusty day's travelling… and Dora the perfect hostess. The house is over a century old and its soothing air of quiet grandeur flows throughout. The egg-shell blue or salmon pink bedrooms are blessed with deep carpets (best appreciated with bare feet) and river views. One has a little balcony and two have their heavy, iron baths planted in the bedroom behind discreet screens. Come supper-time, Dora modestly questioned whether her food was up to our "gourmet cuisine" symbol standard. I assured her it most definitely was, tucking into baby sole that cut like butter. She's as keen on classical music as she is on cooking and I was serenaded with Rachmaninov at dinner. Pavarotti sang to me at breakfast before a gentle wander along the riverbank, open daily to tea-drinkers and cake-eaters. The water flows lazily past a row of coral trees just five metres from the house, and from the jetty I watched a cormorant drying his wings. Dora asked if there was anything I thought she could improve on. Not really….

Rooms: 4: all doubles with en-suite bath, or bath and shower.
Price: R330 – R600 pp sharing. Single supplement 50%.
Meals: Full breakfast included (included if you are self-catering too).
Directions: From Mossel Bay take N2 towards George, exit 409 signed left into Great Brak River. Follow past 2 stop signs. House on right before bridge.

Botlierskop Private Game Reserve

The Neethling and Wiggett Families
PO Box 565, Little Brak River 6503
Tel: 044-696-6055 Fax: 044-696-6272
Email: botlier@mweb.co.za Web: www.botlierskop.co.za
Cell: 083-628-1105

The Garden Route is best known for its scenery and sea life, so the last thing I expected to see as I navigated the back roads was a rhino. But there it was, chewing the cud like a contented cow. Time to take a closer look. Botlierskop is a private game reserve that, for those with limited time, brings the big five south. It's not as wild as its northern counterparts (the lions are in a sanctuary) but it's a magical place to stay, set in 2,400 hectares of grassy plains and forested sandstone hills. The park is open to day visitors but it's skillfully co-ordinated to ensure your paths never cross. One of the highlights (well two of them actually) are Sam and Totsi, orphaned elephants trained not only in giving rides, but also as actors. Did you see Far of Place? Or Elephant Boy? Trust me, they were great! Elephant back rides and elephant picnics are a big pull at Botlierskop. Overnighters are appointed their own private guide and I had Hentie, an animal almanac and rock art aficionado. A short quad-bike ride from the cavernous hilltop restaurant, he ushered me into a dinghy and we drifted off down the wooded, Moordkuil river to the guest tents. More of a marquee than a tent, each is set on its own patch of decking with steps leading to a floating jetty (a great spot to fish from). It's luxury with a capital 'L' and inside, deep armchairs, a writing desk and a room-for-two bath accompany the mosquito-netted four-poster. One tip though, zip it closed when you leave – the vervet monkeys have a penchant for coffee and cookies.

Rooms: 8: 7 kings and 1 twin luxury tents, all with en/s bath.
Price: R1,290 – R1,790 pp sharing. Rates include game drive, activities and all meals.
Meals: Fully catered.
Directions: From Mossel Bay and CT on N2 take Little Brak River exit (401). Heading inland turn R to Sorgfontein. Continue 4km and after causeway turn R for 4km along gravel road to Botlierskop.

Map Number: 5

Entry Number: 124

The Waves

Liza and Iain Campbell

7 Beach Rd, Victoria Bay, George 6530
Tel: 044-889-0166 Fax: 044-889-0166
Email: thewaves@intekom.co.za Web:
www.gardenroute.co.za/vbay/waves/index.htm

Iain and Liza have an amazing photo from 1906 when The Waves was the only house on the beach, used as a holiday home by an Oudtshoorn farmer. It is not surprising a few others have since joined the club. The hamlet is closed to vehicles – only residents hold the key to the gate, so you can park your car securely at night. I'm no surfer, but the waves here are enticing, rolling up the perfect arc of the small bay at a height that is challenging, but not scary. Iain will arrange a wetsuit and surfboard or fins and a snorkel. Or if you like your activity less damp, there is horse-riding nearby, dolphin- and whale-watching in season and walks along the bay front. The house is right on the sea (see above) and all three bedroom suites (each with its own lounge) look out, although you may spend more time on the verandah watching the waves roll in. They are hypnotic. Breakfast is served here in the sunshine and often goes for hours. The Outeniqua Choo-Tjoe (yes, it's a steam train) runs through Victoria Bay twice a day. Both Iain and Liza are consummate hosts, love what they do and share a great sense of fun. Bay life could be addictive. *Fully no-smoking anywhere. Children over 12 only.*

Rooms: 3: all doubles with extra beds, 1 with en-suite shower, 2 with en-suite bath and shower.
Price: R375 – R650 pp sharing. Singles R495 – R850.
Meals: Full breakfast included. Dinner can be ordered in and a table will be set for you.
Directions: From Mossel Bay on N2 past George exits where highways merge. 1km signed Victoria Bay to right – follow down hill 3km. Park and walk along beach road to collect the key for the gate.

Malvern Manor

Sandra and Michael Cook

Nr Fancourt, Blanco, George 6530
Tel: 044-870-8788   Fax: 044-870-8790
Email: malvernmanor@msn.com Web: www.malvernmanor.co.za
Cell: 084-867-6470

If you are having any difficulty understanding why the area is called the Garden Route, well, have a trundle up Michael and Sandra's drive. Much more colourful and vibrant than anything visible from the public thoroughfares. I drove past cows and dams onto a redbrick road overflowing with thick tangles of foliage that hide Malvern from view – and all this perfectly framed by the imposing Outeniqua Mountains. Here is another English couple who fell in love with South Africa, upped sticks and bought their country idyll. Both of farming stock, this 21-hectare dairy farm was perfect. But despite being just a hop, skip and a jump from George, it was no easy task converting the Manor House, the keep at the heart of the farm, into a guest house; just ask Michael about the basin palaver. But it's all come together so nicely. My room opened onto the garden through French doors, and lavish Greek-style pillars pick out the bath – the perfect place to unwind after a round of golf at Fancourt (recent host of the President's Cup). For non-golfers, two dams offer blue gill and big-mouth bass fishing or else there's endless scope for pre-breakfast walks. Play your cards right on your return and Michael might don his apron and prepare his speciality 'chocaccino'. Delightful people in an enchanting setting.

Rooms: 3: 1 queen, 1 twin or king, 1 double with single bed. All have en-suite bath and shower.
Price: R320 – R540 pp sharing. Singles on request.
Meals: Full breakfast included. Restaurants nearby and deliveries can be arranged.
Directions: From N2 take George airport exit onto R404 and follow signs to Oudtshoorn for approximately 8km. After Fancourt Golfing Estate, sign to Malvern Manor on left. Follow signs.

Map Number: 5

Acorn Guest House

Colin and Esther Horn

4 Kerk St, George 6529
Tel: 044-874-0474 Fax: 044-884-1753
Email: info@acornguesthouse.co.za Web: www.acornguesthouse.co.za
Cell: 083-539-7398

With birds chirping in the tree-lined street and church bells chiming (Kerk is Afrikaans for Church), I approached the pink, ivy-clad walls utterly unaware of the riches hidden within. Acorn Guest House is a veritable treasure trove and Esther was quick to explain: "where some people go to casinos, we go to auctions." Almost everything in this Edwardian house is second-hand and antique. Persian rugs are strewn over bare floorboards; battered wooden trunks are scattered throughout the bedrooms; mirrors and ornaments adorn the available wall space; every nook and cranny arrests the eye. The bedrooms are equally ornate, the master room boasting a large en-suite bathroom separated from the grand sleeping area by a gold-coloured curtain. Had I stayed a little longer (and deprived the Horns of even more of Esther's delicious home-baked cake) I could have joined Colin on a fishing trip… although not the leisurely pipe-and-picnic fishing I had envisaged. "If guests are able to swim 4km in the sea with a snorkel, they're welcome to join me," he proclaimed, re-emerging with his weapon of choice, a spear gun. If all this sounds a bit too James Bond for you, he also offers more serene tours of the estuary in his boat. Those with spoils to share come evening do so on the braai, whilst bargain hunters furiously jot down Esther's top tips.

Rooms: 4: 2 doubles, 1 with en-suite bath and shower, 1 with en-suite bath; 1 twin with en-suite shower; 1 family unit with en-suite shower.
Price: R200 – R350 pp sharing. Singles R350 – R450.
Meals: Full breakfast included. Picnic basket by arrangement.
Directions: Take York Street exit off N2 towards town. Go through town on York Street until the roundabout. Turn right (signed to Knysna) and Kerk Street is third turning on left. Second property on right.

Fairview Historic Homestead

Philda Benkenstein
36 Stander St, George 6530
Tel: 044-874-7781 Fax: 044-874-7999
Email: benkenstein@mweb.co.za Web: www.wheretostay.co.za/fairview
Cell: 082-226-9466

This picturesque, listed Victorian house on the eastern edge of George is an intriguing place to stay. With its high ceilings and abundant Victoriana, Fairview has the feel of an old English rectory, although the vivid colours owe more to African than Anglican themes. All the bedrooms are a treat: the two on the ground floor still have their original 1880s floorboards, beams and fireplaces; the Orange Room, complete with dashing white trim, bathes in afternoon sunlight, while the Yellow Room soaks up the morning. The sitting room has the same high ceilings and wooden floors, with shuttered sash windows and enormous linen press. The whole place has a happy family atmosphere, enhanced by the original home features, which have been retained wherever possible. Philda loves to host and have people in her beautiful home. She will cook too and if you do eat here, as the GG guests visiting were, then you'll enjoy mainly South African fare. Husband Desmond is a green-fingered doctor and the creative force in the glorious garden. There are tropical fruit trees, an immaculate veggie patch, swathes of clivia and plans for much more.

Rooms: 4: all doubles with an extra bed. All have en-suite shower, 1 has en-suite bath.
Price: R250 – R320 pp sharing. Singles plus 50%.
Meals: Full breakfast included. Dinners by arrangement.
Directions: From CT on N2 take York St turn-off to George. Turn right at T-jct into Courtenay St. Over railway bridge and turn left into Second Street and turn left at stop sign into Stander St, house on right.

Map Number: 5

Entry Number: 128

Strawberry Hill Country Lodge

Di and Bill Turner
Old George-Knysna (Seven Passes) Road, Wilderness, PO Box 4822,
George East 6539
Tel: 044-877-0055 Fax: 044-877-0055
Email: getaway@strawberryhill.co.za Web: www.strawberryhill.co.za

Bill and Di wouldn't swap this for all the animals in Africa. Their hill-marooned farm looks across to the mountains and, though shrouded in mist when I arrived, the view here has previously had guests applauding and trying to order prints! The garden plunges straight from the pool and lawns to two deep gorges and nothing spoils the unfettered vista. The area is home to afro-montane forest and over the years Di has identified 56 species of fern while Bill has hacked his way through the bush to create numerous hiking tracks down to the deepest pools. He will happily be your guide – as he was for me – striding along, identifying the astonishingly diverse plant and bird life and pausing for well-earned breathers at stunning, log-bench lookouts. Di was away trekking through the Scottish highlands at the time (as you do), but when at home, she and Bill invite their guests to join them every evening for wine and snacks on the verandah or beside the enormous log fire. The lodge is luxurious and homey and no details have been overlooked. The fully, self-contained cottage is available to rent too, tailored to children with a playground and tree house in the fenced garden, pretty country furnishings and animal murals in an upstairs bedroom. *Great hiking and well-situated for exploration of the Garden Route.*

Rooms: 6: 3 doubles in house; 1 suite (sleeps 2 extra on divan) with en/s shower; 2 doubles with en/s bath & sh; 1 self-c house with 3 doubles sharing bath & sh.
Price: For B&B: R250 – R500 pp sharing. For self-catering: R300 – R1,000 for cottage (sleeps 9).
Meals: Full breakfast included. Light self-service supper provided (request in advance). Cottage less R30 if self-catering for breakfast.
Directions: From George head towards Wilderness on Knysna Rd. L onto old George-Knysna road signed Saasveld Technikon (Pine Lodge on corner). Strawberry Hill after 7.5km on R.

Moontide Guest House

Maureen Mansfield

Southside Rd, Wilderness
6560
Tel: 044-877-0361
Fax: 044-877-0124
Email:
moontide@intekom.co.za
Web: www. moontide.co.za

It's a rare pleasure for us to stay somewhere on *holiday* and to experience it over a period of days. And Moontide was a palpable hit with all five of us. Its position is hard to beat, right on the banks of the lagoon, its wooden decks shaded by a 400-year-old milkwood tree. Here you can sit out for bountiful breakfasts or with an evening drink from your bar fridge, and watch giant kingfishers diving for fish – well, we saw one anyway. Bird life is profuse on the lagoon. The long, white-sanded Wilderness beach is only a one-minute walk from the house, but you can also take a canoe straight from Moontide up the lagoon into the Touw River and then walk along forest trails to waterfalls to swim in fresh-water rock pools. Whatever we did it was a pleasure to return, play cards in a relaxed sitting room, or read in the cool of a bedroom. I was delighted with 'Milkwood' because I'm a sucker for dozing on a futon, in a loft, under thatched eaves, with river views by my head. But I would like to return and try them all. Since we descended *en masse*, Maureen has built herself a tree-top sanctuary. The deck, day-bed, even the free-standing bath, look out across thatched roofs to the river. Sportingly, she's decided it's too nice to keep for herself!

Rooms: 5: Don River luxury suite (king & 2 twins); Treetop (queen, bath & outside shr); Milkwood (double & 2 singles & shower); Stone Cottage (twins & shr); The Boathouse (double & bath).
Price: R280 – R460 pp sharing. Single rates on request.
Meals: Full breakfast included.
Directions: From George on N2 ignore Wilderness turn-off. Cross Touw River bridge, first left signed Southside Rd. Moontide at the end of cul-de-sac.

Wilderness Manor

Johan and Marianne Nicol
397 Waterside Rd, Wilderness 6560
Tel: 044-877-0264 Fax: 044-877-0163
Email: wildman@mweb.co.za Web: www.manor.co.za

Marianne has a flair for interiors. You won't need one of the hundreds of books (African art and history, its wildlife and architecture, war memoirs, children's classics and psychology texts) that rub sleeves throughout the house to find this out. Overlooking the lagoon, the glass-encased sitting room is coir-carpeted with Afghan kilims, a low-slung ivory sofa and a pair of Morris chairs, given to the Governor of Gauteng. There's an old billiard table, too, somewhere under a pile of maps. African artefacts have been begged, borrowed or bought: Ndebele pipes and beads, bartered-for carvings and stones from the Cradle of Mankind. The bedrooms have similar horn-and-hide hues, all the luxurious trappings you could wish for, and room for Indonesian chairs and chests, chocolate leather sofas, slipper baths and dark canopied beds with reading lights. In the morning, linen tables were dressed with bone-handle cutlery and lilies in a square metal vase placed on an old country bench next to fruit and muesli. Your hosts are discreet and attentive, and after serving up a faultless (and greaseless) breakfast, will give you a map and bountiful beach-bag and set you off to explore your surrounds. Bird life is rampant in the area and walks in the surrounding forests are a must. It is only a five-minute stroll along lagoon-side boardwalks to the beach, town and some good restaurants.

Rooms: 4: 2 kings with en-suite bath and shower; 2 twins, one with en/s bath and shower, one with shower only.
Price: R390 – R490 pp sharing. Single supplement plus 50% (100% in summer). Rates greatly reduced in winter.
Meals: Full breakfast included.
Directions: From George, follow N2 to Wilderness (beware of speed cameras on descent). Turn left into Wilderness Village and follow road to T-junction. Turn right along lagoon to Wilderness Manor on left.

Eden B&B

Bev Campbell

Erica Rd, PO Box 623, Wilderness 6560
Tel: 044-877-0149
Email: bcampbell@telkomsa.net Web:

At GGHQ, we consider it a good sign if we make notes *before* we visit a place. One phone call to Bev and I'd taken down first-class directions, remembered old acquaintances, talked elephants and admirals and assured her that I was half the man my predecessor was (Guy is 6'10, whereas I was designed to be fired from a circus canon). Bev used to live on a citrus farm in Addo, but has now relocated to this hilltop wilderness. Amongst the homes of golf stars and polo players, Eden is something out of the ordinary. But then so is Bev. Not many people can lay claim to having built (and sold) a village. Now she's perched between forest and sea, in a house hand-made by a 'wood expert', with individually painted walls, where you join her for breakfast. You sleep in the uncluttered woodcutter's cottage next door, which has a quaint little kitchen, old wood-burning stove, beds that embrace you and a shower that steams with hot water. Her two dogs – one a pedigree Jack Russell, the other a jolly good effort – will accompany you round the garden. The legacy of the previous owner, it teems with irises, watsonia, strelitzia, clivia and an incredible selection of succulents. Further afield, toward the mountains, you can gambol through lush meadows and pine forests, wildlife in full song. "I make no apologies for the noises off," says Bev. "This is Africa!"

Rooms: 3: all twins, 1 with en-suite shower, 2 sharing bath and shower.
Price: R200 – R250 pp sharing.
Meals: Full breakfast included. Plenty of restaurants 5 mins away in Wilderness.
Directions: From George turn off N2 into Wilderness Village. Left past Wilderness Hotel to T-junction. Stay left on Heights Road, up hill, past Bundu Café and map of Africa settlement. Erica Rd on left, right fork to Eden on right.

The Dune Guest Lodge

Gary and Melisa Grimes

31 Die Duin, Wilderness 6560
Tel: 044-877-0298
Fax: 044-877-0298
Email: info@the dune.co.za
Web: www.thedune.co.za
Cell: 083-941-1149

Gary Grimes is both consummate host and chief breakfast-maker at The Dune and when I pulled up (carefully avoiding parking in the space marked "for my girlfriend/wife") he and Melisa had just finished feeding the hordes with a man-stopping fry-up. "Anything you can do with eggs, I do it," he tells me. I made a note to arrive a little earlier next time. By most standards, he is greedily tall, but at 6'7" he insists he was pretty average among his basketball contemporaries and after years as a pro in Switzerland he dropped the ball in favour of a dishcloth, dinner plates and the wildness of Wilderness. If you're looking for a beach-house then you couldn't get much more beachy than this. As the name suggests it's smack-bang in the dunes and, to be numerically fastidious, exactly 85 wooden steps lead down to 7.5km of pristine sandy beach stretching away to both east and west. The whole place has a wonderfully soothing, seaside feel. Walls hung with seascape oils are whitewashed or sea blue. Driftwood sculptures surround the fireplace and bedside sofas look south through wall-to-wall windows for round-the-clock whale-watching. Best of all though, wherever you are in the building, you can hear the surf heaving, sighing, thumping and crumping against the beach.

Rooms: 4: 2 doubles, 2 twins with 3/4 beds, all with en/s bath and shower.
Price: R350 – R700 pp sharing.
Meals: Full breakfast included.
Directions: From CT pass Wilderness on N2. Cross the Touw river and turn right into Die Duin 700m later. Take the right fork and The Dune is first on the left.

Forget-me-not B&B

Mary and Derek Woolmington
21 Boekenhout St, Upper Old Place, Knysna 6570
Tel: 044-382-2916 Fax: 044-382-2913
Email: mary@forget-me-not.co.za Web: www.forget-me-not.co.za
Cell: 083-505-4225

Derek and Mary, a warm and down-to-earth English-Irish couple, embody all that we look for in hosts. Having built businesses and raised family, they're starting out on their own again. Hence Forget-me-not (Self-catering and B&B, to give it its full title), with its sloping slate roof, dormer windows and gravel drive set behind a picket fence. The house is edged with wisteria, primroses and forget-me-nots and other flowers Mary can't quite put a name to (and nor can I obviously) – she puts it down to "Outeniqua rust", a lethargic malaise blamed on easy living. Inside the sweep of a maranti staircase leads to two bedrooms. Iris has pine floorboards, leaning walls, blanket box and hanging space. There's a cushioned window-box from which to sit and stare. The rose room, more feminine in shades of pink with floral motifs, has Oregon pine furniture. An elongated bathroom harbours a bath tucked under the eaves. Everyone eats at the house (usually outside above the lawn and pool), even those in the self-contained flat, whose wooden deck faces the lagoon, Knysna Heads and the hills. All guests get use of the pool and the braai area and the house is within walking distance of the Waterfront and a short drive to the beaches. The long list of activities, both on water and inland, can be booked on your behalf by Derek and Mary.

Rooms: 3: 1 king and 1 queen both with en/s bath and shower; 1 self-contained apartment.
Price: R170 – R270 pp sharing. Singles on request.
Meals: Full cooked or Continental breakfast and variety of fruit and fruit/veg juice boosts. Plenty of local restaurants.
Directions: Head east out of Knysna and turn left onto Old Toll Rd, Upper Old Place. At T-junction turn right and take first left into Boekenhout St. Forget-me-not on right.

Glenshee

David and Fiona Ramsay

Eastford Downs, Eastford Nature Reserve, Welbedacht Lane, Knysna 6570
Tel: 044-382-3202 Fax: 044-382-3202
Email: glenshee@mweb.co.za Web: www.gosouth.co.za/glenshee/
Cell: 082-789-5062

David and Fiona were the first to build up here on the mountain, their pink-washed home blessed (not by chance) with majestic valley views down the steep sides of the Eastford Nature Reserve to the curve of the Knysna River far below. Views they couldn't resist sharing with others… which is where you come in. They built the house themselves, the hundred-year-old windows and doors salvaged from Karoo farms, and the wide wooden deck has become the irresistible focal point of the house. And now they have built a grey fibre-glass plunge pool too, further inducement to spend at least one lazy day at Glenshee. The three bedrooms are fresh, light, airy and countrified with wicker bedsteads, excellent linen, your own private deck and viewpoint. David and Fiona really enjoy their guests and operate in traditional B&B fashion, offering much expert advice, over sundowners or tea, on secret spots they have found all along the Garden Route. Or they will point out the best walks from the house through the forests and fynbos. Fiona spends at least an hour each morning preparing the breakfast (Health, Continental or English) and these are taken on the deck with the invigorating view as backdrop. A real home and delightful hosts. *Despite Glenshee's imperious mountainside position it is just 8 minutes from the town centre.*

Rooms: 3: 1 double with en/s bath; 1 twin with en/s shower; 1 double/twin with en/s bath and shower.
Price: R200 – R450 pp sharing. Singles on request.
Meals: Health, Continental or English breakfast included. 3-course dinner by arrangement: R100 – R150 pp. Local restaurants in Knysna.
Directions: From George, before Knysna, turn left into Welbedacht Lane, go straight for 2km to crossroads. Go right signed Eastford Downs follow for 250 metres, then straight through the gateposts into Eastford Downs. Glenshee is 800 metres down on the left.

Gallery Guest House

Lolly Hahn-Page
10 Hill St West, Knysna 6570
Tel: 044-382-2510 Fax: 044-382-5212
Email: gallery.guesthouse@pixie.co.za Web: www.galleryguesthouse.co.za
Cell: 083-309-3920

Lolly manages the happy trick of combining her work as an artist with running a friendly, laid-back guest house in a peaceful part of Knysna. She is a strong force for the promotion of arts and crafts in the town, itself a honeypot for those that can hold a pencil steady. Thus the "Gallery". Her own and local artists' paintings and sculptures dot the walls and cover the carpets in the guest house, one of the longest-running in Knysna. When she can, Lolly steals away to her private studio, handing the reins to the charismatic Miriam, grand-daughter of the King of Lesotho (!). The main room where breakfast etc happens is upstairs and the adjoining wooden deck has tremendous views out over the Knysna Heads, Leisure Isle and Pledge Park nature reserve. There is lots to do in town, what with sunset boat rides, the Outeniqua Choo-Tjoe, sea swimming, canoeing etc and Lolly is very knowledgeable. Best of all she has special private places – sunset spots, music venues, beaches, walks and restaurants – you will only find with her help. The bedrooms themselves are simple, showcasing more local artwork, but cater for all your needs. Choose Gallery Guest House for the irrepressible personality of both house and hostess. *Nine good restaurants within 2 mins.*

Rooms: 4: 2 twins and 2 doubles; 1 with private bath, 3 with en-suite bath or shower.
Price: From R200 pp sharing. Single rates on request.
Meals: Full breakfast included and served from 8 to 10 am.
Directions: From George take N2 to Knysna. At 2nd lights turn left into Grey St, then 2nd left into Hill St West, to end of cul-de-sac. Map on web site.

Narnia Farm Guest House

Richard and Stella Sohn
off Welbedacht Lane, Knysna 6570
Tel: 044-382-1334 Fax: 044-382-2881
Email: narnia@pixie.co.za Web: www.narnia.co.za
Cell: 083-325-2581

Narnia combines just about every element we search for in a place to stay. It's defiantly itself – the style (luxuriously ethnic, but never overdone) is so unusual and so genuine that you know it is the extension of real people, not some pretentious interior design job. Stella (graphic design graduate, protea farmer, mother of two) is one of those people and Richard (lawyer, 'architect' and father of four) the other. Narnia is entirely their creation, a dream slotted round one or two key requirements: the house should have a deck with a clear view to the Knysna Heads; and there should be a big, open, friendly entrance hall. Otherwise the house has grown organically into some mad ship with wooden decks, gangways and staircases, swing chairs, heavenly colours of tropical brilliance ("In a previous life I must have been a Mexican," says Stella), a prize-winning garden, long views in all directions, and smaller surprises everywhere. This year they have added a decking-clad, black-painted pool (of swimming – as opposed to plunging – dimensions) and are busy creating a new cottage next to it. Stella and Richard amaze me with their great energy and skill with people, despite holding down so many jobs. *Bushbuck are often spotted by the dam on the farm and visitors to the garden include porcupine, monkeys, bushpigs, lynx and 85 species of bird.*

Rooms: 3: 2 doubles with en-suite bathrooms; 1 cottage with 1 twin and 1 double and shared bathroom (self-catering or B&B).
Price: R295 – R495 pp sharing. Seasonal rates and singles on request. Children under 12 half-price.
Meals: Full breakfast included and served from 8.00 – 9.30 am.
Directions: On N2 from George turn into Welbedacht Lane just before Knysna. Then follow signs to Narnia Farm Guest House.

Entry Number: 137

Map Number: 6

Spring Tide Charters

Stephan and Evelyn Pepler

34 South Jetty, Knysna Quays, Waterfront Drive, Knysna 6600
Fax: 044-382-5852
Email: info@springtidesailing.com Web: www.springtidesailing.com
Cell: 082-829-2740

As I took the helm on board the Outeniqua, 50 feet of shimmering beauty somehow suddenly under my command, and sailed her across Knysna lagoon at a leisurely six knots, I felt very special indeed. The Outeniqua is sailed daily by Stephan and his young friendly crew who clearly love what they do and it's not hard to see why. The coastline around Knysna is spectacular, with regular sightings of marine life and pelagic birds. The vessel itself is also exceptional, and I'm not just saying that because Stephan spent four and a half years building and fitting her out! Every immaculate thing on board, excluding the hull, is his own work. Anyone who has climbed aboard will agree, from President Mbeki to baby son Alix. The day starts with a call to the harbourmaster to raise the bridge, as you head off across the lagoon to the Heads, two majestic sandstone cliffs that lead out to the open sea and a whole world of excitement. Various day trips include a 4-hour day sail with lunch, a 2.5-hour sail and the 3-hour sunset cruise where you can indulge in Knysna's famous oysters, seafood and sushi all washed them down with a fine South African bubbly. Evenings are spent anchored in the calm lagoon where a private chef conjures up a gourmet dinner from the galley. A wonderful experience. Advance bookings essential.

Rooms: 2 cabins – ideal for a family or two couples. Day sails and champagne sunset cruises available.
Price: Overnight charters from R2,400 pp. 2 1/2-hour cruise from R340 pp. Also offer 3-hour sunset cruise and day sailing with lunch.
Meals: Full breakfast and dinner included.
Directions: Knysna Quay Marina is on the Waterfront Drive. Park on the waterfront, next to the station. Yacht moored next to 34° South restaurant.

Southern Cross Beach House

Sue and Neill Ovenstone

1 Capricorn Lane, Solar Beach, Plettenberg Bay 6600
Tel: 044-533-3868 Fax: 044-533-3866
Email: southerncross@robbergbeach.co.za Web:
www.southerncrossbeach.co.za Cell: 082-490-0876

…and relax. With this dreamy, whitewashed, wooden house at the quiet end of Robberg Beach's long arc, it is impossible not to. Plettenberg Bay is a lively town, with lots of restaurants and bars, but people really come here for the sea, and you would seriously struggle to get closer to it than at Southern Cross. During the Christmas holidays the beach is packed, but for the rest of the year there are more signs of life in the sea. Dolphins race by all year round, revelling in their position at the head of the food chain, with southern right whales often wallowing just in front of the house from June to November. The house itself is just up a wooden gangway from the beach. Wood predominates, with blues and white echoing the ocean. The brochure says 'plantation style', but I would plump for classic Massachussetts beach house. Wooden decking looks across the bay to the Tsitsikamma Mountains to the left and the Robberg Peninsula opposite, which is geologically identical to the Falklands, bizarrely… and a fantastic place to walk. Inside is the breakfast room and living room, and set around the garden on the ground floor (Sue and Neill live upstairs) are the five lovely rooms. Barefoot, laid-back luxury.

Rooms: 5: 1 double, 1 queen, 2 twins, 1 king; all with en-suite shower, 2 with baths as well.
Price: R375 – R595 pp sharing. Single supplement R150.
Meals: Full breakfast included. Kitchenette available for putting together salads and light meals.
Directions: From roundabout in Main St, go down hill past Central Beach, over Piesang River bridge. Over the circle, past shops (Kwikspar), right into Longships Ave. Straight over 3 speed bumps (2km). Left into Gris Nez Dr. Over stop street, left into Gemini, 3rd street on L. Turn right and then left into Capricorn Lane.

Beacon Lodge

Al and Clo Scheffer

57 Beacon Way, PO Box
1694, Plettenberg Bay 6600
Tel: 044-533-2614
Fax: 044-533-2614
Email:
beaconlodge@worldonline.co.
za Web:
www.beaconlodge.co.za

Garden Route, Western Cape

This is a small (just two rooms), personal, friendly and involving B&B – and I mean B&B in the proper sense where you share the house with your hosts. (Both rooms have their own separate entrances, mind you, if you want to slip about more furtively.) The patio (for breakfasts, garden bird-watching or reading) has long views out to sea and it's only a short walk to the beach and the lagoon, presumably where you will want to spend at least some of your time. To this end Al and Clo have all beach necessities at the ready – umbrellas, towels and the like. The larger of the two rooms was my favourite (and also the more expensive – my wife will tell you this is typical) with sea views through a huge window and anti-glare solar blinds. There is seagrass on floors, plenty of immaculate seaside white in walls and towels and colour is added in the form of fresh flowers. The Scheffers take the greatest care of their guests. *Fridge facilities provided. Great restaurants within walking distance. Whales and dolphins in season. Closed mid-Dec – mid-Jan and either June or July. Enquire first!*

Rooms: 2: 1 twin and 1 double, both with en-suite bathrooms with showers.
Price: R165 – R350 pp sharing. Single rates on request.
Meals: Full breakfast included. There are good restaurants in town for other meals.
Directions: From Knysna take the N2. Take the second turn into Plett at the Engen 1-stop garage – the house is 600 metres on your left.

Bosavern

Vivienne and Gerald Dreyer

38 Cutty Sark Ave, Plettenberg Bay 6600
Tel: 044-533-1312 Fax: 044-533-0758
Email: info@bosavern.co.za Web: www.bosavern.co.za
Cell: 082-922-4721

The striking S-shaped waves of Bosavern's timbered ceiling mimic the sea and combine with minimalist white interiors and mirrors to strike a harmonious note with the blue ocean far below. Glass doors lead off the open-plan sitting room and onto the balcony where you can treat yourself on wicker chairs to a regal cliff-top view of the Robberg Peninsula and the white beaches of Plettenberg Bay. Powerful binoculars will pick out whales and schools of dolphins which are (can be!) plentiful in the clear water. The bedrooms downstairs have the same sliding doors that disappear smoothly into the wall and the sea breeze wafts in through a square gap of sky as if from a bright blue painting. The view from your room and private balcony is no less spectacular. Comfort is a priority, with goose-down duvets on enormous beds, fine cotton sheets, a welcoming bottle of Nederberg, gowns and slippers. Vivienne and Gerald are natural hosts, who provide great breakfasts and also picnic hampers for the beach or Robberg hikes, and mountain bikes and canoes for the madly active (a pool caters for loungers). They will also point you in the right direction for golf, and recommend a number of restaurants within easy walking distance.

Rooms: 5: 4 twins/doubles & 1 double; 3 with en-suite shower, 2 with en/s bath and hand showers.
Price: R385 – R620 pp sharing. Singles plus 50% out of season, 80% in season.
Meals: Full breakfast included and served from 8 – 9 am.
Directions: From Knysna take N2. Right at Shell garage into Plettenberg Bay. Turn 1st right into Cutty Sark Ave. Follow road round, then turn right again into cul-de-sac. House on left.

Cornerway House

Dee and Robin Pelham-Reid
61 Longships Drive, Plettenberg Bay 6600
Tel: 044-533-3190 Fax: 044-533-3195
Email: cornerwayhouse@mweb.co.za Web: www.cornerwayhouse.co.za

Robin and Dee recently moved from my Wiltshire school-town (as it happens) to start Cornerway House, and fantastic hosts they make too. Although new to Plett, they've wasted no time in unearthing its treasure – Robin is active on the tourism board – and will ably point you off to the beach with sundowners or to the Robberg Peninsula walk, an exhilarating experience. After drinks in their English drawing room, we repaired for dinner, where wine flowed and conversation roamed. Dee uses what she can from the garden, herbs of course, but artichokes and strawberries too on the day I visited. When a professional cycling team came to stay they were so well fed they failed to win a single race (… not that professional then!). I retired to my room – wooden antiques, comfy bed and sash windows looking onto the garden – and at dawn joined Ocean Blue to spot whales, dolphins and sharks, returning to a proper breakfast, courtesy of Robin. Dee teaches art in the township and throughout the house there are colourful quirks, to wit the yellow-washed and lilac shutters of the house, the petunias bathing in a bath, a purple TV sitting room with bright blue cushions and the pink and yellow mohair in the garden suite. I left Robin and Dee among the frangipani, gardenia and orange trees as I wrenched myself away.

Rooms: 5: 4 twins and 1 double; 2 with en-suite shower, 3 with en-suite shower and bath.
Price: R250 – R495 pp. Singles plus 50%. Low season rates can be negotiated.
Meals: Full breakfast included. Lunch (salads & sandwiches) from R60; 3-course dinner from R120, includes pre-dinner drinks & bottle of wine per couple.
Directions: From N2 heading east, turn right into Plett. Continue to circle and go straight over. Road descends to river and crosses it. Over circle, turn right onto Longships Dr. Continue down 0.9km to Cornerway House on right.

Map Number: 6

Entry Number: 142

Gulls View

Noel and Pam Mills

32 San Gonzales St, Plettenberg Bay 6600
Tel: 072-343-7217 Fax: 044-533-3498
Email: info@gullsview.co.za Web: www.gullsview.co.za

Gulls View is named for the feathered athletes who riot and curl in the thermals that funnel up the cliff at the sea-facing end of the garden. From the verandah, upstairs main bedroom and from rooms there are views in bands of searingly simple colour; a spread of blue sea, white beaches on the peninsula, then the green of a lawny (and wholly indigenous) garden filled with birds including the Knysna Loerie. Noel and Pam (who also have a (GG) guesthouse (Rockwood) in the Cederberg) have coaxed the second oldest house in town into the 21st century and built a whole new one too. This way you can live in the new house if there are only two of you, or use both if you are more numerous. The new house has an open feel with polished timbers, nice curvy wicker chairs, soft white, cream and turquoisey-green tones and billowy ivory-coloured curtains framing the view. All of which are right and proper for the sea. The little things haven't been forgotten either; TV and VCR, stereo set, CD player and, of course, a top-notch kitchen. The house is equidistant to several beaches (down a fairly steep hill) and a five-minute walk to the vibrant and trendy town where there are excellent restaurants. Louann lives next door and will meet and greet you and look after you as much or as little as you wish.

Rooms: Self-catering house let as a whole, with 6 bedrooms.
Price: Low season: R600 per night for 2 sharing, + R100 per extra person; Mid: R1,000 per night as above; High (1st Dec – 20th Jan): R2,500 per night. Rates include week-day servicing.
Meals: Breakfast ingredients can be supplied on request at a cost of R30 pp.
Directions: Turn off N2 into Plett' at Shell Garage. Turn right at the roundabout, then left into San Gonzales St. Gulls View is 2nd last house on the right before Signal Hill.

Bitou River Lodge

Sue and Paul Scheepers

Wittedrift Rd,Plettenberg Bay 6600
Tel: 044-535-9577 Fax: 044-535-9577
Email: info@bitou.co.za Web: www.bitou.co.za
Cell: 082-978-6164

For well-heeled South Africans "Plett" is *the* place to summer and its sophisticated buzz can border on the frenetic. Which is why Bitou River Lodge is such a find. Just east of town, it's close to Plett's glass-plated beach houses, bijou shops and restaurants, yet feels a million miles away. Paul and Sue wanted to make the most of the natural environment and have created a peaceful haven for nature lovers. The drive sweeps past a citrus orchard and horse paddock to the whitewashed lodge, which sits on five hectares of neat flower-filled gardens, with pool, chipping-green and river frontage. Behind pepper trees and honeysuckle, stable-style bedrooms have river-facing patios, where dazzling sunbirds congregate. The lime-washed, painted-pine rooms have slate-floored kitchenettes and bathrooms, and sliding doors keep them light-filled. Farmhouse feasts are served in the breakfast room, which adjoins a warm lounge where you can settle into birding books (there are 134 species in the area to tick off). Outside, the liquid-smooth lawn gathers all before it – boulders, benches and flowerbeds – as it slips silently toward the lily-leafed river. While away some time out here, watching busy weaver birds build upside-down nests and lazy ones sway in the reeds, while the ripple of canoe paddles, the splash of a kingfisher and whiz of a fly-reel provide a soothing summer soundtrack. *In season the bay hosts whales, dolphins and seals.*

Rooms: 5: 3 kings and 2 twins, all with en-suite bath and shower.
Price: R275 – R475 pp sharing. Singles on request.
Meals: Full farmhouse breakfast included. Plenty of restaurants in nearby Plett.
Directions: Head east from Plettenberg Bay on N2. Immediately after bridge, turn left onto the R340. Bitou River Lodge is signed on left.

Tarn Country House

Guy and Erica De La Motte & Mark and Lanice Thorp
N2, The Crags 6602
Tel: 044-534-8806 Fax: 044-534-8835
Email: info@tarn.co.za Web: www.tarn.co.za

Ah, this is the life… 100 acres of bucolic bliss. Picture the scene if you will: frogs croaking contentedly, birds chirping merrily in the afternoon sun, and a smug inspector enjoying the top tea spot on the Garden Route. From the shade of a pine tree I overlooked the reservoir onto a forested valley and up to the Outeniqua Mountains stretching away into the hazy distance. My thoughts were only lightly disturbed by a lone guinea fowl clucking about in search of food and an ephemeral twinge of guilt as ruddy-faced guests returned from hikes through the foothills of the nearby Tsitsikamma Mountains in time for a fireside apéritif and a hearty dinner. But I quickly discovered that I'd also somehow earned a four-course Erica special. The restaurant enjoys the same views as my favoured tea spot, through the full-length French doors that flood the room with morning sunshine. Blissfully settled beside the ceramic wood-burning fire, I chomped my way through Camembert-filled filo pastry parcels, a succulent fillet of beef with a mustard cream sauce, sorbet, rounded off with grilled plums, and all washed down with a local wine from Tarn's extensive collection. The sprawling, bungalowed building is surrounded by a brilliant moat of flowers, and as I slopped around in my over-sized tub, contemplating the king-size bed that awaited me, I realized that after only a few hours here I already felt refreshed, revitalized and raring to go.

Rooms: 9: 6 doubles all with en-suite bath and shower; 2 twins both with en-suite bath and shower; 1 family room with shower.
Price: R350 – R690 pp sharing. +50% single supplement.
Meals: Full breakfast included. Light lunch on request from R45. Dinner at Erica's Restaurant, R130 for 3-course meal, R160 for 4 courses.
Directions: On N2, 15km east of Plettenberg Bay, sign to the left. Coming from PE direction, 19km from Toll Gate, sign to the right.

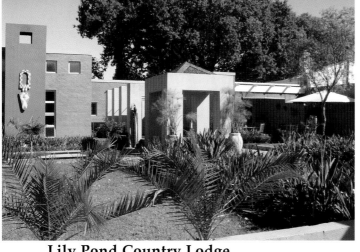

Lily Pond Country Lodge

Niels and Margret Hendriks

The Crags 6602
Tel: 044-534-8767 Fax: 044-534-8686
Email: info@lilypond.co.za Web: www.lilypond.co.za
Cell: 082-746-8782

Niels and Margret come highly (and frequently) recommended and, tracing their mentions all the way back to Cape Town (Lézard Bleu, in fact), I was confident of a great stay; no disappointment there. For ex-naval officers who "never meant to run a guest house", they are expert hosts, dashing out to greet me with an umbrella when I arrived in the pouring rain. Their home is a monument to mathematical modernity. Straight lines and strong angles prevail and sandy yellow or terracotta walls contrast strikingly with the surrounding greenery of Nature's Valley. And green it is! Lily Pond's lily ponds provide a lush home to a mesmerising array of flora and fauna, most noticeably the frogs, which serenaded me with their croaky chorus as I strolled beside the water and along winding, wooded paths. In summer, the ponds are a carpet of colour and balmy evenings are set aside for drinks and nibbles or even a candle-lit dinner on the miniature island. Margret is a supremely good cook – Niels her dashing waiter – and I was treated to mouth-watering springbok carpaccio and kingklip in Thai coconut and coriander sauce. Come breakfast-time and my reluctant departure, the rain was still hammering down, but it did nothing to spoil a cracking stay with a kind and charismatic couple.

Rooms: 6: 4 doubles, 1 twin, 1 king/twin; 4 with en-suite bath/shower, 2 with en-suite bath and separate shower.
Price: R400 – R600 pp sharing.
Meals: Full breakfast included. Picnic lunch and four-course dinner on request.
Directions: Off the N2. From CT take first exit to Nature's Valley, from Port Elizabeth take second exit after the toll. Then follow R102 for 3km and turn right at the sign.

Map Number: 6

Hog Hollow Country Lodge

Andy and Debbie Fermor
Askop Rd, The Crags 6602
Tel: 044-534-8879 Fax: 044-534-8879
Email: info@hog-hollow.com Web: www.hog-hollow.com
Cell: 082-411-6003

It was a little rude, but I said hello to no one when I arrived at Hog Hollow and made a beeline straight for the view point, a tree-perforated deck that juts out over mile upon mile of tantalising, tumbling, Tsitsikamma forest. "Don't worry, everyone does that," said Jo, one of the bubbly team of local staff that make this place so special. Back inside, I ran out of scribbling space listing intriguing oddities: the tobacco-leaf sofa, the mounted outboard engine, the sewing-machine lamp. I loved the irrepressible spontaneity of it all. Returning guests suggest a pool? Andy and Debbie make it a 15-metre one. Others want a sauna? That's just been finished too, along with three new forest cottages. They're hidden among the trees down snaking brick paths and their mezzanine lay-out make the view equally good from bed or bath. There's bags of space for kids too and with buckets, spades and bed-time stories they couldn't be better catered for. That leaves you free to join other guests for a communal supper, care of Big Joe. I thumbed through a menu of crayfish thermidor, rack of lamb and pesto-crushed line fish, praying a miracle flat battery might force me to cancel my other appointments and stay the night. No such luck.

Rooms: 15: 14 king/twins and 1 queen, all with bath and shower.
Price: R690 – R960 pp sharing.
Meals: Full breakfast included. 4-course dinner from R180, lunch also available.
Directions: 18km east of Plettenberg Bay, Hog Hollow is signed off to the right.

The Armagh Guest House

Johan and Marion Brink

24 Fynbos Ave, Storms River, Tsitsikamma 6308
Tel: 042-281-1512 or 042-281-1587 Fax: 042-281-1510
Email: armagh@mweb.co.za Web: www.thearmagh.com
Cell: 082-296-2000

Johan and Marion are not ones to sit on their laurels. When I popped in this year the paint was still drying on the latest project. What started life as a potting shed is now a snug, self-catering cottage with its own private garden – "A place to commune with nature," Marion tells me. And once you've finished communing you can explore the rest of the Armagh. It remains a fiercely unpretentious guest house, where the milk of human kindness prevails. The exterior is face-brick, while the rest is made almost entirely of pine with a towering roof adding to the feeling of space – the whole place is soundly eco-friendly. The main part of the building combines the bar and restaurant (the zesty Rafters, famed for its strongly home-cooked Cape-Malay menu), and a little loft sitting area up wooden steps, which looks down over the scene and provides the perfect spot to relax and observe guest house life. In the bedrooms, painted walls, snoring peacefully in low-key colours, are rudely awoken by dandy-bright cushions and abstract pictures. Each room opens out onto vine-covered patios and a view of the conical Storms River Peak, in the Tsitsikamma range, which looms over the pool and indigenous garden, patched with small flower-bordered lawns. The beach is minutes away, as is the world-famous Tsitsikamma National Park.

Rooms: 6: 3 doubles and 2 twins, 3 with en/s baths, 2 with en/s showers; a self-catering cottage with one queen and en/s bath and shower.
Price: R250 – R525 pp sharing. Single plus 50%. We advise you book in advance.
Meals: Full breakfast included. Meals available all day in Rafters Restaurant and traditional dinner every evening.
Directions: 165km from Port Elizabeth and 65km from Plettenberg Bay. Turn off the N2 Highway into Storms River Village and you'll see The Armagh on the right.

Honeysuckle Lodge

Lhana and Steven Keyser
Oudtshoorn
Tel: 044-888-1658 Fax: 044-888-1658
Email: honeysucklelodge@mweb.co.za
Cell: 082-426-3451

For a genuine South African experience farm stays are often the most rewarding of all, and if the Keysers are your hosts, you've chosen doubly well. This isn't fancy, five-star accommodation, but it's a ten-star welcome. Stephen, like generations before him, farms ostriches, mohair goats and cattle... "and dogs," groans Lhana. He's passionate about it and you and your kids are welcome to muck in, zooming around inspecting the farm and Stephen's gleaming, John Deere tractors. There are 13 in his prized collection, the oldest dating from 1938. The farm buildings are centuries older and littered with history. The drawing room was once a stagecoach stopping point, the barn a former classroom and an ancient grammar book with hints on using "the noble English language with correctness and elegance" still sits next to the downstairs loo. Honeysuckle Lodge itself is an amalgamation of two farm cottages connected by a newly-built, open-plan sitting room and kitchen. The beds are cast iron, the sink was once a pig-feed, the stove is wood-burning and the whole place, with its provençale blues and whites, has a rustic charm that's hard to beat. This is a place to unwind in the open air and, after a hard day on the farm, everyone can meet for an evening dip. The pool's not heated, but Stephen says that in summer "you need ice lumps to cool it down".

Rooms: 2: Honeysuckle Lodge has 1 double with en/s bath and shower, plus a double and a twin with shared shower; 1 double and 1 twin in the house sharing a bath and shower.
Price: R150 – R180 pp.
Meals: Breakfast (R35) and dinner (R55) on request for self-caterers.
Directions: From George take the N12 north towards Oudtshoorn for 45km and turn R to Heimersrivier (35km from Oudtshoorn). Follow dirt road for 7km and turn R at crossroads towards Herold. Farm is 500m further, on the right.

Red Stone Hills

Petro and Hermanus Potgieter

Oudtshoorn 6620
Tel: 044-213-3783 Fax: 044-213-3291
Email: redstone@pixie.co.za Web: www.redstone.co.za

The humbling sense of the passage of time pervades this 3,000-hectare veld, whose desert colours swirl with Van Gogh vibrancy. For a start, the current Potgieters are the fifth generation to farm this land (ostrich, vineyards, cattle and fruit), but that lineage is put into perspective by the red stone hills. They date to the enon-conglomerate period, formed 65 million years ago when the earth twisted and a torrent of sanguine mud-stone settled and solidified; a few million years later, bushmen hid in the hills' stone pockets and painted wildlife; and in the 1790s Karoo cottages completed the picture. It's all been authenticated by erudite visitors: botanists, geologists and a chap from Roberts who identified 185 birds here, including eagles, black stork and five varieties of kingfisher. But you'll find Hermanus and Petro plenty knowledgeable themselves. We drove out along dusty tracks leading past the schoolhouse his father donated to the mixed community (which still congregates there), through babbling brooks to Chinese lanterns and blankets of fynbos and medicinal succulents. Hermanus will name them all. Petro says he lives in the past, whereas she's an artist facing the future. She's currently planning open-air opera for their natural stone auditorium. There are many ways to enjoy the scenery, cycling, hiking, riding, fishing… and ostrich-rich Oudtshoorn is minutes away. When you're tired out, your sleepy cottage, with original Oregon pine doors and floors and farm-made furniture, awaits.

Rooms: 6 cottages: all fully self-contained with one, two or three bedrooms and shared bathrooms.
Price: R190 – R290 pp self-catering. Singles on request.
Meals: Meals on request. Full breakfast R55, Continental breakfast R45.
Directions: Red Stone is half way between Calitzdorp and Oudtshoorn on the R62. Head west from Oudtshoorn for 28km, then take the Kruisrivier turn-off. Red Stone is 6km down this road. There is another well-signposted entrance between the foot of the Swartberg mountain and the Cango caves via Matjiesrivier.

Map Number: 5

The Retreat at Groenfontein

Marie and Grant Burton

PO Box 240, Calitzdorp 6660
Tel: 044-213-3880 Fax: 044-213-3880
Email: groenfon@iafrica.com Web: www.groenfontein.com

A tiny gravel road twists along the sides of this idyllic valley, beside the river that gives the Retreat its name, while abandoned Cape Dutch farm buildings line the route, which eventually leads to the Burtons' Victorian-colonial homestead. They ran a popular wilderness lodge in Namibia before trawling southern Africa for a new Eden, and it took years to find Groenfontein. It was worth the wait. The view from the verandah, where meals are served (and where I tucked into a bowl of Grant's excellent mutton broth), crosses a valley and climbs the Burtons' own mountain before joining the vast Swartberg Nature Reserve. What with hiking trails and mountain bikes, the opportunities for merry traipsing are limitless. If (when!) it gets hot, you can swim in river or pool, or collapse inside the gloriously cool house. The original marble fireplace and pine and yellowwood flooring remain, but much has been built by Grant himself. He designed the two slate-floor, reed-and-mud roof rooms (away from the house), with French-window views to the Swartberg. Airy bedrooms benefit from simple combinations of yellow, beige and cream. It is an incredible area to explore with kloofs, mountain wilderness, half-forgotten roads, with many animals to look out for – klipspringer, reedbuck, mongoose, jackal, caracal and porcupine among them. But, best of all, you come back to delicious dinners, welcoming hosts and a truly relaxed household. You'll want at least two nights.

Rooms: 6: 2 doubles and 2 twins (in house), 1 with en/s bath and shower, 3 with en/s shower; 2 king/twins, 1 with en/s bath & sh'r, 1 with en/s sh'r.
Price: R450 – R650 pp sharing for dinner, B&B. Singles plus R80.
Meals: Full breakfast and 3-course dinner (without wine) included. Light lunches and picnics from R20.
Directions: From Oudtshoorn take R62 towards Calitzdorp for 30km. Turn R onto dirt rd signed Kruisrivier. After 17km keep L at fork as rd gets narrower & follow for 10.7km until see sign for Burton's to your R. From Calitzdorp L at Groenfontein sign – 19km to house. Drive slowly!

Merwenstein Fruit and Wine Farm

Hugo and Heidi van der Merwe
8km from Bonnievale on Swellendam Road, PO Box 305, Bonnievale 6730
Tel: 023-616-2806 Fax: 023-616-2806
Email: merwenstein@lando.co.za Web: www.merwenstein.co.za
Cell: 082-377-6638

The van de Merwes are simply the kindest people you will ever meet. After scoffing a plate-full of Heidi's *koeksisters* on arrival, Hugo took me for a stroll around their beautiful fruit and wine farm. It was a stunning springtime evening, rows of peach trees were in full blossom and the air vibrated with the hum of busily pollinating bees. Rolling across the valley floor from the Breede river to the feet of the rocky Langeberg range, Merwenstein is perfectly placed to make the most of the Robertson winelands. And once the car is suitably packed with clinking bottles there's everything from guided river trips and golf to horse riding and hot springs to enjoy. Heidi is an expert on the area and will happily take guests to a local crèche she helped set up or on a tour of nearby Bonnievale. She's also a great cook and rustled up a feast of traditional SA fare on my visit. "Here we don't decorate your plate, we fill it!" an aproned Hugo told me. Gloriously full, I slept like a log in my huge room. All four spots here have patios looking onto the garden. Come the morning I was out across the lawn for another birding walk (90 species to spot), savouring every moment at one our most relaxing finds. *Hier wird Deutsch gesprochen.*

Rooms: 4: all en-suite shower including one family suite with double bed and adjoining room with single bed and cot.
Price: R225 – R250 pp. Single supplement plus R50.
Meals: Full breakfast included. Dinner R95 pp.
Directions: Use the same turn-off as for the Merwespont Wine Cellar, 8km from Bonnievale on the road to Swellendam.

Mimosa Lodge

Fida and Bernhard Hess

Church St, Montagu 6720
Tel: 023-614-2351 Fax: 023-614-2418
Email: mimosa@lando.co.za Web: www.mimosa.co.za
Cell: 083-787-3331

Continuing the Swiss influence at Mimosa, Bernhard and Fida have just taken over this two-storey Edwardian townhouse in the middle of mountain-marooned Montagu. It helps that I adore Art Deco as there's a lot of it about: chandeliers, wardrobes, cabinets, revolving bookcases, chairs re-upholstered in daring colours. The bedrooms bear little resemblance one to the other. Some are in the house, others in the dazzling flower garden, with its herbs and vegetables, orchard and black marble swimming pool. Colours are used with imagination throughout, some bold, some demure, but all give a true sense of luxury and space. Each suite has a CD player and all the rooms have a host of little extras: a decanter of Muscadel, books, magazines, fresh fruit, chilled water for example. An old shop counter has become the bar where guests congregate (and salivate) before dinner. Bernhard is a chef extraordinaire who used to run restaurants in Jo'burg and is well known in his native Switzerland. By the time you read this he will be blending his own Mimosa wine, the perfect accompaniment to cuisine prepared using only the freshest of ingredients, many originating from Mimosa's own lovingly-tended garden where more than 200 plant species thrive. I am very happy to be able to continue recommending Mimosa for a special treat. *Children by arrangement. Off-peak dinners by arrangement.*

Rooms: 16: 7 twins, 9 classic rooms, all with en/s bathrooms; 7 with bath & separate shower, 5 with shower, 4 with bath/shower.
Price: R405 – R725 pp sharing. Singles R554 – R1,022.
Meals: Full breakfast included. Dinner (table d'hôte) in the restaurant R145 – R155.
Directions: From Ashton side on R62, Church Street is 3rd on left after entering Montagu. From Barrydale, Church Street is 5th turning on right. Mimosa Lodge is clearly sign-posted.

Villa Victoria

Keith and Yvonne Foster

26 Berg Street, Montagu West 6720
Tel: 023-614-3219 Fax: 023-614-3219
Email: info@villavic.com Web: www.villavic.com
Cell: 083-227-5476

An offer of home-made lemonade (and that's home-made in the lemons-from-the-garden sense) won't guarantee entry into our book, but it's a pretty good start. Barely was I through the door at Villa Victoria than Keith, back from a hike and happily padding around in his socks, slipped a glass of the ice-cold, citrus nectar into my hand and herded me onto a blissfully shaded verandah. When it comes to keeping cool, the Victorians knew what they were doing and this house, with its high, Oregon pine ceilings and large airy windows, is perfectly designed for escaping the scorching, summer sun. The Fosters themselves are effervescently energetic. Keith has built two wonderfully light attic guest bedrooms, a separate staircase up the outside of the house, a new verandah and a garden shed for good measure. Yvonne has been just as busy. When not working at the local farm school teaching crafts and running the library they set up (she'll happily take you there to visit), she's usually beavering away in her painstakingly-clipped garden. It's a stunning array of colour from which I proudly identified petunias, sweet-peas, lavender and the lemon tree before my thin knowledge of flowers petered out and I sheepishly returned to my lemonade. Please, if you are in this area, don't miss Villa Victoria. It's a true gem and its owners utterly delightful.

Rooms: 2: both doubles, one with en/s bath and separate shower, the other with en/s bath and hand shower.
Price: R220 – R300. Singles on request.
Meals: Full breakfast included.
Directions: From Worcester or Oudtshoorn take R62 to Montagu. Arriving in town on Long St, turn into Barry St. Continue to the end and bear L over a bridge. Berg St is second on the L.

Onse Rus

Lisa and Gary Smith
47 Church St, Prince Albert 6930
Tel: 023-541-1380 Fax: 023-541-1064
Email: info@onserus.co.za Web: www.onserus.co.za
Cell: 083-629-9196

The official pamphlet does a good job of conveying the delights of Onse Rus, but it modestly fails to bear testament to the biggest plus, the Smiths themselves. They fell in love with Prince Albert and the 150-year-old Cape Dutch Onse Rus in 1999 and their enthusiasm for both town and house has not abated since. Guests who have come down over the Swartberg Pass are given a whisky for their nerves and trips to The Hell, a famously isolated community 57km down a dirt track, are easily arranged. Back at the house, the large living room is hung with a permanent exhibition of local artists' work. The four thatched bedrooms all have private entrances, high ceilings, white walls and simple Karoo furnishings. One used to be part of the bakery, another was the printing room for a local newspaper. The house has some history! Outside there's a brand-new swimming pool (a thing of particular beauty in such a hot climate) and also a gazebo, a focal point for relaxing in the garden. Here guests are brought food and drink while leisurely hours are whiled away with good books. If the weather permits – which it usually does – you can sit out on the verandah and enjoy fig ice cream in the shade of the Cape ash and Karoo pepper trees.

Rooms: 4: 2 doubles and 2 twins (one twin sleeps 4). All with en-suite shower.
Price: R220 – R300 pp sharing. Single prices enthusiastically given on request.
Meals: Breakfast included. Light lunches and coffee shop open. Traditional dinners on request
Directions: On the main street (Kerk or Church St) on corner of Church and Bank Sts.

Collins House

Tessa and Sheila Collins

63 Kerk St (Church St), Prince Albert 6930
Tel: 023-541-1786 Fax: 023-541-1786
Email: collinsh@tiscali.co.za
Cell: 082-377-1340

Collins House stands out on Kerkstraat, unusual as a fine two-storey Victorian townhouse among so many Cape Dutch gable buildings. The open-plan kitchen/sitting room is the warm heart of the house – check out the beautiful tile and wood floor – and when I arrived Tessa was in her 'office', an old desk in the middle of the room, creating wire topiary and listening to the cricket on the radio. There are french doors out to the flower garden, and the very large swimming pool and air-con in all the bedrooms are a blessing during Karoo summers. The town is full of Cape Dutch national monuments and snoozes right at the foot of the spectacular Swartberg pass. You must not fail to experience this and Tessa takes guests up there with evening drinks – or you can hire your own scooter in town. Collins House is long on luxury. Bedrooms are upstairs (almost a rarity in itself in South Africa) and you are mollied and coddled with fine-quality linens and lotions. Tessa herself has been with us from the start, is refreshingly outspoken and likes grown-ups who she can have a drink with and get to know. Luxury is one thing, but character is inimitable... and Tessa, Sheila and Collins House have that in spades. *No children. DSTV is available in the upstairs guest sitting room.*

Rooms: 3: all twins; 1 with en-suite bath, 1 with shower and 1 with bath and shower.
Price: R250 – R400 pp sharing. Single supplement R100.
Meals: Full breakfast included and served till 9.30 am.
Directions: On Kerkstraat in the middle of town.

Lemoenfontein Game Lodge

Ingrid Köster
Beaufort West 6970
Tel: 023-415-2847 Fax: 023-415-1044
Email: lemoen@mweb.co.za Web: www.lemoenfontein.co.za

Lemoenfontein, in the shadow of the Nuweveld Mountains, is one of those places where whatever your mood on arrival – and after a tiring drive down the N1 mine was ropey – a calmness envelops you like magic vapour. I was suddenly enjoying a cool drink on the vast wooden verandah, gazing over measureless miles of veld and chatting happily to Ingrid about the history of the place. It was built as a hunting lodge in 1850, then became a sanatorium for TB sufferers (the dry Karoo air was beneficial), a farm and finally (and still) a nature reserve. Everything has been done well here, no corners cut and the result is a most relaxing, hassle-free stay. Rooms are stylish and understated with top-quality fabrics and completely comfortable beds. Outside, lawns, a new pool, bar and braai area and the veld are all segregated by high dry-stone walls. You *must* go on a game drive through the reserve before dinner – to look at all the buck and zebra of course, but also to be out in such scenery as the sun goes down. And one final thing: dinner when we got back was at first mouth-watering, then lip-smacking. A real South African experience. *All rooms are air-conditioned.*

Rooms: 12: 7 doubles and 5 twins all en-suite, 7 with baths and 5 with showers.
Price: R295 – R330 pp sharing. Singles on request.
Meals: Full breakfast included. A set dinner is available every night.
Directions: From the N1, 2km north of Beaufort West. Go left at the sign to Lemoenfontein. Go 4km up dirt track, following signs.

Ko-Ka Tsara Bush Camp

Diana Köster
Loxton Road, Beaufort West 6970
Tel: 023-416-1666 Fax: 023-416-1667
Email: info@kokatsara.co.za Web: www.kokatsara.co.za

"Drive slowly. Wild animals", announced a sign as I turned into the craggy gorge below the Nuweveld Mountains. On cue, a herd of wildebeest emerged from the crunchy-dry undergrowth to inspect the stranger. Seemingly satisfied, they allowed me to continue into the heart of the 30,000 acres of Karoo veld, where stone-and-thatch A-frame chalets are dotted camp-style around a dung-strewn lawn – evidence of zebra and buck coming to graze the night before. Even my tracking skills were up to that diagnosis. Sliding glass doors open into the stone-floored chalets and a rustic wooden ladder leads up to the kids' galleried sleeping area. Although each has a fully-fitted kitchen and a private braai and camp-fire area, the guests basking by the pool when I arrived were busy digesting the breaded zebra fillet, marinated in garlic, ginger and soy sauce they'd enjoyed in the star-lit boma the previous evening. As well as guided game drives up the hairy-looking mountain pass, or a gentler self-drive 'game amble' in a converted golf buggy, Ko-Ka Tsara is nirvana for bird-watchers. Alongside rare 'Big Four' birds such as the cinnamon-breasted warbler and the African rock pipit, there are 195 other species to keep eyes peeled for. A camp for lovers of the great outdoors.

Rooms: 7 chalets, all with 2 beds and two singles in the loft. All chalets have en-suite showers.
Price: R650 – R700 per night for up to 4 people. Game drives R90, self-drive game buggy R100 per hour.
Meals: Full breakfast R50, 3-course dinner R95. Light lunch on request.
Directions: Take N1 from Cape Town. Go through Beaufort West. Turn left at Loxton and Ko-Ka Tsara sign (opposite Wagon Wheel Motel) and travel for 7km.

Entry Number: 158

Eastern Cape

Timbila Bhejane Game Reserve

Philip and Adriana Theunissen

Groot River Valley, Near Willowmore, 6539
Tel: 044-923-1816 Fax: 044-923-1816
Email: info@timbila-bhejane.com Web: www.timbila-bhejane.co.za
Cell: 084-508-0754

Some may scoff at a game reserve that lacks big cats and heavy grey creatures, but I think it's great. At Timbila you can merrily tramp far and wide over their 10,000 acres, safe in the knowledge that among the zebra, giraffe and wildebeest, the most dangerous animal you'll meet is Madiba, the arthritic great Dane. So I did just that, setting out for a sunrise stroll armed only with a list of local four-legged residents. Weaver birds whistled all around me, vervet monkeys scampered through the sweet-thorn trees and I did my best to work out which of the 28 hoofed species I had spotted – failing comprehensively. Cue the expert. Thirty-something Philip runs the reserve and accommodation with wife Adriana, while his brothers host visiting hunting parties. From the 4x4 he pointed out majestic eland and kudu as we climbed to a rocky sundowner spot, overlooking 3,700 hectares of true Karoo wilderness. Far below lay the riverside chalet that I had staggered back to the night before, tummy full of springbok lasagne and ready for a moonlit wallow in the tub before being swallowed whole by the enormous double bed, built of contorted eucalyptus. Both chalets and bush camps are fully set up for self-catering, but Adriana's vast brunch and hearty dinners will feed as many kids as you can provide. And trust me, with endless game drives, horse-riding, fishing and walking on offer, they'll need it.

Rooms: 4: 2 luxury chalets, each with 1 double & en/s shower, 1 twin with single & double kids' beds & en/s sh'r; 3-tent bush camp: 1 luxury en/s double and 2 twin dome tents sharing shower; 6-tent bush camp: 2 luxury doubles & 4 twin domes.
Price: Chalets from R900 pp. Bush camps from R800 pp. Meals and activities R350 pp.
Meals: Brunch and supper available. Braai packs and picnic baskets can also be provided.
Directions: From N9 north of Willowmore take R329 towards Steytlerville. After 30km turn L to Klipplaat. Continue 10km and Timbila is well signed all the way. From Steytlerville Timbila is signed off the R329 after 31km.

Map Number: 6

The Cedars Guest House

Linden and Jeanne Booth

Matjiesfontein Farm, Baviaanskloof, Willowmore 6445
Tel: 044-923-1751 Fax: 044-923-1751
Email: jeanne@baviaan.co.za Web: www.baviaan.co.za

Just when I thought I had got to the middle of nowhere I turned off the beaten track into a cul-de-sac! Here you are surrounded by nature reserve mountainous wilderness on all sides. When you go for a hike amongst the stillness, silence and crystal-clear mountain pools you won't bump into another human soul for miles. You are truly 'out there'. On the numerous trails your rewards are bushman paintings in caves, beautiful kloofs and waterfalls, and then a relaxing home to come back to and a swim in the enormous, round, spring-water swimming pool. Linden and Jeanne make this an exceptionally special place with their warmth, calmness and enthusiasm for their piece of paradise. Jeanne insisted on giving me an aromatherapy massage and I certainly didn't object. Her fourteen years as a practising aroma- and massage therapist is manifested in a magical touch and the treatment was heavenly – be gone tense driving forearms! Come evening, I sat under the stars watching Linden turning the organic lamb ribs on the braai and then partook of a finger meal of roasted home-grown vegetables and walnut bread from yonder tree. The Cedars is simply delicious whichever way you look at it.

Rooms: 4: 2 twins, 2 doubles, 1 bathroom with bath and shower, 1 with bath.
Price: Self-catering R250 – R300 pp.
Meals: Simple organic dinner and breakfasts by prior arrangement.
Directions: From Willowmore on N9 head towards Uniondale. After 2km turn left on R332 to the Baviaanskloof. Stay on this dirt road, following all signs to Baviaanskloof, go through Nuwe Kloof pass and after 8km turn right at sign to Cedars Guest House.

Oyster Bay Lodge

Hans and Liesbeth Verstrate-Griffioen

Oyster Bay, Humansdorp 6300
Tel: 042-297-0150 Fax: 042-297-0150
Email: info@oysterbaylodge.com Web: www.oysterbaylodge.com
Cell: 082-700-0553

Here's yet another film-set masquerading as a B&B… this one is for the beach scenes! Hans and Liesbeth have the very envy-inducing run of three and a half kilometres of pristine beach to themselves, the fine white sand of the dunes as pure as it is wind-driven (but for the odd monkey footprint). They have fifteen horses, eight of which are rideable, which roam free on the 235 hectare nature reserve, and the first time I visited there simply wasn't time for a beach ride. So I dreamt hard for two weeks and managed to dream it into reality, returning to experience for real the wind in my hair, salt air in my face and sun shining down… amazing. But there's more: Hans and Liesbeth have made hiking trails from the sand dunes through the fynbos where you'll have a chance to see some of the 140 species of bird on their land and maybe vervet monkeys. I could hear them, but didn't quite catch a glimpse. There are only two guest rooms in the house so your stay is very personable and relaxing with use of the swimming pool and self-catering facilities if you choose. Otherwise, supper could be some Oyster Bay rump steak from their cattle farm or the fresh catch of the day. Come here for the empty beach, the horses and walks along an unspoilt coastline. *Day-tours can be taken to nearby Tsitsikamma Nature Reserve and Baviaanskloof.*

Rooms: 2: 1 self-catering double room and 1 twin, both with bath and shower.
Price: R250 – R500 pp sharing, depending on season. Booking advisable, but walk-ins welcome.
Meals: Full breakfast included, lunches by arrangement, 3-course evening dinner R125.
Directions: From Cape Town on N2 turn off at exit number 632 Palmietvlei and follow signs to Oyster Bay Lodge. From Port Elizabeth take exit to Humansdorp and then follow signs to Oyster Bay Lodge.

34 Lovemore Crescent

Monica Johnson
PO Box 85, St. Francis Bay 6312
Tel: 042-294-0825 Fax: 042-294-0825
Email: dolfinvu@intekom.co.za Web: www.b-b.co.za
Cell: 082-695-3395

34 Lovemore is an unpretentious B&B and an absolute delight. This has everything to do with Monica's warm hospitality and the character of her home, built 20 years ago, though the beachside location is an added bonus. A cuppa appears on arrival and you are then shown up to your quarters, two large rooms under a high thatched roof, with a living area between them, all looking out to sea. The aloe-filled back garden is a bird-watcher's paradise where even the neighbours pop over for the viewing. The front garden has weaver-birds' nests in the trees and possibly Africa's most southerly baobab tree, a tenacious little thing brought down from Zimbabwe by the family in the '80s. And on the other side of the garden there is another separate flat, which can be rented on a B&B basis or as a self-catering unit (but you'd be missing out on an unforgettable breakfast of delicious home-made breads, scones, jams and all…). It lacks the sea views, so Monica feels duty-bound to offer it at give-away prices. With a sweeping vista across St. Francis Bay, where southern right whales can be seen in season and dolphins year round, you cannot fail to relax here. Keen surfers will be interested to note (they will in fact salivate over the news) that Bruce's Beauties are at the end of the garden.

Rooms: 2 rooms in the house: 1 double with en/s shower and 1 twin with private shower and bath; 1 flat sleeping up to 6 with 1 bathroom.
Price: Rooms in the house: R250 – R300 pp sharing. Flat: R170 pp self-catering, R200 with breakfast.
Meals: Full breakfast included for B&B in the house. Flat, as above.
Directions: From the Humansdorp road take 1st right into Lyme Rd South, then 3rd right onto St. Francis Drive, then 5th left onto Lovemore Crescent. 34 Lovemore is sign-posted at each of these turns. 34 is the last house on the left.

Duxbury

Sheila Beckett

8 George Rd, St. Francis Bay 6312
Tel: 042-294-0514 Fax: 042-294-0514
Email: duxburybb@worldonline.co.za

Duxbury makes no claims to being anything more than a very friendly, dyed-in-the-wool B&B. You stay in Sheila's comfortable, white-walled, thatched cottage in this quaint seaside village where strict planning regulations have ensured that almost all the other houses are thatched and white-walled too. Meet Sheila. She has an impish sense of humour and you are soon settled in, sipping a cup of tea, a co-conspirator in her tales of local, national and international matters. The guest rooms have private entrances and there is also a cottage in the garden. The white-washed walls of the interior contrast with the cheerful décor and this lends the house a fresh and enlivening feel. A leisurely breakfast, made to order by Sheila, is quite a spread and guests have been known to try and cajole Sheila into accepting more money for their stay, refusing to believe that such good value can still be found. Sheila is adamant though, and won't put her prices up. She loves her guests and wants them to experience fantastic SA hospitality. The best B&Bs are places where both owner and guest get as much out of the experience as each other. I give you Duxbury. *Sheila will sort out Kromme River and Marina Canals cruises and golf. The house is just 100 metres from the sea for safe beach bathing.*

Rooms: 2: 1 family suite (1 twin with private bath and shower, 1 king with en-suite bath); 1 cottage (twin with en-suite shower).
Price: R160 – R180 pp sharing.
Meals: Full breakfast included. Restaurants nearby.
Directions: Take Humansdorp off-ramp on N2 freeway from Cape Town 80km short of Port Elizabeth. Proceed down Humansdorp Main Street to T-junction opposite caravan park. Turn L to St. Francis Bay (18km). Take first turning L, 2km after crossing Kromme River Bridge, and follow signs to Duxbury.

The Dunes Guest Farm

Chantelle and Brent Cook
PO Box 25, St. Francis Bay 6312
Tel: 042-294-1685 Fax: 042-294-1687
Email: reservations@dunesstfrancis.com Web: www.dunesstfrancis.com
Cell: 082-324-3484

After fourteen years in the madding metropolis of LA, St. Francis Bay represents a vivid and welcome contrast for Chantelle and Brent: 600 hectares of thrumming nature on the doorstep and tranquillity in abundance. At the end of a sandy road through coastal fynbos the guest house sits surrounded by indigenous garden with thick grass – the kind that crunches underfoot – aloe trees and strelitzias. Brent is a walking guide and takes guests through the farm on foot (or horseback). He explains what they are doing for nature conservation while pointing out and expanding your knowledge of any critters spotted en route, including zebra and various species of antelope. A two-hour walk takes you to Thula Moya (the adjoining coastal reserve), via bird-watching hides and waterholes. Here, tea, scones, lunch or a well-earned sundowner will be waiting before you're whisked back to the comforts of the guest-house. Reminiscent of an old Cape farmhouse, the guest-house is part of the conservation effort with its Oregon wood floors, doors and window frames all reclaimed from an old school. The theme of comfortable splendour extends into the bedrooms, with their marble counter tops, percale linens on beds, underfloor heating, ball-and-claw baths and French doors, which open onto the verandah.

Rooms: 4: all doubles with en-suite bath and shower.
Price: R475 – R675 pp sharing. Single supplement R150. Winter specials available on request.
Meals: Full breakfast and tea and scones included. Light lunches R16 – R34. Dinners by arrangement.
Directions: From N2 take St. Francis Bay exit. Follow signs to St. Francis Bay onto R330. Past St. Francis village and follow signs to the right.

Aquasands

Richard and Deborah Johnson

No. 7, 11th Avenue, Summerstrand, Port Elizabeth 6001
Tel: 041-583-3159 Fax: 041-583-3187
Email: greenwood@aquasands.co.za Web: www.aquasands.co.za
Cell: 082-462-6774

Aquasands is glamorous. Deborah, in red lipstick and a white linen dress, is glamorous. By the time I left, even I felt a bit glamorous too. She is a food stylist and husband Richard is a philatelist (a stamp dealer – but glamorous too!). And their open-plan contemporary home is a repository for an ever-changing, rotating collection of fine art. The guest rooms, with their own separate entrances, are blessed with crushed velvet or silk bedspreads, percale cottons and mohair blankets, red gerberas in fish-bowls and cactus-style soap dishes, an echo of the real cactus garden out there next to the tranquil koi fish pond. Breakfast is served on the architecturally spectacular grey-slate-tiled patio under steel and wood, offset with vibrant splashes of pink, purple and cobalt paint blocks. This is surrounded by a lush garden where palm trees intermingle with indigenous plants and giant aloes… and beyond is the ocean, with safe bathing and sandy beaches a mere two minutes' walk away. If that's too far there's always the large heated saline pool, sauna and steam room within flopping distance of the breakfast table. I met grandpa too – another asset of the house – a champion fly-fisherman with photos to prove it. Come here for a holiday and not just a stopover!

Rooms: 4: 2 queens, 2 king/twins, 3 with en-suite bath and shower, 1 with en-suite shower.
Price: R400 – R550 pp sharing. Singles from R450.
Meals: Full breakfast included. Dinner on request.
Directions: From Cape Town take N2 to Port Elizabeth. Take exit 751B at sign for Settlers Way, follow signs to Summerstrand. Keep left onto Marine Drive along the sea front until 11th Avenue.

Broadlands

Rob Whyte
R336, Kirkwood 6120
Tel: 042-232-0306   Fax: 042-232-0306
Email: Info@broadlandsch.co.za Web: www.broadlandsch.co.za
Cell: 082-445-8837

Broadlands had me won over before I had even negotiated the drive: citrus orchards on either side, an avenue of palm trees, pink, purple and orange bougainvillaea, roses in profusion, an explosion of colour. The sweet aroma of nectar filled the country air. The lake opening out from the house overhung by weeping willows and orange grevillias beyond made my munching on home-made cookies all the more pleasurable. I can imagine the serenity at night, with the lanterns lit at the end of the deck and light dancing on the water. The farm here has been in the family since 1885 and apart from the thousands of citrus trees and the pack-house, it looked quite different back then. Today, luxury rooms with chaise-longues, Victorian baths and an anglicised sitting room and fireplaces provide well-appreciated comfort. Freshly-squeezed orange juice for breakfast is, of course, a certainty. The house is just 25 minutes drive from the Addo Elephant Park and for an African bush experience in the real Africa, Rob will take you up to his nearby mountain lodge for a night spent in the wilderness with sounds of the wild experienced from the traditional boma. Alternatively he'll take you on a sundowner game drive amongst kudu, nyala and zebra.

Rooms: 4: 2 kings, 2 twins, 3 with en-suite bath and shower, 1 with en-suite bath.
Price: R450 – R490 pp sharing. Singles + 50%.
Meals: Full breakfast included, picnic lunches and dinners on request (3 courses R110).
Directions: From PE take R75 and take second turn off to Kirkwood onto R336. After 10km turn right onto a dirt road for 200 metres.

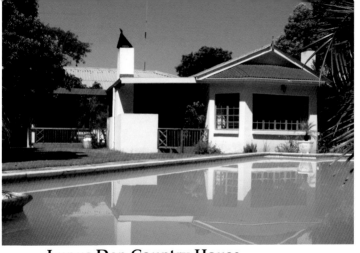

Lupus Den Country House

Priscilla and Noel Walton

Addo,near Sunland 6115
Tel: 042-234-0447 Fax: 042-234-0447
Email: info@lupusden.co.za Web: www.lupusden.co.za
Cell: 072-1814-750

Priscilla and Noel have not needed to learn any tricks about how to host. They are just naturally hospitable people who make you feel instantly at home and relaxed. When I arrived, lunch was waiting on the table and with a cool drink in hand I already felt part of the furniture. Priscilla and Noel have been living in their farmhouse for 40 years now – although the land it stands on has been in the family's hands since 1894 – and have recently made some adjustments to make the rooms all the more comfortable for their guests. Their citrus and cattle farm is found on the friendly dirt roads between Addo and Kirkwood. And when I say friendly, I mean locals waved hello to me all the way there! The garden, surrounded by citrus groves, blooms with bougainvillaea and an abundance of other flowers and trees. The tiled swimming pool – the type I am particularly fond of – and an enormous tipuanu tree are two of the gardens greatest assets, while vine-shaded terraces are the perfect places of repose after a rendezvous with the elephants in Addo (only 20 minutes away). When staying at Lupus Den you can be a tourist by day out in the parks and feel a local when back in the fold. Breakfast includes freshly-baked bread (naturally). A true farm B&B with home cooking – hard to beat.

Rooms: 3: 1 twin and 2 doubles, 2 with en-suite bath and shower, 1 with en-suite shower. All rooms are air-conditioned.
Price: R200 – R250. No single supplements. Children under 10 no charge. 10 – 12 years 50 % adult rates. Teenagers (13 up) full price.
Meals: Full breakfast included. Dinners (R85) and light lunches (R35), both by arrangement. Reduced rates for children.
Directions: From PE take R335 towards Addo. Cross railway line in Addo, then turn left into R336 towards Kirkwood. At Sunland turn right at Lupus Den B&B sign and follow signs.

Map Number: 7

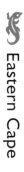

The Elephant House

Clive and Anne Read
PO Box 82, Addo 6105
Tel: 042-233-2462 Fax: 042-233-0393
Email: elephanthouse@intekom.co.za Web: www.elephanthouse.co.za
Cell: 083-799-5671

The bush telegraph gave advance notice of the many charms at Elephant House. Many tourists and other guest house owners had urged us to visit, with a sincerity you could not ignore. It's a stunning house, the brainchild of one night's sleepless pondering by Anne who mapped the whole thing out in her head – a small lawned courtyard surrounded on three sides by thatched and shady verandah. The house is in a sense inside out. The drawing room leads to a dining room outside on the verandah (with antiques and Persian rugs). All the bedrooms open onto the verandah too and dinner (advertised with an African gong) is served there on silver and crystal. Evening meals are lit to stunning effect with lampshades made of Tuareg bowls. Lawns, indigenous trees and the racehorse stud (Clive used to run one in Natal too) surround the house and when I was there the paddocks were full of mares with their foals. The bedrooms are luxurious with antique furniture, carpets, thick duvets and deep beds; and morning tea or coffee is brought to your bed, if so desired. There is also the Stable Cottage, which, separate from the main house, retains the same charm, just a little cosier. The Elephant House also runs open-vehicle game drives in Addo, a few minutes away, morning and afternoon.

Rooms: 9: 4 twins, 4 doubles, all with en-suite bath and shower; 3 have outdoor showers. Also 1 cottage with en-suite shower.
Price: Seasonal. R800 – R1,250 pp sharing, Stable Cottage R360 – R550 pp sharing.
Meals: Full breakfast included in Elephant House. Self-served Continental for Stable Ctg. Lunch & dinner provided. 3-course dinners R150 – R170.
Directions: From P.E. R335 through Addo 5km on the road towards the park – you will see a sign off to your left for The Elephant House.

Quin Sculpture Garden and B&B

Etienne and Maureen Du Plessis
5 Suid Street, Alexandria 6185
Tel: 046-653-0121 Fax: 046-653-0121
Email: info@quin-art.co.za Web: www.quin-art.co.za
Cell: 082-770-8000

Visitors willingly pay an entry fee to wander through the Quin Sculpture Garden, marvelling at the array of beautiful sculptures that stand on plinths, peek from behind trees, graze on the lawn, guard a fountain or glower down from walls. 'Perfect synergy between sculpture and garden', as the brochure puts it, is spot on. For only a little more (and this really is outstanding value), you can stay in a private section of Maureen and Etienne's house. The apartment has its own entrance and consists of two comfortable bedrooms with their own en-suite bathrooms and lounge areas. Here you are left to your own devices, but everyone ends up in the lush garden, inert in imitation of the sculpture, cool and thoroughly relaxed in the plentiful shade. Maureen is well known nationally and frequently asked to exhibit all over the country. You must visit her studio of 30 years standing, where you can watch her at work, and there is a gallery at the bottom of the garden (extended since our first edition). You may not be able to resist a purchase. Etienne welcomes guests with natural warmth and modestly smiles away the many compliments that pass his way. Muffins, freshly-made each morning, are the breakfast speciality.

Rooms: 2 units: 1 double with en-suite bath & lounge area; 1 twin with en/s shower and lounge area.
Price: R150 pp sharing.
Meals: Continental breakfast included. English breakfast on request.
Directions: From Port Elizabeth take the N2 eastwards. At 50 km turn off on to the R72 to Port Alfred for another 50 kilometers. Enter Alexandria, see sign to Quin Sculpture Garden and B&B. Follow signs.

Map Number: 7

The Safari Lodge on Amakhala

Justine and Mike Weeks
PO Box 9, Paterson, 6130, Amakhala Game Reserve
Tel: 042-235-1608 central reservations Fax: 042-235-1041
Email: safari@amakhala.co.za Web: www.amakhala.co.za
Cell: 082-448-2971

As I soaked in my double bath, candles lit, the late sky glowing pink with pleasure, birds twittering, bush buck barking in the surrounding hills and lions roaring from afar (or so I chose to think…), it crossed my mind that this was perhaps not the toughest assignment of my life thus far. Amakhala Safari Lodge is surely the luxurious way to experience the game parks of the Eastern Cape. Beds, equipped with mosquito nets, are super-comfortable and there's a sofa area inside each thatched hut whose canvas fronts and terraces look onto the valley brush and the waterhole below. The bedrooms and the communal hut are decorated with Cape antiques and furniture carved from the wood on Mike's farm. Mike and Justine aren't always at the camp, but Mnoneleli and Riaan, their rangers, are sure to take good care of you. After a delicious meal – usually served round the fire outside – and a good night's sleep, an early wake-up call takes you to the Addo Elephant National Park to admire its ponderous pachyderms at close quarters. Game drives to Amakhala Game Reserve follow in the afternoon, with its beautiful and varied scenery of bushveld, savannah, cliffs and animals… lots of animals, including the big 5. *Day trips to the neighbouring Shamwari Game Reserve are included in a 3-day package. Closed June*

Rooms: 6: 4 doubles with en-suite double baths with shower attachment and outside showers, 2 luxury with private plunge-pools.
Price: R1,480 – R2,380 pp sharing. Singles plus 30%. All inclusive (meals, local beer & house wine, safari activities).
Meals: All included.
Directions: From PE take N2 for 60km towards Grahamstown. Turn left on gravel road to Paterson and follow signs.

Woodbury Oxwagons on Amakhala

Giles and Jennifer Gush
PO Box 57, Paterson , Amakhala Game Reserve 6130
Tel: 042-235-1608 Fax: 042-235-1041
Email: centralres@telkomsa.net Web: www.amakhala.co.za

A Voortrekker would instantly recognize the authentic canvas-covered wagons but perhaps not the giraffe-setting or the trimmings of comfort, even luxury, that have been woven into the camp. Beds are enticing these days with cotton linen and down duvets, which are – like magic – toasty when the night air is cold, but cool on hot nights. In the modern mode of things, each wagon has its own private bathroom down the wooden steps, just a few paces away, lamp-lit. Giles's ancestors were in the oxwagon transport business, so it is perfectly meet and right that the wagons should come to rest on his family land that was once sheep farm, now game reserve. And, yes, what is extra fantastic about the camp is that just a few hundred metres away are the giraffes, zebra, rhino, elephant and antelope of the Amakhala Game Reserve. Sitting on the large sundeck, while breakfasting or dining, the savannah-land and its grazing animals are clearly visible and audible – and just a few metres away, I was thrilled to see a vervet monkey with her baby. Game-drives and river-cruises are utterly recommended and also pop in to visit Jennifer at the conservation centre. She has a PhD in zoology and facilitates the monitoring of the game from here. *Dinners are sometimes served at Woodbury Lodge, also located in the reserve. Plans are afoot to add 3 luxury tents.*

Rooms: 3 oxwagons, each with private bathrooms with showers.
Price: R575 pp sharing dinner B&B. In winter cost per night includes a game drive. Game drives R300 pp in summer.
Meals: Breakfast and dinner included. Picnic lunch by arrangement.
Directions: On N2, 80km from PE towards Grahamstown. Woodbury Lodge sign on the right.

Leeuwenbosch on the Amakhala Game Reserve

The Fowlds Family
Off N2 between Port Elizabeth and Grahamstown,
Tel: 042-235-1252 Fax: 042-235-1252
Email: leeuwenbosch@amakhala.co.za Web: www.amakhala.co.za
Cell: 083-383-2921

Leeuwenbosch has gone from strength to strength since the first edition and remains a real South African find offering an unbeatable colonial safari experience. Firmly established as the senior partner in the Amakhala Game Reserve, it is a place full of zest and character, which has steadily been building its portfolio. There's a whole lot more in the game reserve now and with lion, rhino, cheetah and elephants as new additions the 'big five' is complete. Game drives and river cruises for birding and fishing are a must and if you are staying for a few nights a bush dinner is also recommended. Meals are generally served in the Dutch settler's house and remain intimate, convivial and delicious. For their accommodation, guests can either choose the Victorian mansion with its antique furniture, antique full-sized billiard table and antique photographs of Fowlds ancestors, or the contemporary shearer's lodge. This now houses four luxury rooms each with its own stoep, ideal for lounging in wicker chairs and watching Shamwari game across the way. Bill's tiny cellar pub remains an intimate forum for story-telling and a mini-chapel rounds off the Leeuwenbosch 'village', constructed in time for William Fowlds junior's wedding. All the family chip in to make your stay personable and memorable.

Rooms: 8: 4 rooms in the manor house, 2 twins, 2 doubles all with en-suite bathrooms. 3 twins, 1 double in lodge all with en/s shower and bath.
Price: R1,480 – R1,950 inclusive package of two reserve activities (game drive, river cruise, night drive, canoeing, guided walk) breakfast, lunch and dinner. Dinner B&B from R730. Off-season and last-minute specials.
Meals: Full breakfast included. Dinners are included in the price. Lunches included in package.
Directions: From P.E. take the N2 to Grahamstown (do not take Paterson) for 67km where you'll see signs for Leeuwenbosch on your right only 1.5km beyond Shamwari turn on the left.

Entry Number: 172

Map Number: 7

Reed Valley Inn on Amakhala

Rod and Tracy Weeks

Amakhala Game Reserve
Tel: 042-235-1287 Fax: 042-235-1287
Email: reedvalley@bulkop.co.za Web: www.amakhala.co.za
Cell: 082-782-2506

Reed Valley Inn just oozes history. The 1806 homestead, complete with wattle and daub walls and wonky floors, sits on the old mail wagon route from PE to Grahamstown, where weary messengers would change horses and quench thirsts. Following in their hoofsteps (but in a car), I found Rod and Tracy had made some slight changes since the farm came into Weeks' family hands in 1898. There was no 'Big 5' game viewing in those days, and what was once the Inn are now charming guest quarters, with the original roof and a gaping fireplace retained. I hear your cries of anguish: "But where do we get our booze then?" Don't despair... Rod has merely moved the pub next to the dining room, far more convenient. Before joining Rod and Tracy for supper in the colossal, chandeliered and wooden-floored dining room (unless it's being served under the stars out in the bush) you can soak up the history on display in the pub. Old farming tools dangle from the walls alongside black-and-white photos of the farm from the 1920s, and a selection of pipes and a chessboard await those of a more ruminative disposition. Days of course are spent out on the range looking at animals. The perfect stopover before I was back in the saddle and galloping on towards Grahamstown.

Rooms: 4: all doubles or twins on request, all with en-suite bath and shower.
Price: R475 – R675 pp sharing. +30% single supplement.
Meals: Full breakfast included. Lunch and dinner available.
Directions: From PE take N2 for 60km towards Grahamstown and see sign to Reed Valley on the right.

Hlosi Game Lodge

Sharon and Will van Duyn
Bushmans River Conservancy, Amakhala Game Reserve
Tel: 042-235-1253 Fax: 042-235-1253
Email: res@hlosilodge.com Web: www.hlosilodge.com
Cell: 082-327-9705 or 084-867-1231

Will is an avid conservationist – "humans in cages and animals wandering free," he murmurs with a wistful smile – and he spends much of his time releasing animals into the wild and keeping tabs on them. When I visited, he had a caracal (aka African lynx) in the lodge boma, ready to be set free. The van Duyns keep close tabs on their guests too, thoroughly spoiling them. The lodge itself is built around the ruins of an old Trek-boer homestead, with wooden bridges connecting the thatched rooms. Four-poster beds, open fires, yawning sofas… and I am fast becoming a sucker for outside showers; it is hard to resist a sprinkling by starlight. In the evening Sharon offers a variety of places to eat dinner depending on the night: an African-themed meal in the boma with Xhosa dancing; or a port and poetry evening under a lanterned tree perhaps. Rest assured, wherever dinner is served, the animals are never far away. As I reluctantly left I took a detour up to a ridge that looks out over the lodge and the Bushmans River meandering slowly into the distance. I was a little sad not to have spotted the cheetahs after which Hlosi is named (in Xhosa) but I guess that just means I'll have to go back next year – shame.

Rooms: 4: all doubles, 2 twins on request, all with en-suite bath and shower and all with outside showers.
Price: R1,850 – R2,500 pp sharing. +50% single supplement.
Meals: Full breakfast, lunches, snacks, 4-6 course dinners included.
Directions: N2 from PE towards Grahamstown. After 70km turn right onto R342 towards Alexandria. 4km on the left is Bushmans River Management Centre and reception. You will then be transferred to the lodge.

The Cock House

Belinda Tudge
10 Market St, Grahamstown 6140
Tel: 046-636-1287 Fax: 046-636-1287
Email: cockhouse@imaginet.co.za Web: www.cockhouse.co.za
Cell: 082-820-5592

The Cock House offers a warm and friendly welcome and fine dining in the setting of a historic old house in downtown Grahamstown. Nelson Mandela has stayed three times and current President Thabo Mbeki has also been a guest (their visits are recorded in photos on the walls of the bar). The recent death of Peter Tudge has been a huge blow to the whole staff, but they have pulled together and it is clear that they enjoy working here. Belinda has taken Peter's place behind the delightful yellowwood bar, a favourite with the locals, and there's always an opportunity to strike up a conversation. The house dates back to 1826 and was one of the first built in Grahamstown. The rooms are named after previous owners, most recently South African author André Brink. A stone-floored verandah stretches along the front of the house (mirrored by a wooden balcony upstairs) and the interior is full of yellowwood beams and broad planked floors. I can recommend the restaurant, which offers an international cuisine with a South African flavour and has its own herb garden, using local and seasonal ingredients wherever possible. The home-made bread is a particular treat. The two large rooms in the main house have glass doors opening onto the balcony and the six converted stables open onto the garden. Personal and fun.

Rooms: 9: 6 doubles, 3 twins; 7 with en-suite bath and shower, 2 with en-suite shower.
Price: R330 – R420 pp sharing. R390 – R480 singles.
Meals: Full breakfast included and served any time. Lunch and dinner available in the restaurant (except Sunday lunch). Dinners from R120.
Directions: From P.E. take 2nd exit from N2 signposted "Business District/George Street". Take off-ramp L, turn L at bridge into George St. Continue down long hill into Grahamstown. At 4-way stop with Market St turn R and you will see the Cock House on the right corner.

Rivermead

Karen and Paul Davies
Bond Street, Grahamstown 6140
Tel: 046-636-2727 Fax: 046-636-2728
Email: helbom54@global.co.za Web: www.rivermead.co.za
Cell: 082-343-5665

As the heavy gates groaned open, I had no idea what to expect from Rivermead, so efficiently was the property concealed behind them. I parked by the (all-weather) tennis court and climbed the brick path that wends its way through beautiful terraced gardens and lush lawns, past stone steps that descend to the swimming-pool terrace (salt-water), and up to the titanic trees that shade the entrance. From this summit, the views over the trees of the Rhodes University campus and the Grahamstown valley are nothing short of imperious. On the opposite hillside is the 1820 Settler Memorial (I'm told it resembles a ship, but you have to squint quite a bit…). Naturally the most is made of these views throughout the house, with solid sliding glass doors and private verandahs attached to all the bedrooms. Cool tiled floors sweep you through the extensive open-plan kitchen, dining and lounge area with their black granite work surfaces and whitewashed walls. Space is in abundance. Karen and Paul have provided the finest linens on beds, marble tiles and glass doors in the bathrooms and there are mod cons aplenty. The suites both have sitting rooms too. But for all the luxury Rivermead is still at its heart a very friendly bed and breakfast. So there you are, that's what's behind those gates.

Rooms: 3: 2 suites with double beds and lounge area with sofa-beds, 1 with en-suite shower, 1 with en-suite bath and shower; 1 double with en-suite shower.
Price: R280 – R375 pp sharing. Singles R300 – R400.
Meals: Full breakfast included. Self-catering option available for other meals.
Directions: From High St, turn right into Summerset St. Turn left into Leicester St (immediately before St Andrew's Prep School). Continue until Bowles St. Turn right. Rivermead is signed from here. Map can be faxed or emailed.

Dovecote

Angela Thomas
17 Worcester St, Grahamstown 6139
Tel: 046-622-8809 Fax: 046-622-8809
Email: anthomas@imaginet.co.za Web: www.grahamstown.co.za/dovecote/
Cell: 082-695-4262

From the charming garden cottage off her quiet Grahamstown street, Angela runs a good old-fashioned B&B: very comfortable and very friendly. Even as I drove up Worcester Street, I knew I was going to like Dovecote – joggers, dog-walkers and garden potterers all offered a nod and a wave. Angela, an avid bridge player, was the most friendly of the lot, opening up her cottage to guests simply because she loves doing it. And guests quickly become devoted. Her most famous returnee, Emeritus Archbishop Desmond Tutu, often stays when he's in town – there's a photo of him and his wife standing in the Dovecote garden. Perhaps it's this small garden with pebbled paths and a stone table in the shade of the bougainvillaea; perhaps it's the quiet privacy of the studio-style cottage, with its stable door and small kitchenette; or perhaps it's Angela's delicious home-made baking that lures him back time after time. Big, warm, freshly-baked scones were just one small scratch on the surface of Angela's impressive breakfast repertoire. I surreptitiously held one back to savour later in the day, they were so good. All of this has certainly whetted my appetite for a return visit.

Rooms: 1 cottage with twin beds and sleeper-couch and en-suite shower.
Price: R165 – R180 pp sharing. +R10 single supplement.
Meals: Continental breakfast included. Selection of restaurants in Grahamstown.
Directions: On N2 from PE take first Grahamstown exit signed Beaufort Street. At lights turn left into Summerset Street. Go over three stop-streets and as road curves left, turn left into Worcester Street.

Map Number: 7

Entry Number: 177

Settlers Hill Cottages

Marthie and Don Hendry

71 Hill Street, Grahamstown 6140
Tel: 046-622-9720 Fax: 046-622-9720
Email: settlershill@imaginet.co.za Web: www.settlershillcottages.co.za
Cell: 082-809-3395

Marthie Hendry's passion for Grahamstown and its history is infectious and will envelop you too, if you stay in one of her delightful cottages, built and originally inhabited by British settlers in the 1820s. Sheblon, an intimate, thatched cottage, is a national monument near the evocatively-named Artificers Square, the city's original artisan quarter. Jasmine, with its separate garden cottage, and Belhambra cottages are larger, but similar in charm and character. Martie's pride and joy is the latest addition to her collection, Settlers Hill Manor. This Victorian house has been recently renovated and has shining yellowwood floors and spacious rooms with en-suite bathrooms, plus a rose garden fronting it despite the trials and tribulations of rose-planting in South Africa. The decoration throughout is a blend of original features and modern where these matter (i.e. in bathrooms and kitchens…), but the notable lack of ostentation only adds to the authenticity. You will be hard-pushed to take any of it in, however, if you attempt everything on Marthie's Things-to-Do-in-Grahamstown list, which is as long as a man's arm. She loves taking people around the imposing Victorian buildings in town or to the witch-doctor shop nearby, where a Xhosa herbalist can mix you up some good luck potions.

Rooms: 4 cottages: 2 are self-catering; Jasmine cottage and Settlers Hill Manor are B&B, and have 7 en-suite bedrooms.
Price: R275 – R330 pp B&B. R200 pp self-catering.
Meals: Full breakfast included for B&B. There are a number of restaurants within walking distance.
Directions: Marthie meets guests at 71 Hill St, which intersects the High Street at the Cathedral.

Château Blanc

Ann White
32 Westbourne Road, Kenton-on-Sea 6191
Tel: 046-648-1271 Fax: 046-648-1271
Email: annwhite@telkomsa.net Web: www.kenton.co.za
Cell: 083-354-8189

I imagine Ann standing on her balcony, drinking in The Bushman's River opening out onto the Indian Ocean before the house, the fine white sand, the turquoise-blue water, the sand dunes, an intoxicating vision that fills the senses, and thinking, "I really should share this with as many people as I can!" Ergo Château Blanc. She moved here from a farm near the Winterberg Mountains and, as she says, once a farm lass, always a farm lass. She has bought her warm hospitality and baking with her (I had some yummy carrot cake) and she has even secreted a bonsai herb and vegetable garden where you wouldn't have thought one could exist. She has no lawn or vines but just three paces from her house is the beach where blue river meets blue ocean meets blue sky and gives you the best kind of garden you could wish for. In the area you can try out a variety of water-sports (water-skiing, boating, canoeing, surfing, diving), fishing, golfing, horse-riding, or simply enjoy a sunbathe and picnic on the beach. I'm not quite sure why Ann's home is called Château Blanc as it is a camouflaged, sandy-yellow colour and has no castle-like pomp or grandeur. Here you are simply a guest within an unpretentious home with a light-filled room and an ocean view. 100% personable B&B at its best.

Rooms: 2: I double with en-suite bath and shower, I twin with private bathroom. Single party bookings only.
Price: From R220 pp sharing. Whole cottage available from R1,500 per day.
Meals: Full breakfast included. Dinners on request. Restaurants nearby.
Directions: From PE take R72 and turn right into Kenton-on-Sea. Go down Kariega Road until 3-way stop, turn right down River Road and continue until the river. Turn left into Westbourne Road.

Coral Guest Cottages

Cynthia and Alf Kleinschmidt

Jack's Close, Port Alfred 6170
Tel: 046-624-2849 Fax: 046-624-2849
Email: cynthia@coralcottages.co.za Web: www.coralcottages.co.za
Cell: 082-692-3911

Staying in Cynthia and Alf's settler's cottage was like being transported back in time, a charming old structure with an unlikely and rather romantic history. Once upon a time, in the mid-1800s, it housed the consulting rooms for a Doctor Jones-Phillipson, having previously been transported to Port Elizabeth from England, then to Grahamstown and then by ox-wagon express to Port Alfred. Our own Alfred, of the Cynthia-Alf variety, discovered the cottage in disrepair and decided to dismantle it, treat the wood and resurrect it body and soul in their front yard. Quite a mission, but well worth the effort! So thank you Alf for your entrepreneurial spirit. Now guests can sleep in a well-travelled Oregon pine cottage, which is quite an exclusive experience. Cynthia's daily and delicious contribution is breakfast, her speciality in both variety and eclectic style. She can cook different breakfasts every day for two weeks, so what you have depends on her creative inspiration on the morning in question. I sampled her eggs benedict africano with cheese sauce and grated biltong, but you may get her crêpe speciality with potatoes, mushroom, bacon and sausage. The beaches nearby are not to be missed so make sure you allow enough time to enjoy them in a relaxed way.

Rooms: 2: 1 twin and 1 double, both with shower.
Price: R185 (in winter) – R245 (in summer) pp sharing.
Meals: Full breakfast included.
Directions: Off the R72 in Port Alfred.

The Lookout

Louise and Alan Corrans

24 Park Rd, PO Box 2809, Port Alfred 6170
Tel: 046-624-4564 Fax: 046-624-4564
Email: info@thelookout.co.za Web: www.thelookout.co.za
Cell: 073-273-2912

It was only after I returned to the office that I found Louise's answer-phone message inviting me to join her and Alan for lunch. Shame… I know I would have eaten well. And also as it turned out, I'd only limited time to explore everything the Corrans have done with their perfectly positioned pad. After sifting through the old photos, I can see that they've done a lot. Not for nothing is The Lookout so named, with a sight line down to the Indian Ocean over the head of a toy town Port Alfred fragmented over its harbour islands below. The breakfast table, strategically placed in front of vast sliding glass doors, makes the most of the hillside setting, and each of the alluring suites downstairs opens directly onto the garden, where a royal palm and an aloe bainesii sway above the pool. Although each guest has their own red-tiled verandah from which to soak up the views, I recommend what now looks like an innocent braai area. This is to become the beer garden for Alan's African-themed pub. Ok, the pub itself is only a storeroom for the time being, but with the concept already bubbling away in the melting pot of Alan's ambitious mind, I don't expect guests to be abandoning their posts at The Lookout in search of social lubricant for much longer. Perhaps by the time you get there it will be done.

Rooms: 3 units: 1 king with en-suite shower; 1 twin with private bath and shower and open plan dining/kitchen/lounge area; 1 twin with en-suite shower and open plan dining/kitchen/lounge area. All have sofa-beds.
Price: R200 – R260 pp low season. R330 – R400 pp high season. Extra guests on request.
Meals: Full breakfast included. Other meals self-catering.
Directions: R72 from PE into Port Alfred. Turn first left after bridge into Pascoe Crescent, then immediate right into Park Road. House is signposted on the right.

Map Number: 7

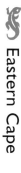

Fort D'Acre Reserve

Mel and Rory Galley
Fish River Mouth, Port Alfred 6170
Tel: 046-675-1091 Fax: 046-675-1095
Email: mel@fairgame.co.za Web: www.fortdacre.com
Cell: 082-559-8944

When the sun's gone down, you're running late and, whether you admit it or not, are ever so slightly lost, some sort of a signal is much appreciated. On cue, the Fish River Lighthouse that stands in the middle of the reserve lit up the night sky like a beacon to guide me in (or so I like to think). The lodge, where guests stay, is a mammoth thatched affair, entered via heavy sliding glass doors from a pretty redbrick garden path. It's immediately obvious that this was a lodge designed for hunters: the rustically tiled floor is strewn with animal skins and the local taxidermist has not been idle. Even the great central hearth is framed by elephant tusks. A galleried landing overlooks the communal lounge, where a cavernous leather sofa almost prevented me from making it to bed that night. The next morning I was able to see the Fort D'Acre Reserve in all its glory. Opening the curtains in the bay windows that dominated my bedroom, I looked beyond the milling herd of zebra to the Great Fish River stretching out below me towards the Indian Ocean and the Reserve's private stretch of beach. I enjoyed my breakfast on the sun-drenched terrace, but the open-walled, thatched, outside bar could be equally appealing. Oh, and just in case you were wondering, the fort was built by the British during the wars against the Xhosa.

Rooms: 4: 3 doubles and 1 twin, all with en-suite showers.
Price: R450 pp sharing. Game drives an optional extra.
Meals: Full breakfast included. Dinner by arrangement or selection of restaurants nearby.
Directions: On R72 20km from Port Alfred towards East London. First turning to right after Great Fish Point Lighthouse.

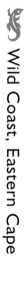

Umngazi River Bungalows

Terry and Tessa Bouwer
PO Box 75, Port St Johns 5120
Tel: 047-564-1115/6/7 Fax: 047-564-1210
Email: stay@umngazi.co.za Web: www.umngazi.co.za
Cell: 082-321-5841

The wild coast may be South Africa's most spectacular and yet least touristy region with its rocky coastline, indigenous forests, secluded coves and many river mouths. And all this is on your doorstep at Umngazi, a lively family holiday resort where the only time you will spend indoors will be to sleep and eat. The relaxed and informal lodge is on the banks of the Umngazi estuary so you can choose between swimming in the pool, the river or the sea, fishing off rocks or boats, and walking in the forests. Bird-watching cruises are also organised for sunset. Ferries transport guests over to the beach from a river jetty. Meanwhile, back at home you will be missing out on tennis, snooker and table tennis. I guarantee that a week here, however lazy you are, will see the colour back in your cheeks and a bit of muscle on the arms and legs. And your sense of time will go haywire. Children are well catered for with trampoline, fort, sandpit and designated dining room. You have a choice of sea-, river- or garden-facing cottages and there are three honeymoon suites with working fireplaces, sliding doors onto private patios, sea views, a big spa bath and double outside shower. Weekly fly-in packages are available Friday to Friday from Durban where you fly at 500 feet above sea level along the beautiful coastline – a wonderful experience to start a holiday.

Rooms: 65 bungalows: twin or double on request, all have en/s bathrooms, most with baths and showers.
Price: R395 – R595 pp sharing all-inclusive. Fly-in package R4,500 – R5,050 pp includes flight, 7 nights, all meals & transfers from Virginia Airport. Pick-up/transfer from Durban Int R200 pp.
Meals: All included.
Directions: From the south, Umngazi lies 90km due east of Umtata. From the north, via Flagstaff and Lusikisiki to Port St Johns on a tarred road. There is also a transfer service from Umtata and a private flight service between Durban and Port St Johns.

Comfrey Cottage

George, Gerda and Grant Freeme
51 Stephenson Street, Lady Grey 9755
Tel: 051-603-0407 Fax: 051-603-0407
Email: info@comfreycottage.co.za Web: www.comfreycottage.co.za
Cell: 082-576-7224

Spectacular views, passes and geological formations sculpted by volcanic action, such are the Witteberg Mountains on the Maloti route. This is not known as the most scenic route in SA for nothing! Glancing out over magnificent mountains, windy roads, oh and watch out for the goats, made me a bit late – sorry about that – but instantly a cup of tea and sandwich sprang forth for a hungry traveller. Hospitality here rules ok. The three G's have recently renovated their hundred-year-old cottages into high-comfort Porcupine's Place, with its wooden floors and French doors onto the garden; Comfrey Cottage, with its Queen Ann coal fire, old retro fridge and pink-and-green stove; Robin's Nest, with its wrap-around balcony and benches on the verandah; Apple Crumble, still to come; and the newly-built, smart-yet-relaxed lounge and dining room. The garden is filled with fifteen different species of fruit trees – pears, figs and walnuts amongst others – and someone was swinging in a hammock contemplating the mountain as I passed. Mountain rambles, bird-watching, visiting the art academy and George's geological tours are favourite activities here. There are unique geological features and alpine flowers at the south-western edge of the Drakensberg and they merit an explanation. What's more, Tiffindell, the only ski resort in SA, is nearby, so be prepared for breathtaking snow-capped mountains come winter.

Rooms: 10: 6 doubles and 4 twins, 2 with en-suite baths, 8 with en-suite showers.
Price: R280 – R300 pp sharing for dinner B&B. Self-catering possible.
Meals: Full breakfast and 3-course dinner included.
Directions: From Jo'burg, take N1 to Bloemfontein, then take N6 to Aliwal North and R58 to Lady Grey. Then follow signs to Comfrey Cottage.

Leliekloof Valley of Art

Dries and Minnie De Klerk

Burgersdorp 9744
Tel: 051-653-1240 Fax: 051-653-1240
Email: sanart@intekom.co.za Web:

What a place! Magnificent Bushman art and high-altitude wilderness to nourish the soul; log fires and home-cooked meals to look after earthier parts. Dries and Minnie have landed on their feet at Leliekloof, a farm adjoining their own property which they acquired a few years ago. The river here has chiselled a tortuous gorge through the sandstone and ironstone hills and the many caves host thirteen remarkable sites of Bushman art, many of the paintings of indeterminable age. Dries took me for an exhilarating morning drive and we visited two of them, Eland and Dog Caves. The quality of the paintings is superb, Dries a full reservoir of information about both the images and their artists. There is also a two-day scenic 19-kilometre hike around the valley, and a large dam for canoeing and trout fishing. Art apart, the countryside will extract from you superlatives you never knew you had. Single guests usually stay, for reasons of sociability, at the De Klerks' farm, while others have the run of Leliekloof House nearer the valley. The magnificent main room is 22 metres long, with sitting area, yellowwood bar, fireplace and huge antique Oregon pine dining table. You can self-cater, but given the stellar quality of Minnie's food (and the variety of things to do), I strongly suggest that you ask her to prepare your meals. Two-night minimum stay recommended. *Plains Game hunting and wing shooting available May – August.*

Rooms: 1 farmhouse with 3 bedrooms (2 dbl and 1 twin, 2 with en-suite bath, 1 en/s shower) plus a loft sleeping 4; also 1 extra bathroom with bath & shower.
Price: Full board rates: R380 – R440 (for three or more). R400 – R460 for 2 people. Single rates on request.
Meals: Breakfast, lunch and dinner included. Dinner is 3 courses including bottle of wine.
Directions: 6km south of Jamestown on N6 turn towards Burgersdorp. Turn right after 10 km. After another 5.5km fork right and Leliekloof is another 1km. Map can be faxed.

Map Number: 7

Entry Number: 185

The Stagger Inn

Robin and Berta Halse & Sean and Ann Bryan

Carnarvon Estate, Sterkstroom 5425
Tel: 045-966-0408 Fax: 045-966-0408
Email: carnarvon@worldonline.co.za Web: www.carnarvon-estate.com
Cell: 082-445-1032

So nice to arrive somewhere and instantly know that the people there will make your stay all the more enjoyable. I wasn't even asked if I'd like lunch… it was assumed and presented. Tea? That came too. Smiling, warm faces are a given at the Stagger Inn and all three generations of the family that help on the estate exude a contagious enthusiasm for it. So here you are in the great outdoors with 25,000 acres of pristine wilderness at your beck and call. You can bird-watch, fish for rainbow trout and large-mouth bass, swim in the weirs of clear spring water, go boating on the dams, do some clay pigeon shooting and spot some of the fifteen species of antelope on game-drives (also lynx, jackal, genets, black eagles, fish eagles and vultures). Or you can just walk among the indigenous shrubs and wild flowers. Ruddy-faced and hungry from the fresh air and activities, guests cosy up by the blazing log fire before a hearty, healthy dinner of home-cooked produce fresh from the farm (cows, sheep, pigs, sawmill and a dairy). And then to bed, hunting-lodge-style in farmhouses with comfortable (rather than luxurious) rooms for a well-needed night's sleep. As I discovered in the morning, the quality of light up here is a phenomenon, and the views breathtaking. The rolling ridge-country and grassy plains reach as far as the eye can see. Make sure you stay for long enough.

Rooms: 6: 1 double, 4 twins with en-suite bathrooms; 1 double for self-catering with en-suite shower.
Price: R300 – R400 pp dinner B&B.
Meals: Full breakfast and dinner included.
Directions: From Queenstown, take N6 for 50km and turn right on the R344 towards Dordrecht and follow signs to Stagger Inn (gravel road for 13km).

Redcliffe Guest Farm

Johnnie and Carol Morgan
PO Box 137, Tarkastad 5370
Tel: 045-848-0152
Email: info@dtours.co.za Web: www.dtours.co.za

Johnnie and Carol kindly adopted me for the night when I couldn't – or rather didn't want to – leave their unspoilt country idyll in the depths of the Winterberg Mountains. Not many tourists have yet found the Winterberg, but surely it is only a matter of time. This is an escape from everything apart from cows, sheep, birds and the natural environment that supports them. The simplest way to enjoy the area is to go for a hike across the rolling grassland hills. The gorge on a neighbouring farm is, I think, the most spectacular spot I have been privy to in South Africa and it goes virtually unvisited. The plateau folds in on itself and plummets hundreds of metres down, waterfalls dropping from terrace to terrace. Or you can go swimming, trout-fishing, mountain-biking, horse-riding, bird-watching, or play tennnis back at the house. Carol may cook you her speciality stuffed leg of lamb for dinner and Johnnie will happily show you around his shearing shed. He is especially proud of his merinos whose pure white wool is used to make smart Italian suits. Guests here have all the space they could need both outside and inside the five-bedroom farmhouse, including a light-filled sun room. A real home and the area of highland farms is still to be discovered even by the more adventurous overseas traveller.

Rooms: 1 farmhouse: 1 double and 4 twins, 3 en-suite and 2 with private bathrooms.
Price: R525 pp lunch, dinner, bed and breakfast minimum 2 people, R150 pp self-catering minimum 3 people. Phone to discuss group prices.
Meals: Breakfast, lunch and dinner on request. Self-catering also an option.
Directions: On R344 between Tarkastad and Adelaide. Directions faxed or emailed.

Cavers Country Guest House

Kenneth and Rozanne Ross
R63, Bedford 5780
Tel: 046-685-0619 Fax: 046-685-0619
Email: ckross@intekom.co.za Web: www.cavers.co.za
Cell: 082-579-1807

I can't be the first to call Cavers an oasis, but it is irresistible. There in the distance a stand of tall oaks shimmers unconvincingly in the haze. And then suddenly you are among well-watered and mature gardens, an Eden of lawns and vivid flowers. The fine stone, ivy-encased farmhouse was built in 1840 and has been in Ken's family for four generations. The bedrooms, with wooden floorboards, high ceilings and voluptuously draped windows, are refined and elegant. From one of the upstairs rooms I got an impression of living in the trees with an hadeda nesting at eye level and yellow orioles twittering and fluttering about. Two grand upstairs rooms with pressed-metal ceilings have balconies overlooking the profusion of flowers below. The thatched cottage also has long views over the lawns and up to the Winterberg Mountains. Rozanne is a maestro in the kitchen, cooking with fresh produce from the farm and the surrounding area and all her meals are mouth-watering feasts. The memory of that salmon cheesecake is even now a Pavlovian trigger that gets the mouth watering. There is a clay tennis court, hiking and riding or even cricket on the magnificent ground nearby. Swimming is in the pool or a big round reservoir.

Rooms: 5: 4 rooms in the manor house: 2 twins & 2 king/twins, 2 en-suite shower, 1 bath, 1 shr & bath; 1 cottage has 1 twin & 1 double sharing bath & shower.
Price: R300 – R450 pp sharing, B&B.
Meals: Full breakfast included. Dinner and lunch on request.
Directions: 8km from Bedford on the R63 towards Adelaide, turn left at the sign and follow the dirt road for 8km.

Die Tuishuise

Sandra Antrobus
36 Market St, Cradock 5880
Tel: 048-881-1322 Fax: 048-881-5388
Email: tuishuise@eastcape.net Web: www.tuishuise.co.za

Unique accommodation indeed! Sandra has a raptor's eye for historic detail, laced with an antique dealer's nose and the heart of an interior designer – unparalleled in my experience of South Africa. There are 25 houses along Market Street, all antiquely furnished to reflect different styles, eras and professions. The houses were once lived in by bank managers, teachers, wagon makers etc, and you step into their 19th-century shoes when you stay – although the bathrooms, perhaps, retain a little more modernity. Each house is an antique shop in its own right, but modern comforts include fans, heaters and fireplaces. I was lucky enough to visit them all and it is no exaggeration to say I was struck dumb – reason enough for Sandra to have gone to the effort (some might feel). The hotel, a Victorian manor at the end of the street, has a further 19 rooms similarly done out in the style of the time and sherry is served in the drawing room before buffet dinners (my Karoo lamb was delicious). Sandra and her daughter Lisa are dedicated to presenting South African history in a way you can touch and feel. They do cultural performances epitomising the Xhosa and Afrikaner culture – ask in advance. *Closed 24th & 25th December.*

Rooms: 25 restored 19th-century houses, each rented out as one 'unit'. There is also a hotel.
Price: From R270 – R300 pp sharing. No single supplement.
Meals: Breakfast served 7 – 9 am in summer, 7 -10 am in winter. Traditional dinners available.
Directions: From PE take N10. When you arrive in Cradock at 4-way stop turn left into Market St. Die Tuishuise is 3rd block on left.

Somerset House

Vega and Stephen Niekerk

88 Paulet St, Somerset East 5850
Tel: 042-243-1819 Fax: 042-243-1207
Email: djmsales@lantic.net
Cell: 073-154-6199

Everyone I met in the Eastern Cape seems to have stayed at Somerset House, or at least knows someone who has. Comments such as: "You're staying at Vega's? You'll love it!" were becoming run-of-the-mill. Well, they weren't wrong. I did love it. Vega and Stephen have completely renovated a century-old school building, using old photos to restore the deep verandah. Now scattered with cushioned chairs and coffee tables, the verandah looks out over lawns and garden up to the looming Misty Mountains. The living room, where I found a glass of wine tapping its watch, boasts high Oregon pine ceilings, painted white to reflect the sunlight that streams in through French doors, and is dotted with family heirlooms. Vega has lived in Somerset East most of her life, so over a drink and with the invisible tendrils of roasting Karoo lamb wafting out of the kitchen, she revealed her passion for this historic town. Stephen, meanwhile, chipped in with some of the more gruesome tales of betrayal and bloodshed that make frontier country so intriguing. Guests amble over to friend and neighbour Janet Telian, founder chef of Cape Town's Savoy Cabbage, and have dinner there. A luxuriously decorated house and a gorgeous setting, but Vega and Stephen are a super-hospitable couple and bind it all together.

Rooms: 3: 1 double with en-suite shower, 2 twins with en-suite bath and shower.
Price: R250 – R350 pp sharing. Singles R350.
Meals: Full breakfast included. Dinners provided on request either by Vega or Janet Telian at an extra cost.
Directions: From PE on the N10, take R63 signed to Somerset East. In Somerset East, turn left and head down Main Street. Turn right opposite the church and follow signs to Somerset House.

Wheatlands

Diana and Arthur & Kirsten and David Short

Route R75, PO Box 325, Graaff-Reinet 6280
Tel: 049-891-0422/4 Fax: 049-891-0422
Email: wheatlands@wam.co.za Web: www.wheatlands.co.za
Cell: 082-414-6503

Guests at Wheatlands are thoroughly spoilt. I had read that the main house had been built on the profits of ostrich feathers in 1912 (a so-called 'feather palace'). I'm not sure why, but this led me to expect a humble farmhouse… and to get my shoes muddy finding it! But no. I found instead a gigantic manor house with a façade dominated by three extravagant gables. The house, designed by Charles Bridgeman, mingles Cape Dutch and Edwardian styles with a lovely white-pillared verandah at the back and then a green lake of lush lawn where heritage roses grow like weeds. Park your wagon (or whatever you are driving these days) in the huge sandy courtyard and enter a long, cool, wood-panelled hall, an instant pleasure as you leave the desert heat of the Karoo. It's an appropriate home for the piano, all the antique furniture and the Persian rugs. The corridors are lined with books, there is a snug for reading and guest bedrooms are not converted outhouses, but an integral, lived-in part of the house. There are wonderful wanders to be had in the revelation of a back garden. Diana and Arthur are astoundingly nice people, brimful of the hostly arts. Diana and Kirsten cook delicious dinners, which are eaten at one large oak table. Arthur, meanwhile, is a serious wool and mohair farmer and cricketer… they even have their own ground.

Rooms: 3: all twins, 2 with en-suite bath and shower, 1 with private bath and shower.
Price: R280 – R320 pp sharing.
Meals: Full breakfast and dinner included (Karoo lamb a speciality).
Directions: 42km on the R75 south of Graaff-Reinet – Wheatlands turn-off to the left, 8km up a gravel road.

Map Number: 6

Cypress Cottage

Hillary Palmé
76 Donkin St, Graaff-Reinet 6280
Tel: 049-892-3965 Fax: 049-892-3965
Email: info@cypresscottage.co.za Web: www.cypresscottage.co.za
Cell: 083-456-1795

Everyone from Greenwood Guides has now been to stay at Cypress Cottage and it is a pleasure to recommend it to you too. After a hot – and possibly bothersome – drive to this historic Karoo town, it is an immense relief to be welcomed by people as easy-going and instantly likeable as the Palmés… and to be installed in a beautiful, early 1800s Cape Dutch cottage… and to find yourself minutes later, cold beer in hand, on a stoep with magnificent mountain views. The bedrooms in the cottage are understatedly decorated with a (highly developed) taste for the natural and comfortable, thus the high reed ceilings, solid pine and slate floors, antique chests, fresh flowers and free-standing baths. Breakfast is laid up outside on the terrace – free-range eggs from house chickens, succulent figs, peaches, prunes and apricots from the orchards. Everything is as fresh and natural as possible. Guests can swim in the bore-hole-fed reservoir, which has been converted into a swimming pool. The garden is an extraordinary feat of will and clever engineering – Hillary has managed to turn desert into lush vegetation despite the difficulties of brackish water. Graaff-Reinet is worth at least two days' stopover in my opinion – Cypress Cottage many more.

Rooms: 3: 2 doubles and 1 twin. All with en-suite bathrooms; 1 with bath, 1 with shower, 1 with both. All with aircon and heating.
Price: R250 – R400 pp sharing. Singles on request.
Meals: Full breakfast included.
Directions: From south: enter the town and pass the police academy on L and go over bridge. Two filling stations on L – take the road between them (West St). Follow to the very end, turn R into Donkin St, guest house first on L. From north: R at T-jct (Caledon St). 4th Left is Donkin St. House last on R.

Auberge Caledonia

Johann Swiegelaar and Michael Smit
61 Somerset Street, Graaff-Reinet 6280
Tel: 049-892-3156 Fax: 049-892-3157
Email: info@caledonia.co.za Web: www.caledonia.co.za
Cell: 082-774-1795

In one of the oldest towns in South Africa, this is the oldest hotel. Built in 1854, it was renovated in 1881 by a hotelier who had it "comfortably fitted up" so that it would "be found cool, clean and comfortable". 123 years later, Johann and Michael have embarked on a fresh overhaul that would make that Victorian owner proud. The flat-fronted, wooden-shuttered building sits right on the street and has something of provincial France about it. Double-doors sweep you into a broad and breezy hallway whose smoothed-and-grooved floorboards lead out to a dappled courtyard, its table settings shaded by an ornamental vine. The bedrooms are arranged in adjoined outbuildings, one accessed through the garden, by way of rose parterre and plunge pool, the other from the street. Rooms have honey-coloured wood and whitened walls and are simply furnished with enough space for a film crew to sprawl out in (as they did when I visited). The rooms offer a cooling refuge when the Karoo turns up the heat. One place you won't feel the heat is in the kitchen. That's strictly Johann and Michael's domain. In a Provençal-style dining room that matches the cuisine, they serve up culinary sensations. In 1881 Mr McMurray was determined that the "requirements of the inner man… be strictly attended to"! Johann and Michael espouse this admirable motto as their own.

Rooms: 6: 4 double suites with en-suite shower and bath; 1 double and 1 twin both with en-suite shower.
Price: R225 – R310 pp sharing. Singles on request.
Meals: Full breakfast included. There's an à la carte restaurant on the premises serving dinner daily, mains from R50.
Directions: Faxed when booking.

Trymore Cottage

Marion and Robert Rubidge
Wellwood Farm, Nr Nieu-Bethesda, Graaff-Reinet 6280
Tel: 049-840-0302 Fax: 049-840-0302
Email: wellwood@wam.co.za
Cell: 082-379-0131

The first Rubidges started farming at Wellwood in 1838 (the visitors book, to which I proudly added my name, even dates back to 1873) and today it is a well-known merino sheep farm. Everything from the main homestead to workers' cottages are in picturesque keeping with the arid landscape – white gables, shady trees, white wooden fences and a backdrop of Karoo koppies. Trymore Cottage was built in the 1950s for Robert's grandfather, Sidney Rubidge, on his retirement, a place to clean the fossils that he found on his land. These are kept in a museum at the main farm today, and what a collection! Only staying guests have access to this, so ask Marion to give you a very knowledgeable guided tour of some of Gondwanaland's finest pre-dinosaur monsters. But this pre-Jurassic feast is only half the Wellwood Farm experience. A smiling Mieme (who grew up on the farm) will ensure that you are settled into the gabled cottage, showing you through the pine-floored bedrooms and keeping the large, open fireplace well stocked with wood. I spotted in the hall a bottle of Marion's homemade kumquat liqueur, which I duly sampled (powerful stuff and on sale). Dinner itself is a true Karoo farm affair – good old-fashioned meat and veg, with house specialities of venison pie or local roast lamb, all served in the cottage. A farm experience with a difference.

Rooms: 1 cottage with 3 twins and 1 double, separate bath and shower room. The cottage is for one group at a time only.
Price: R290 – R310 pp for adults. Children under 12 half price.
Meals: Full breakfast and dinner included.
Directions: Take N9 from Graaff-Reinet towards Middelberg. 32km from Graaff-Reinet is a sign on the left saying R. Rubidge, Wellwood.

Ganora Guest Farm and Excursions

JP and Hester Steynberg
Nieu-Bethesda, near Graaff-Reinet 6280
Tel: 049-841-1302 Fax: 086-680-0884
Email: info@ganora.co.za Web: www.ganora.co.za
Cell: 082-698-0029

JP and Hester, along with visiting palaeontologists and guests, are thrilled with the historic finds on their farm, which together demonstrate a South African heritage spinning back in time from the Boer War to the Bushmen dynasty, to the pre-dinosaur era. 'Give us one day and we will give you 240 million years,' says the brochure. They originally bought their 4000-hectare Karoo property to farm Dohne-Merino sheep, famous for their fine wool (shearing and grading fleeces demonstrated in the shearing shed) and excellent meat. Then JP hit the Jurassic jackpot, so to speak, finding a horde of fossils in an ancient mud slide; and a tip-off from the previous owner led to Louis and Reiner (JP and Hester's teenage sons) finding a cave with not only the engravings from an escapee of the Boer War, but also bushman and Khoi paintings. Hester pointed out the image of a tortoise, the only one found in SA, and explained to me the methods and significance of the art. If history is your thing (and it will be), you can go horse-riding (only for the proficient) to the nearby canyon, bundu-hike up the Compassberg Mountain, swim in the Karoo river pools or visit Helen Martins' weird and wonderful Owl House. Guests stay in newly renovated former labourers cottages, with bare stone walls and large, powerful showers. After an activity-filled day, a four-course supper and a bout of star-gazing, a good night's sleep is had by all.

Rooms: 4: 3 twins and 1 double, all with en-suite shower.
Price: R250 pp sharing dinner, bed and breakfast. Visits to Boer War engravings, bushman rock shelter, fossil museum/walk and woolshed visit from R35 each.
Meals: Breakfast and dinner included. Lunch available on request.
Directions: Off N9 between Graaff-Reinet and Middleberg, turn towards Nieu-Bethesda (second turning to Nieu-Bethesda if coming from Graaff-Reinet). Directions on web or emailed.

Map Number: 6

KwaZulu Natal

Plumbago

Mick and Libby Goodall

546 St Ives Ave, Leisure Bay
Tel: 039-319-2665 Fax: 039-319-2665
Email: begood@mweb.co.za
Cell: 082-561-6993

I think the coast of KwaZulu Natal gets better and better the further south you head, and Leisure Bay is testament to that. It's just stunning, and, buried in the banana plantations between bush and beach, is easily missed by those hammering along the N2 to more on-the-beaten-track destinations. Plumbago itself is on the crest of a hill on sandy St Ives Avenue (just off Torquay Avenue, naturally), a gentle stroll from the sea. It's an airy double-storey home, hidden from its neighbours by the thick foliage of Libby's indigenous garden, indigenous that is "except the rosemary and the lemon tree for G&Ts," she admits. The birds are amazing and hop around right under your nose, and while they chattered in the trees, we chattered (over lunch) at a long, central dining table made from an old jetty post. Downstairs the house is open-plan with large windows, high ceilings and soft, blue walls – the perfect antidote to sizzling summer days. Upstairs a wrap-around verandah keeps the main bedroom equally cool and if you do get over-heated you can just jump in the outside shower. There are endless sea or land-based activities to keep you busy in the area, but with a beautiful beach on hand, well, I'd be just as happy focusing on some serious R&R.

Rooms: 2: both doubles, one with bath and shower, one with bath, outside shower available to both.
Price: R250 – R300 pp sharing.
Meals: Full breakfast included. Other meals on request.
Directions: Follow N2 and R61 south from Durban towards Port Edward. About 5km north of town take the Torquay Ave/Leisure Bay turn off. Follow Torquay Ave to the crest of hill and turn L into St Ives Ave. Plumbago is 100 yards down on the R.

Nolangeni Lodge

Bev and Herbert Hirschboeck
3 Nolangeni Ridge, St Michaels-on-Sea 4265
Tel: 039-315-7327 Fax: 039-315-7327
Email: nolangeni@mweb.co.za Web: www.nolangenilodge.co.za
Cell: 082-660-9045

Staying the night with Bev and Herbert was a true pleasure, particularly as they spoilt me rotten with a superb supper (a reliable fast track to my affections). "It's a team effort," Herbert told me. "Bev cooks, I watch." And the system works very well. We ate together in the glass-walled dining room and, by moon and candlelight, put paid to excellent chicken with rosemary, lemon and feta on a risotto bed, then cheesecake in an indulgent, strawberry coulis. It's hard to think that when they moved here just a few years ago Nolangeni was little more than a structural time-bomb. Bev shudders at the memory. These days the two-storey, hillside house (three including the pool down below), exudes a relaxed, lived-in feel and its owners a doors-always-open attitude. But then the Hirschboecks are seasoned pros (Herbert came from Germany in 1979 to run the room service at the (in)famous Sun City resort). At Nolangeni, rooms offer something for everyone: a self-catering unit downstairs, a family room above and two kings both with smart, wrought-iron furniture and a popular patch of slated balcony. I lingered after breakfast to enjoy mine and "do some paperwork". Needless to say I ended up wedged in a sofa in the open-fronted living room just gazing out at the sea, the birds, the river, the garden, the sky… well, you get the idea.

Rooms: 5: 1 self-catering unit with 1 queen, a 3/4 sofa-bed & shared shower; 1 king/twin with shower; 1 king with bath; 1 queen with combined bath & shower; 1 family unit with twin & double rooms & shared bath & shower.
Price: R260 – R300 pp sharing. Singles on request.
Meals: Dinners and light lunches on request.
Directions: Faxed or emailed on booking.

Wailana Beach Lodge

Rene Tobler

436 Ashmead Drive, Ramsgate 4285
Tel: 039-314-4606 Fax: 039-314-4606
Email: wailana@iafrica.com Web: www.wailana.co.za
Cell: 082-379-0922

The pace of life at Wailana is about as relaxed as you'll find anywhere on KZN's sub-tropical south coast and when I turned up Rene Tobler (pronounced as in Toblerone) was moseying around in shorts and flip-flops trailed by his chirpy young daughter/assistant Joya. He's a well-travelled chap and after countless trips to Thailand and Laos – his eyes light up at the slightest mention of them – he's swapped his Swiss homeland snow for SA sun and a modern, chill-out zone, hidden among the palms just a stone's throw from the Indian Ocean. This is a place to kick back and mooch, whether you're slabbed out on the pool-side deck, ploughing through a good book in the hammock or inventing cocktails in the half-inside, half-outside bar. I loved the bright colours and arched doorways, and the individuality of each room. How to choose between them? On the upper deck I liked the sea-view, sea-blue Captain's Cabin, but wanted the open shower that tumbles from the Master room's bathroom ceiling. And then there's the Oriental room down below with its koi carp prints and driftwood swing on the balcony. Oh… I don't know. How about a night in each? There's so much more I could tell you, but I'd be cheating if I uncovered everything, so you'll just have to visit and discover the rest for yourself.

Rooms: 5: 2 kings, 3 queens. 2 rooms have bath and shower, 3 have shower only.
Price: R300 – R490 pp sharing.
Meals: Full breakfast included.
Directions: From N2 and Durban take the R61 south until Margate/Ramsgate off-ramp (exit 29). Head towards the sea. Turn L at T-junction. Pass Spar and Total garage then turn R onto Ashmead. Wailana is 200m on, on R.

Map Number: 8

Lindsay Loft

Caroline Jankovich

26 Lindsay Avenue, Morningside, Durban 4001
Tel: 031-207-1634 Fax: 031-208-3227
Email: caroline@lindsayloft.co.za Web: www.lindsayloft.co.za
Cell: 083-490-0963

If you're loft is anything like mine it's a dark and dusty dumping ground for old junk. Caroline's loft, I can enviously assure you, is NOTHING like mine. It's enormous. Walls are whitewashed and go up forever, floors are tiled to keep it cool in summer and there's a lengthy, decked verandah, of which more later. Actually no, I can't wait. The verandah is great, accessed from both the living- and bedrooms it peaks through the trees and across the city from its hill-top look-out. Bottle-brush, mango and avocado all tickle its handrail and you're encouraged to pick the fruit to avoid it crashing down onto the neighbour's tin roof. Sadly, my visit was a little early for those fresh treats so I was duly filled up with tea and toast instead. Back inside, the bedroom is cavernous and calming with (besides a bed of course) caramel armchairs and a beautiful old writing desk. The living area too is dotted with mahogany antiques and separated from the kitchen by a breakfast bar. For the chef, there's all the cooking kit you need and Caroline will supply the essentials to get you started. This is a great base from which to explore KZN. The Drakensberg mountains are a few hours inland, the game reserves a short drive up the coast and there are excellent beaches and golf courses.

Rooms: 1 double/king with en/s combined bath and shower.
Price: R275 pp sharing. Singles R450.
Meals: Starter supplies provided.
Directions: From M4 to Durban take exit 2, Moore Rd. Follow to traffic lights and turn R into Manning Rd which becomes Essenwood Rd. 100m after feeding into Montpelier Rd take Lindsay Ave up a steep hill. Lindsay Loft is just over the brow.

Ntengu Lodge

Andrew and Kathryn Buchanan

24 David McLean Drive, Westville, Durban 3630
Tel: 031-266-8578 Fax: 031-266-8026
Email: ntengu@intekom.co.za Web: www.ntengulodge.com
Cell: 083-777-2644

That Andrew was sloping around barefoot was an immediate sign of the pace of life at Ntengu: gloriously slow. A couple of recently-arrived guests were sipping a chilled glass of wine, installed in poolside wicker armchairs; another, here on business, was tapping at the computer in Andrew's office. Everyone seemed happily ensconced as if in their own homes. Like so many of the owners in this book here is a man "too creative for the corporate world" who has opted for a change of track and these days spends his time hammering and sawing in his workshop, building striking kiaat wood furniture to fit his house. And he's got his work cut out after expanding from one to six rooms in as many years. Ntengu Lodge is a two-storey house squarely planted on one of the jungly ridges that fold back from Durban's beachfront. Up here the trees rustle with a constant breeze that makes for a welcome escape from sweltering city-centre summers. In fact, the city couldn't feel further away. The breakfast room opens onto the decked pool and a wall of greenery, and from wrought-iron bedroom balconies there is a stunning view down into the Palmiet nature reserve that protects the surrounding hillside. Staff are easy smilers, rooms have silk curtains, walk-in showers or other twists of luxury, Shiane the Ntengu chef will excite your taste buds… need I go on?

Rooms: 6: 2 king/twins and 2 doubles with showers only, 2 extra length queens, one with separate bath and shower, one with bath and shower combined.
Price: R345 pp sharing. Singles R480.
Meals: Full breakfast included. Dinner on request.
Directions: From Durban follow N2 north towards Stanger. After 20km take N3 towards Pietermaritzburg. Take next exit, M32 to Pavilion shopping centre and turn R at top of ramp to Westville. Continue 2.1km to T-junction, turn R for 1.2km to BP station. Turn L into David McLean Drive and house is number 24 on L.

Fairlight B&B

Bruce and Michele Deeb

1 Margaret Bacon Avenue, (Corner South Beach Rd), Umdloti Beach 4350
Tel: 031-568-1835 Fax: 031-568-1835
Email: bdeeb@mweb.co.za Web: www.fairlight.co.za
Cell: 082-775-9971 or 082-443-8529

I got my first taste of Bruce and Michele's laid-back hospitality as soon as I arrived. It was another hot KZN day and I was bustled off for a joyous dip in the sea just across the road – "We can talk later". And we did. This newly-refreshed 'inspector' was soon sipping a cold beer by the pool and tucking into some delicious Lebanese pastries and thoroughly South African boerewors as Bruce tended the braai. The garden behind the house is dominated by two large milkwoods, a great place to shelter from the sun, although there are also sun-loungers around the swimming pool. The front of the house has a wooden deck running all along it, from where you can watch the surfers – all the rooms open onto it. Dolphins love the surf, too, and if you're lucky you can swim with them. Bruce can lend you a boogie board and flippers. Inside, it is effectively a family home and luxury guest house rolled into one – plenty of light and air as befits a beach house, family snaps on the wall and a warm, welcoming vibe to it. Rays of positive energy emanate from Michele and Bruce and their long-standing housekeeper Maria. Soak it up, then go forth and fish, surf or swim with a big smile on your face. Ten miles of heaven, a.k.a. Umdloti Beach, are but 40 paces from the house. *Durban and the airport are both within half an hour's drive.*

Rooms: 6: all sea-facing with en-suite shower (3 with bath and shower). 4 have aircon.
Price: R350 – R500. Singles from R450.
Meals: Full breakfast included.
Directions: N2 exit to Umdloti. Follow down to roundabout. Keep right past Total garage and Fairlight is 500 metres along South Beach Rd.

Uthula

Candy Jessel and Avril Tucker

PO Box 793, Umdloti Beach 4350
Tel: 031-568-2104 Fax: 031-568-2104
Email: cjessel@t-online.de Web: www.zimbali.de
Cell: 082-349-7380

"Uthula" means peace in Zulu and if you don't leave this house feeling peaceful I'll personally pay you a refund. Well, I might…. Down to the hanging chains that replace plastic drainpipes, every architectural detail has been meticulously thought out to create a two-storey haven of Zen-like tranquillity. It's part of the private Zimbali estate, just north of Durban, where homes have been built to melt into rather than stand out from their surroundings. Candy's house overlooks sand and surf and has a private stairway leading down to the beach. Either side of the covered entrance, water trickles into a Japanese pond, home to a lone but enormous coy carp, looking suspiciously as if he had gobbled his companions. Inside, the roof-high hallway is lined with family prints of Candy as a nipper. Dark, mahogany woodwork and cream-coloured walls run throughout. Two of four bedrooms face seaward and wall-to-wall windows upstairs and down mean the whole house can be opened to the huge deck and fabulous weather through the summer months. I absolutely loved it and reckon it just as suited to a gang of pals as a family (the kids will love the pool and bunk-beds). Candy's mum, Avril, looks after the place and meets you on arrival. She's hugely friendly and helpful and will organise a cook or buy enough starter goodies to keep the wolf from the door (or pool). Golfers, by the way, have their own golf cart (included in the price) to go out and play from the doorstep.

Rooms: 4: 1 king with en/s bath and shower, 1 twin with en/s shower, 1 double and 2 bunk-beds (i.e. sleeps 4!) which share bath and shower.
Price: From R3,000 per night, rates negotiable.
Meals: Self-catering, but a cook is available.
Directions: From Durban take N2 north until Ballito exit. Take first R onto M4 (heading south). Pass Zimbali Country Club entrance. Take next off-ramp and turn L signed Zimbali Coastal Forest Estate. Gate guards will instruct you from there.

Seaforth Farm

Trevor and Sharneen Thompson

Exit 214 off N2, Salt Rock, Umhlali 4390
Tel: 032-525-5217 Fax: 032-525-4495
Email: ttastym@iafrica.com Web: www.seaforth.co.za
Cell: 082-770-8376

Seaforth Farm is a full-blown treat of a guest house. Trevor and Sharneen have many interests, talents and motivations and Seaforth is a constant source of stimulation. Trevor is an official tour guide and will advise you on the 'must-do's' in the area. Dolphin trips are very popular with guests. One is whisked out through the surf on a "Rubber Duck" and if lucky, one can get close up to these wonderful creatures that abound along this stretch of the coastline.Sharneen is a water-colourist and has also won medals for flower-arranging, so the house blooms with extravagant displays and paintings. Trevor is a skilled craftsman and much of the furniture has been made in his workshop (his latest piece, a huge lychee-wood bed) – and it is highly accomplished work. The garden is lush and wild and envelops everything at Seaforth in tropical colour. There are brahman cattle, chickens, pawpaw and pecan trees, and the dam and its abundant bird life. Trevor is coaxing it in with a cunning plantation of pond weed, lilies and islets, and you can bird-watch from a hide overlooking the dam. The guest house provides large, well-equipped bedrooms, a pool and thatched summer-house with dam-view for heavenly breakfasts and candle-lit curry evenings. Finally, the staff have a stake in the success of their venture. A pioneering guest house indeed…. *Zulu spoken.*

Rooms: 4: 1 family cottage with 2 bedrooms, each with en/s shower; 2 doubles and 1 twin with en/s shower and bath.
Price: R290 pp sharing. Family suite (sleeps 5) from R720.
Meals: Full breakfast included.
Directions: From Durban take the N2 north. Exit on the 214 signed Salt Rock. Go 200m and take the 1st right into Old Fort Road, then 1st left into Seaforth Ave – the house is at the end.

Nalson's View

Wendy and Kelvin Nalson
10 Fairway Drive, Salt Rock
Tel: 032-525-5726 Fax: 032-525-5726
Email: nalsonsview@3i.co.za
Cell: 083-303-1533

After a long, long (long, long) day on the road I finally emerged from my car at Nalson's, wild-eyed and mud-besmattered. I couldn't have pitched up anywhere more perfect. Kelvin and Wendy welcomed me as if I had been living there for years. This was my room, these my beers and friends… I owned the place didn't I? A fantastic shower washed off the mud (don't ask) and I was invited to dinner. I couldn't tell who were guests, who were family friends, such is the open-house air of friendship here, and the meal was out of this world. Kelvin and Wendy have an oyster and mussel licence (guests can go with them and pick their own) and these were by FAR the best I've had in SA. Nalson's is one of those places where guests stop over for one night and have to be prised out of the place days later. Breakfast was sensational (both local baker and butcher are true servants of the community!) and, joy oh joy, freshly squeezed fruit juice. Guests who make the correct decision to stay more than one night will get involved in the sea activities – dolphin- and whale-watching on boats, fishing, bird-watching and the ten kilometres of beautiful Christmas Bay Beach. There's plenty to do on dry land too including golf galore, walking-distance restaurants and the Sibaya casino just 10 minutes away. *Ask about children.*

Rooms: 4: 2 doubles, 1 family and 1 double/twin; 3 with en-suite shower, 1 with en-suite bath and shower.
Price: From R300 pp sharing. Singles on request.
Meals: Full breakfast included and served when you want it. Dinners by prior arrangement. Price depends on what you have.
Directions: From Durban take N2 north. Take exit 214 (Salt Rock/Umhlali). Right at T-junction signed to Salt Rock, follow road round to the right past Salt Rock Hotel (on your left). Fairway Drive is next right.

The Chase

Jane and Jonathan Chennells

PO Box 45, Eshowe 3815
Tel: 035-474-5491 Fax: 035-474-1311
Email: thechase@netactive.co.za Web: www.thechase.co.za
Cell: 083-265-9629

Jane and Jonathan have so much to offer their guests that you hardly have to leave the premises. The weather-boarded house is gargantuan (Mrs Chennells senior had a penchant for large, open spaces) with long views of the farm's sugar cane plantations on overlapping mounds of distant hills. On clear days you can even see 90 degrees of sea. (They also have ducks, chickens, cows, sheep and goats like a proper farm should, of course.) The garden is an orgy of barely controllable tropical growth, lush and colourful (check out the tulip tree and the Indian mahogany), its trees often weighed down by parasitic ferns and creepers. Birds are equally irrepressible and there are 70 species in the garden and 280 (!) in the Eshowe area. Kids will love the walled-in swimming pool (13 metres long) where you can swim by floodlight at night too. A hammock swings from a tree, a trampoline is stretched at ground level and there is a hard tennis court. Chennells Chase is an involving, very comfortable, incredibly good-value family home, with huge amounts of space inside and out. Pack a sense of humour and a pair of binoculars.

Rooms: 2: 1 double with en-suite bath; 1 twin with en-suite shower. Also a self-contained farm cottage with 5 bedrooms and 2 bathrooms.
Price: R200 – R300 pp sharing. Singles R300 – R400. Self catering in the cottage (sleeps 5) R450 – R550.
Meals: Full breakfast included (except in the cottage – by arrangement only) and served any time.
Directions: From Durban take N2 north for 1 hour. Turn off at Dokodweni off-ramp. Half an hour to Eshowe. Take first left signed to Eshowe, house 1.8km signed on left.

Entry Number: 205

Map Number: 15

Zimbete Country House

Anne and Nick Nicolson
PO Box 1141, Empangemi 3880
Tel: 035-791-1991 Fax: 035-791-1991
Email: nickanne@iafrica Web: www.zimbete.co.za
Cell: 083-632-0195

Zigzagging through the sugar cane, you probably won't spot Nick and Anne's house until you're actually there. It's surrounded by a tropical garden, bursting with indigenous and exotic plants (and consequently birds – 278 species in fact, including the palm-nut vulture). The palm trees are vast and billowing bougainvillea engulfs the farmhouse. Finally reaching the front door and Zimbete's inner sanctum, I was amazed to hear the plants were all put in just twenty years ago. But then this place is brimming with surprises, not least the family history. Anne and Nick are both descended from Natal Settler families (and are both history buffs). Anne's great-grandfather fought in the Zulu wars before becoming chief architect, city engineer and mayor of Durban all at the same time (clever chap!). Nick – farmer of nuts and veg and bird and tree fundi – is a local lad too. His family are everywhere and visitors to famed food-house Cleopatra Mountain Lodge will meet his sister Mouse Poynton. Food is a major theme at Zimbete too. Anne has a range of devilish desserts and after one of her dinners you'll be glad of a room just a few yards down the corridor. They're great by the way, each with a garden view. But my favourite was a diminutive garden cottage hidden in the vegetable patch between the leeks and the lettuce – eyes peeled for Peter Rabbit.

Rooms: 5: 4 queens, one with shower, others bath and shower; 1 twin with bath and shower.
Price: R375 – R450 pp sharing.
Meals: Full breakfast included. 3- or 4-course dinner on request (R120).
Directions: From N2 take R102 at Zululand University exit north towards Empangemi. After 4km turn R towards Felixton. Zimbete is signed 100m further on to the L.

Maputaland Guest House

Jorg and Penny Orban

Kabeljou Ave, No. 1, Greater St Lucia Wetlands Park, Zululand 3936
Tel: 035-590-1041 Fax: 035-590-1041
Email: bookings@maputaland.com Web: www.maputaland.com

Maputaland Guest House is great value and the perfect launch pad for exploring the World Heritage Site, beaches, reefs and big game of the area. Jorg, who is very modest about his talents, is the bird fundi (430 local species live locally!). His wife Penny runs the house and sister Nicola is a dive-master. Jorg and she are both registered professional game guides too, so you've got no excuse to laze about! They take trips into nearby Hluhluwe-Umfolozi reserve. And, amazingly, Jorg likes to explore the streets of St Lucia itself, taking his guests on night safaris. Hippos, impala and on rare occasion even leopards can be seen wandering about the pavements. Bush babies and chameleons come out during the cicada hours too. The lodge is recently built, homely, relaxed and perfectly comfortable. But you're hardly here to stay indoors! Jorg does a cracking 'bonnet breakfast' (he assures me it's NOT road-kill) for those that go with him on day tours (starting at 4 am and getting back at 6pm – yep – good value alright). Nicola's dive tours are also run on a no-limits basis and you can dive and snorkel as many times as you like. Ask them about turtle-watching tours (two rare breeds come here), deep-sea fishing and fly-casting for 1.5-metre darga-salmon (which Jorg sometimes also cooks on the braai). Exciting, but very friendly with it.

Rooms: 5: 2 doubles and 3 twins with en-suite bath and shower. 1 double with twin in room and en-suite bath and shower.
Price: R250 – R300. Full-day safaris from 4am – 6pm from R450. Half-days from R350.
Meals: Full breakfast included. Dinners by request. Tours include all meals during the day.
Directions: From Jo'burg (7 hrs): take N2 through Bethal, Pongola etc and past Hluhluwe. Turn off to Mtubatuba then left on R618 to St Lucia. From Swaziland (3 hrs): join N2 from Pongola/Mukuzi and head for Mtubatuba. From Durban (3 hrs): N2 towards Mtubatuba, right on R618 to St L. Signs in St. L for guest house.

Makakatana Bay Lodge

Hugh and Leigh-Ann Morrison

Mtubatuba 3935
Tel: 035-550-4189 Fax: 035-550-4198
Email: maklodge@iafrica.com Web: www.makakatana.co.za
Cell: 082-573-5641

Makakatana Bay Lodge is sensational. If only we had space for ten shots, to show you every aspect of the lodge: the gleaming wooden interiors; the bedrooms (including the wonderful new honeymoon suite), connected by walkways through the forest, with their gargantuan slabs of glass and warm, earthy African colours; the pool encased in decking and raised above the grasses of the wetlands; the lake itself and the extraordinary St Lucia waterways. Guests are taken on pole-driven safaris in mokoro canoes, searching for birds (360 species!), crocodiles and hippos. You can also take a boat trip across the lake for lunch on the beach or a game drive to a nearby reserve before returning to a sumptuous dinner with your hosts in the outdoor boma. Safari drives to Hluhluwe Game Reserve are also available if you have a hankering to see the Big 5. The family's old 'Crab House' is the only part of the lodge not raised above the tall grasses. This was once a storeroom for crabs caught in the lake, now a wine cellar with a giant tree growing out of its roof. Huge sliding doors throughout the lodge open onto wooden decks with views over the lake, and the absence of railings just adds to the feeling of openness to nature. The lodge is beautifully welded to its environment. An absolute treat.

Rooms: 6: 1 honeymoon suite with extra single bed, 2 king suites, 3 twin suites; all with en-suite bath and outside shower.
Price: From R2,150 – R2,750 pp sharing. Singles from R2,800 – R3,000. Prices may change after October 2005. Winter rate R1,869 pp sharing (1st May – 30th Sept).
Meals: Fully inclusive of all meals and safaris.
Directions: Take N2 north from Durban for 250km to Charter's Creek. Follow road for 15km (14km on tar) to fork. Take right fork and follow signs to Makakatana Bay Lodge (4 more km or so).

Hluhluwe River Lodge

Gavin and Bridget Dickson

Greater St Lucia Wetlands Park, Hluhluwe 3960
Tel: 035-562-0246/7
Fax: 035-562-0248
Email: info@hluhluwe.co.za
Web: www.hluhluwe.co.za

A short drive through dense bushveld takes you to this friendly, informal lodge overlooking the shores of Lake St Lucia. On arrival, I dumped my kit in a wood-and-thatch chalet and headed straight for the big deck, the centrepiece of the lodge, for a drink and some orientation. The view is straight across the Hluhluwe River flood plain. There's a pool lost in the trees near the Zulu boma (for evening braais), but most will want to make full use of the all-seeing, all-knowing guides (including sometimes Gavin himself) who will take you exploring in this remarkable region. The river is just there for canoe safaris (hippos and crocs are commonly sighted and always a great variety of birds) and you can take boat trips around the lake, eyes peeled for all sorts of land game coming in to drink. There are drives through the Wetland Park sand forests, but I visited nearby Hluhluwe Umfolozi Park. And what a trip, my first real game drive and we spotted a leopard! You can also go on botanical trips or guided walks to old fossil banks and (astounding) bird-watching excursions in the park. Whatever you choose this is an intimate, sociable place, where small numbers and very knowledgeable guides make the experience personal and rewarding. The focus is on the topography, the bird life and the wetland environment as a whole, rather than just the 'Big Five'.

Rooms: 12: 8 twins, 2 family rooms all with en/s shower; 2 honeymoon suites (pictured) with shower & bath. If you want the honeymoon suites, ask when you book.
Price: From R1,194 – R1,499 pp sharing for all meals and tours. From R856 – R1,085 pp sharing for dinner, B&B.
Meals: Full breakfast and dinner included. Lunch on request from R65.
Directions: From Durban take N2 to Hluhluwe. Turn off and follow through town, down hill to T-junc and turn left. After 1.2km turn right and cross railway. After 3.4km turn R onto D540. Follow 5km signs to lodge. The gate guard will direct you (& follow signs).

Bushwillow

Julian and Liz Simon
PO Box 525, Hluhluwe 3960
Tel: 035-562-0473 Fax: 035-562-0473
Email: info@bushwillow.com Web: www.bushwillow.com
Cell: 083-651-6777

Game reserves can be an expensive stopover, so for visitors on a tighter budget we've uncovered some more affordable gems that still offer great access to local highlights. Bushwillow is one such, set in the Weavers Nature Park. With 150 hectares to explore (on foot) you'll spot plenty of wildebeest, zebra and giraffe, setting the mood for the 'Big 5' at Hluhluwe Umfolozi or the St Lucia Wetlands half an hour away. It's hidden in the sand forest and can be reserved for your exclusive use, so you need only battle friends and family for deckchair space (often the toughest battle of all). I arrived to whoops and squeals from the pool on a blisteringly hot day, and was only too glad when Julian shepherded me inside to the cooling waft of the ceiling fans. The four forest-green chalets blend into the bush perfectly, cunningly positioned a stone's throw from a waterhole so you needn't go further than the deck to spot the local wildlife. Bedrooms are peacefully private and just a few steps along the boardwalk from the living area, with its granite worktops for Jacomie, the chef, and a eucalyptus dining table that supports her excellent meals. It seems they've thought of everything.

Rooms: 3: 2 twins and 1 king chalet all with bath and shower.
Price: R450 pp sharing. Bookings can be reserved to one group at a time.
Meals: Self-catering or meals on request. Breakfast R50, dinner R125.
Directions: From the N2 take the Hluhluwe off-ramp and pass through Hluhluwe town. Take the R22 towards Sodwana Bay. Continue 16km after crossing the railway line and Weavers Nature Park is on the L. Bushwillow is signed within the reserve.

Thonga Beach Lodge

Paige and Brett Gehren
Mabibi 3815
Tel: 035-474-7100 Fax: 035-474-1490
Email: info@isibindiafrica.co.za Web: www.isibindiafrica.co.za
Cell: 082-322-1642

I had been eagerly looking forward to my visit to Thonga Beach Lodge since before I had even left Cape Town. I knew it would be great because all the Gehrens' places are (see Isibindi Lodge, Kosi Forest Lodge and Rhino Walking Safaris). So, typically, when I did finally arrive thousands of KZN kilometres caught up with me and, lying down for an afternoon snooze, I didn't wake until six the next morning! Sundowners at Lake Sibaya and a gourmet dinner all passed me by, but I was raring to go for a sunrise stroll. The sky was a soft pink, the surf breaking onto footprint-free sand and looking back to the lodge I could just make out the thatched tops of each rounded room, twelve in all, poking out through milkwood brush. Thonga Beach is sandwiched between forested dunes and ocean, an hour's sandy drive and 4x4 trail from the nearest tar road. Huts are connected by snaking, wooden walkways and in mine a huge mosquito net hung from high rafters, separating the bed from the bathroom, a design marvel in itself. One single piece of sculpted concrete flows past glass-bowl sinks and chrome taps into an oval bath. This is as luxurious and romantic a destination as you'll find anywhere, but it's super-relaxed too. Zoë, Lawrence and all their staff are hugely friendly, the birding, diving, walking and wildlife are superb and – a rare bonus – it's majority community-owned so your pennies help support the local economy.

Rooms: 12: 9 twins, 3 doubles, all with bath and shower and sea or forest view.
Price: R1,900 – R2,240 pp sharing includes all meals, guided snorkelling, guided walks and canoeing.
Meals: Full board.
Directions: From Durban take the N2 north to Hluhluwe and then follow signs to Kosi Bay. 30km beyond Mbazwana follow signs right to Coastal Forest Reserve. Thonga car park (and lodge pick-up point) is 32km on along sandy road.

Kosi Forest Lodge

Brett Gehren
Kosi Bay Nature Reserve, PO Box 1593, Eshowe 3815
Tel: 035-474-7100 Fax: 035-474-1490
Email: info@isibindiafrica.co.za Web: www.isibindiafrica.co.za
Cell: 035-474-1473

Kosi Bay is the sort of place that novelists map out and then construct adventures in. You are picked up by a four-wheel drive, which can negotiate the sand tracks criss-crossing the region. You park up not just your car, but also the modern world you are now leaving. There is no tar and no electricity here. Instead you enter a landscape of raffia palm groves, primary sand forests, mangroves, water meadows, interconnecting lakes (yes, hippo and crocodile like it too and are regularly sighted). And then there is the sea and the mouth of the river for diving, swimming and fishing in 'perfect white sand coves with huge overhanging trees' (says the lodge brochure). The reed-thatched camp itself perfectly balances the wild (your chalet is in the middle of a boisterous forest) with the romantic (candlelit meals and outdoor baths and showers). I loved the deep stillness of the early-morning guided canoe trip and other activities include reef-snorkelling, turtle-tracking, forest walks and bird safaris. I consider Kosi Forest Lodge one of the most rewarding (and therefore best-value) places I have stayed in SA. I recommend a minimum of two or three nights.

Rooms: 8: 1 family 'bush suite'; 6 twins and 1 honeymoon double; all with outdoor bath & shower.
Price: All-inclusive (meals and activities) R1,120 – R1,380 pp sharing. Singles plus 30%. Transfer from police station R15 pp. Children under 12 half price.
Meals: All meals and teas included. Also included guided canoeing on the lakes and walk in the raffia forest. 2-night stay includes 1 full-day excursion too.
Directions: From Hluhluwe take N2 north past Mkuze. Turn R signed Jozini. In Jozini thru' town, L over dam, follow for 37km. Turn R at T-jct & follow for 67km to Kwangwanase. R at Kosi Forest sign & follow tar rd to R & up slope to police station. Turn and park under trees.

Map Number: 15

Entry Number: 212

Tamboti Ridge

Denise and Brian Blevin

Between Pongola and Mkuze, Golela T-junction, Pongola 3170
Tel: 034-435-1110 Fax: 034-435-1008
Email: shayalodge@saol.com Web: www.shayamoya.co.za
Cell: 083-269-9596

What a relief! After days of inland dryness I'd made it to the Pongola valley, a lush expanse of well-watered sugar cane farms, dripping with bougainvillea. And at its heart, Tamboti Ridge, smiling Blevins and a restorative glass of iced juice. Phew. These two are super-relaxed and this shows in a wholesome B&B. Here, there are plenty of farm-based activities for the children and also access to next-door Shayamoya (also owned by the Blevins) for top nosh, fishing and game drives on the Pongola Reserve. Brian runs his farm as holistically and organically as possible, producing everything from sugar and vegetables to yoghurt and cheese for the guests. You can watch the cows being milked, ramble across the farm or fish for bass at the dam. Otherwise, the jacaranda-shaded lawn and pool are ideal for lazing. In the heat of the day I fancied nothing more than a good book on the room-side deck, gazing through a sub-tropical garden to the river far below. But time was not on my side. I had a date at Blevin project number two! A welcome place to water the horses and break long journeys between Jo-burg and the KZN reserves and resorts.

Rooms: 4: 3 twins and 1 double; all en-suite with bath and shower, plus air-conditioning and fans.
Price: R300 – R320 pp sharing B&B. Singles on request. R225 pp for game drives and river safaris. Tiger fishing R600 pp per half-day.
Meals: Full breakfast included. You can also eat lunch and dinners at the main lodge; 3-course meals from R115 (excluding wine).
Directions: When travelling north on the N2, 40km past Mkuze, turn left at the signs directly at the Golela junction. When travelling south on the N2, 30km past Pongola, turn right onto the farm, almost directly opposite the turn to Golela and Swaziland border post.

Shayamoya Tiger Fishing and Game Lodge

Denise and Brian Blevin
PO Box 784, Pongola 3170
Tel: 034-435-1110 Fax: 034-435-1008
Email: shayalodge@saol.com Web: www.shayamoya.co.za
Cell: 083-456-8423

Sometimes, 230 words are just not enough. Shayamoya is the Blevins' fantastic game lodge, offering all the luxuries you could want, but with the family-run atmosphere of a homespun B&B. After a blissful slosh in the pool (research, you understand) I was soon sharing a beer with Brian in the bar and planning a morning fishing trip (more research). From its hilltop look-out the lodge surveys the vast Pongolapoort Lake and 10,000 hectare reserve. Alongside boat cruises, elephant tracking, rhino walks and game drives – as if that wasn't enough – the tiger fishing is superb. But hook and line could wait. First came supper, dining under the stars on fillet steak and a shiraz from the new cellar (wine tastings and food are yet more strings to the Shayamoya bow). You can see across to Swaziland from the dining-room deck, as I could from my chalet, a hexagonal affair with cobbled outdoor shower and funky, ceramic hippo plugs. Come dawn, Nandi, the resident spotted eagle owl, woke me up and I was soon driving past giraffe and wildebeest to the lake with ranger Douglas. For some reason, despite a display of great skill, I caught absolutely nothing, while fellow fishermen were hauling them in truly agricultural fashion! They were staying on the Blevins' twelve-sleeper houseboat "Shayamanzi". That's for rent too, by the way, and with any luck, I'll be chucking my line from that next year.

Rooms: 10 chalets: 2 premium kings, 8 standards including 2 doubles and 6 twins. All rooms have bath and outside shower.
Price: All inclusive (all meals and one activity) R1,150 – R1,350. Dinner, B&B R880 – R1,045. Singles +R250. Self-catering R380 pp, singles +R190.
Meals: As many as you want.
Directions: From Jo'burg take N2 23 km past Pongola to Swaziland/Golela turning on L. Shayamoya is 5km on on the L. From Durban take N2 north. Turning is 40km beyond Mkuze.

Isandlwana Lodge

Pat Stubbs
Isandlwana 3005
Tel: 034-271-8301/5 Fax: 034-271-8306
Email: lodge@isandlwana.co.za Web: www.isandlwana.co.za
Cell: 082-789-9544

Isandlwana Lodge is *the* place to relive Anglo-Zulu War history and approaching through the dust I could see its namesake hill from miles away. The rocky outcrop was throwing a long shadow across the valley, just as it did on January 22nd 1879 when 25,000 Zulus attacked the British soldiers encamped on the hill's eastern slope. The story of the ensuing battle is fascinating and the lodge eats and sleeps it. Rob Gerrard, an ex-Gordon Highlander, leads tours that include nearby Rorke's Drift. Even the lodge itself is designed around a Zulu shield, a thatched, tapered structure that wraps around the hillside and looks across the Isandlwana battlefield. Though steeped in history, it has a refreshingly modern feel. Upstairs, the lounge and bar have leather sofas, ceiling fans and high-backed, hide-backed dining chairs. All twelve rooms are downstairs off a winding, rocky corridor, with very private balconies for enjoying the incredible view. Pat has furnished the lodge in a pleasingly subtle blend of hand-printed bedspreads, copper lampshades and slate-tiled, chrome-tapped bathrooms. Having arrived here from Florida and a life of "peanuts and insurance", she has taken to hosting as a duck takes to water. Once you've waltzed through her to-do list of battlefield tours, walking trails, 300 bird species, cultural tours, horse riding, swimming and gourmet dining, you'll have happily spent at least three nights here.

Rooms: 12: 5 doubles and 7 twins all with showers.
Price: From R1,190 (low season) pp sharing, singles R1,490 for dinner B&B. Battlefield tours R300 per tour. Other activities quoted on request.
Meals: Price includes dinner, bed and breakfast.
Directions: From Durban take the N2 north to Eshowe then the R68 through Melmoth and Babanango. Turn L at 4-way stop in Babanango. Travel for approx 45km to turn-off to Isandlwana Lodge, then another 9km on dirt road.

Isibindi Zulu Lodge

Brett Gehren
Rorke's Drift, Dundee 3000
Tel: 035-474-7100 Fax: 035-474-1490
Email: info@isibindiafrica.co.za Web: www.isibindiafrica.co.za

Driving up to Isibindi in the early evening, the way ahead was intermittently illuminated by a spectacular thunderstorm. It seemed to be following me. Ignoring the portents, I pressed on Homerically to claim my prize, a night at the wonderful (the first line of my notes just reads 'Wow!') Isibindi Zulu Lodge. It's on a hill in the middle of a 2000-hectare nature reserve on the Buffalo river, with six secluded chalets looking out over the bush, a modern spin on the traditional Zulu beehive hut. The best view is reserved for the pool, a great place for daytime dozing before an afternoon game drive with lodge managers Frans and Anne. Frans has been passionate about the wild since he was knee-high to a bushbuck and after years as a Kruger park ranger he's a talking encyclopaedia on anything that moves (and most things that don't too). The game wasn't playing ball on our evening outing but we heard plenty of locals snuffling about in the twilight as we walked back under the stars to the lodge (the game vehicle wasn't playing ball either!). For those not balmy about the bush there are Zulu dancing evenings laid on, daytime tours of the Anglo-Zulu battlefields or even a rafting and abseiling camp on the reserve for the adventurous. From nature, history and culture to adrenaline-pumped excitement… Isibindi has it all.

Rooms: 6: 4 twins, 1 double, 1 honeymoon beehive suite; all with en-suite bath and shower.
Price: R1,075 – R1,150 pp sharing for dinner, B&B. Singles plus 30%. Prices include three meals and game activities.
Meals: Full board includes breakfast, lunch and dinner, hikes and 1 game drive per day. Rafting, Zulu cultural evening, guided battlefield tours and homestead visits extra.
Directions: Take R33 south from Dundee for 14km, then turn left onto dirt road to Rorke's Drift – 25km or so. Follow signs to Isibindi. 5km beyond the village of Rorke's Drift.

Map Number: 14

Mawelawela Game and Fishing Lodge

George and Herta Mitchell-Innes

Fodo Farm, PO Box 21, Elandslaagte 2900
Tel: 036-421-1860 Fax: 036-421-1860
Email: mitchellinnes@mweb.co.za Web: www.mawelawela.co.za
Cell: 083-259-6394 or 082-734-3118

George and Herta are a natural, down-to-earth couple whose veins of hospitality run deep... and staying with them is to enjoy a few days awash with incidental pleasures. Herta, a bubbly Austrian, moved out to South Africa 28 years ago and married George, who is a beef farmer – his boerewors is delicious. He is also a keen historian and leads tours out to the site of the battle of Elandslaagte. His study is full of Anglo-Boer war prints and weighty tomes including a collection of the London Illustrated News. (Ask him to show you his father's beautiful collection of bird-eggs too.) If you stay in the main house the rooms are very comfortable and the bungalow across the jacaranda-filled garden is perfect for families or groups. A short drive away from the farm itself you'll find the thatched hunters' cottage on 1500 wild hectares set aside for game. There is a trout dam at the front into which George has built a waterfall, and there are a shower and a plunge pool to one side. The cane-sided shady braai area faces dam-wards and you can watch the eland and kudu come to drink in the evenings. Finally a toast to Herta's cooking which is wonderful! Many of the ingredients are home-grown and all is served on her collection of fine china and family silver. *Bookings essential.*

Rooms: 4: 2 twins (1 with en/s bath, 1 en/s bath & shower); 1 apartment with double, twins & single (self-catering or B&B); 1 self-catering game lodge sleeps 7.
Price: B&B R250 pp sharing. Singles on request.
Meals: All meals are in the main house. Full breakfast included. 3-course dinners (excluding wine) R80. Main and coffee R50.
Directions: On N11, 35km from Ladysmith, 70km from Newcastle. Also entrance on R602, 35km from Dundee south via Greytown.

Oaklands Country Manor

Jamie and Anna Bruce

PO Box 19, Van Reenen 3372
Tel: 058-671-0067 Fax: 058-671-0077
Email: info@oaklands.co.za Web: www.oaklands.co.za
Cell: 083-304-2683

Jamie was in the British army for many years but bar the military memorabilia that pops up in flags and prints there's no regimentation at Oaklands. Instead the colonial manor, with its original Oregon pine floors and ceilings, is an intimate country hotel set in 260 acres of heavenly highveld countryside that teems with rock art and birds. Kids are well catered for (Jamie and Anna adore them) and when I visited four large ones – namely the Combined British Services polo team – had descended for the weekend. Jamie is super keen on his polo and had organised a tournament of horse-backed fun. Festivities kicked off with a delicious (and very well-lubricated) dinner in the friendly Oaklands pub. The following morning a jaded but jolly British team impressed all with a hopeless performance at the home-grown "polo-pit squash" before smashing balls into the northern hemisphere in a penalty shoot-out. For the non-horsey among you, there are Boer War battlefield tours, a balustraded pool, mountain bikes and a tennis court (with umpire's chair to provoke argument). The stone-walled rooms are fun, converted from old stables and outbuildings. All are different in style, but consistent themes are the colourful duvet covers, bright African art and stunning views from the patios. Here you're in the wilds among mountains, craggy cliffs and paddocks full of galloping horses, and I guarantee you'll love it.

Rooms: 13: 7 twins, 6 doubles all with en-suite baths and shower over the bath.
Price: May – Oct: R540 pp sharing, R570 singles. Nov – April: R660 pp sharing, R690 singles.
Meals: Full breakfast and dinner included. Lunch is also available.
Directions: Take the N3 to Van Reenen, turn right at the Caltex garage. Go 7km down a dirt track – Oaklands is signed to the right.

Montusi Mountain Lodge

Anthony and Jean Carte
Off D119, Alpine Heath, Bergville 3350
Tel: 036-438-6243 Fax: 036-438-6566
Email: montusi@iafrica.com Web: www.montusi.za.net

Montusi feels a bit like a hotel, which just happens to be run by your aunt and uncle. You know… you haven't seen them for years, but no sooner have you stepped from the car than they've got your bed sorted (well, your thatched, Conran-style, country cottage complete with fireplace, selected DSTV and view!) and are fixing you a sundowner on the patio. Yes, the sunsets are every bit as good as the photo suggests. Ant bought wattle-strangled Montusi Farm in the early 1990s. Being a man of X-ray vision, he saw through the undergrowth to a lodge perfectly positioned to catch the surrounding view, he saw fields of galloping horses and he saw lakes to fish in. So he did away with the wattles (via a community project) and a new Montusi emerged. Meals are superb… some examples: lamb with chargrilled lemon and mint, ostrich fillet with garlic and marinated peppers, malva pudding, custard cups. There are many ways to burn off the calories with limitless hiking, horse-riding for all levels of experience, mountain-biking and fishing. But best of all is ex-skiing pro Chris's circus school! It is as professional as they come, with trapezes, bungies, nets, ropes and they sometimes put on shows too. Montusi impressed me because it's a happy family run place with plenty of style. *Golf and massages available locally. Picnics at waterfalls can be arranged.*

Rooms: 14 cottages: 4 are kings with en-suite bath and another twin with en-suite shower next door. 10 are kings with shower and bath.
Price: R650 – R715 pp sharing. Singles plus R100. Price includes dinner and breakfast.
Meals: Full breakfast and 4-course dinner included (wine extra).
Directions: If coming from the south head north through Pietermaritzburg, Estcourt and turn left signed Northern Drakensberg. Continue for 80km through Winterton and Bergville on R74. Follow signs (some small) to Montusi.

Ardmore Guest Farm

Paul and Sue Ross

Champagne Valley, Winterton 3340
Tel: 036-468-1314 Fax: 036-468-1241
Email: info@ardmore.co.za Web: www.ardmore.co.za
Cell: 083-789-1314

It was raining caracals and jackals when I visited Ardmore… so to speak. And the deluge didn't lift for a second, so sadly I couldn't experience the stunning views of Champagne Castle (second highest mountain in SA at 3377m) and the Cathkin Peaks which previous GG visitors have enjoyed. The Drakensberg National Park begins just down the road so bring your hiking boots. Ardmore is a super-relaxed, freewheeling sort of place. Sociable and delicious dinners, eaten by lantern light at long tables in the yellowwood dining room, draw on the farm's organic produce – eggs from happy, roaming chickens and fruit, vegetables and herbs from a pesticide-free garden. Paul will tell you all about the art here, all created by the local Zulu community and much from the famous Ardmore Pottery at the end of the garden. There is masses to do: hike to waterfalls and mountain peaks; watch the rare bald ibis that makes its home here; fish, canoe, mountain-bike; the game farm nearby (1/2-hr drive) offers cheap horse-riding to see the rhino, zebra and giraffe; the Drakensberg Boys' Choir performs on Wednesdays at 15h30; and there are 230 rock-art sites in the area too. The small thatched rondavels are sweet and cosy and the bigger ones have fireplaces. Garden furniture is set out under the giant liquid amber tree, an important focal point for the property, where you can take tea and contemplate the mountains.

Rooms: 5 rondavels: 3 large doubles with en/s bath and shower; 2 small with en/s shower; 2 x 2 bedroom cottages: 1 double & 1 twin with en-suite bath & shower.
Price: Dinner, bed and breakfast: R265 – R330 pp sharing. No single supplement.
Meals: Full breakfast and dinner included.
Directions: From the N3 take the R74 to Winterton and go south along the R600 towards the Central Drakensberg for 18km. You'll see a sign on your left, 5km up partly dirt road for Ardmore.

Map Number: 14

Entry Number: 220

Spionkop Lodge

Lynette and Raymond Heron

R600, Drakensberg Area, Ladysmith 3370
Tel: 036-488-1404 Fax: 036-488-1404
Email: spionkop@futurenet.co.za Web: www.spionkop.co.za
Cell: 082-573-0224/5

A magnificent storm was exploding over the Drakensberg Mountains when I visited and it was a relief to soon be tucked up in an armchair by the fire with a dog at my feet. Raymond is a convivial Scot who grew up on the far side of the Zambezi. He's a registered guide, raconteur par excellence and an expert on the tragic movements of the Battle of Spionkop, a keystone in the Anglo-Boer war. You only have to go to the characterful bar and you'll be sitting right where General Buller camped with 27,000 men (Winston Churchill and Mahatma Gandhi among them). The lodge is built on the old Spearman farm and is now a 700-hectare eco-reserve with 278 bird species and a mass of flowering aloes in June and July. You can stay either in bothy-ish stone cottages, which are comfy and snug with fireplaces for winter and verandahs for summer; or in the colonial farmhouse with its polished floorboards and library full of history books (plus a sunroom to read them in). But the main heart of the lodge is the 108-year-old stone, converted barn, now a massive glass-walled dining room with sinuous blonde branches creeping from floor to ceiling. You'll get to know it pretty well. As well as the history, there are game drives, fishing, birding and bushman art enough to keep you entertained for a week.

Rooms: 8 doubles, all en-suite with bath and shower. Plus 2 self-catering cottages; Aloe has 2 double beds and a bath; Acacia has 3 bedrooms and 2 bathrooms.
Price: R830 – R930 full board pp sharing. Aloe R790 per night. Acacia R990 per night.
Meals: All meals included in B&B price. Meals optional for self-caterers: R65 for breakfast, R45 for lunch and R100 for dinner.
Directions: 20 mins off N3 from either Durban or Jo'burg. See web site for map.

Sewula Gorge Lodge

Graham and Santie McIntosh & Jacquie Geldart

Off R103, 18km from Estcourt, Estcourt 3310
Tel: 036-352-2485 Fax: 036-352-2868
Email: bookings@sewula.co.za Web: www.sewula.co.za
Cell: 082-824-0329

The pictures do not exaggerate. This glorious thatched lodge lives beside a rocky-river gorge filled with cascading waterfalls (the main one is 20 metres high) and swimming pools. As soon as I arrived I realized I had made a significant mistake. I had not organized to stay the night at Sewula and had missed my opportunity to swim under the waterfall looking at the stars. The emphasis is on relaxation and seclusion and only one party stays at a time. Staff live away from the lodge and there is absolutely no one about except you, a very rare treat (even by GG standards). For this far-too-low-really price, you can pretend you own this truly heavenly place. It is self-catering, but with any domestic hardship extracted. Not only does nature spoil you, but the staff do too, washing up, servicing the rooms, lighting fires and bringing fresh milk, butter and cream down from the farm. Under the thatched pitch of the main lodge roof are the kitchen, bush-chic sunken sitting room, a giant fireplace, an oversized chess set and much wildly original carpentry and functional sculpture. Similarly lovely are the cottages, which have sleeping lofts for children and face the falls. You can walk to an iron-age settlement, battle memorials and great fishing spots. Jacqui is a stellar host and constantly thoughtful. 100% (as the locals say)! The rock art sites and white-water rafting are within an hour's drive.

Rooms: 4 cottages (max 8 adults & 10 children): 3 have en/s shower, 2 of which have outdoor shower too; 1 cottage has en/s shr & bath. One booking at a time.
Price: Min. R680 for the whole place per night self-catering. R340 pp for extra guests, but children half-price if sleeping in loft.
Meals: Restaurants are nearby.
Directions: Exit 143 on N3 from Durban to Mooi River. Take R103 to Estcourt, 20.3km from off-ramp, take right turn onto dirt road to Malanspruit and follow signs to Sewula Gorge Camp.

Zingela

Mark and Linda Calverley
PO Box 141, Tugela River
Tel: 036-354-7005/7250 Fax: 036-354-7021
Email: zingela@futurenet.co.za Web: www.zingelasafaris.co.za
Cell: 084-746-9694

Hiking, fishing, abseiling, rafting, swimming, game-viewing, hunting, quad-biking, horse-riding… perhaps I'd be better off listing the things you *can't* do at Zingela. Mark and Linda are delightful and, over twenty years or so, have built up their home/riverside bush camp to offer everything and anything, all the more astonishing given their location. This really is wild country. From a rendezvous in the wee village of Weenen it was an hour's 4x4 drive (not for the faint-hearted) past isolated Zulu villages and down to the Tugela river – worth every bump. There are five palatial double tents overlooking the river, all open to the elements. Showers are more outside than in, branches provide the towel rails and each tent has hefty, iron-framed beds and beautiful wooden furniture from Zanzibar. Those on the romance beat will love the "hitching post" with doubtless the world's largest headboard, a vast, mattress-to-canvas slab of sandstone. There's electricity and gallons of hot water but Zingela is essentially bush living ("don't-forget-the-loo-roll-or-matches kind of country," says Linda). When I visited the place was alive with families (there are zillions of kids' beds in extra dormitory tents). Some youngsters were preparing for a rafting adventure and everyone was thoroughly enjoying the endless fresh air, filling grub and lashings of good, wholesome fun.

Rooms: 5: all tents, 3 doubles and 2 twins, all with shower.
Price: R650 – R750 includes all food plus game drive, abseiling and rafting. Quad-bikes, horse-riding and stalking are extra.
Meals: Full board.
Directions: Faxed or emailed on booking, or just phone en route.

Sycamore Avenue Treehouse Lodge

Bruce and Gloria Attwood

11 Hidcote Road, Hidcote,
Mooi River 3300
Tel: 033-263-2875
Fax: 033-263-2134
Email:
sycamore@futurenet.co.za
Web: www.sycamore-
ave.com

KwaZulu Natal

Tree houses! Need you read any further? …There are not many can weave a whole house into the branches of a giant pin oak, but Attwood senior (you'll meet his son Andrew at the Antbear) has done it not once, not twice, but three times… and no the first two didn't fall down. All three of Bruce and Gloria's arboreal retreats are standing strong, hidden from the house by foliage but overlooking miles of rolling fields. Bruce is a functional sculptor and his weapon of choice is wood. You'll spot his work all over the Midlands, but it's here that he's really gone to town, or rather, tree. From beds and bread bins to window hooks and hinges, everything is crafted from beautifully grained cedar or wattle, or whatever he can lay his hands on. The latest addition, Bottle-tree House, is magnificent. It's spiral staircase winds up from a bottle-walled sitting room to the queen-sized bed, and set into the balcony is an outdoor jacuzzi. Just picture it… enjoying a good soak to the sound of rustling branches and golden orioles, although you might have to turn the bubbles off first. Below the tree is a magical garden where couples love to get married and there are two cracking rooms in the house too, "for those who want to keep their feet on the ground". *Well placed for the arts/crafts region and Giants Castle.*

Rooms: 5: 3 tree houses, 1 queen, 2 doubles, two have jacuzzis and all have showers; also two rooms in the main house, both with en/s shower and bath, one with jacuzzi.
Price: R400 – R500. Single supplement +50%.
Meals: Full breakfast included. Dinner by arrangement: 3 courses from R95 (excluding wine).
Directions: Take exit 152 off N3. From south turn right, from north turn left onto the R103 Hidcote Rd. Travel for 2km and Sycamore is signed right.

The Antbear

Andrew and Conny Attwood

Fernhust Farm, Moor Park –
Giants Castle Road, Estcourt
3310
Tel: 036-352-3143
Fax: 036-352-3143
Email: aattwood@antbear.de
Web: www.antbear.de

Thank goodness Andrew and Conny gave up the corporate rat race in Germany for B&B'ing. They renovated the old farmhouse and, like all the buildings at The Antbear, it is thatched and sits on a hilltop surveying the Drakensberg peaks. Everything here has had the skilled hands of your craftsman-host and his father Bruce laid upon it. Andrew is a canny chap. The lodge and rooms are home to his chairs, tables, doors, staircases, towel holders, candle-sticks – the list of working wooden sculptures runs and runs. This is the hallmark of the Antbear, firmly stamped on the newest room with its quirky bathroom mosaic and carved reading/smoking chair. Just across from the lodge's leafy, colonnaded front patio an old tractor shed has been converted into four other bedrooms. Billowing white curtains frame the view and the rooms have intriguing fireplaces and plenty of humorous sculpture. The first room is superb with a staircase that climbs the right-hand wall, a loft bed-platform in the thatchy peak on the left and a six-foot causeway between the two. Andrew is the chef – Moroccan tajine cooking is his current favourite – and meals will almost be 100% organic if the horses, tortoises, chickens or tame-ish spurwing goose haven't raided Conny's garden. You'd be a fool to stay for only one night. *Birding, rock art sites, river rafting, battlefield tours, local arts and crafts.*

Rooms: 5: 4 en/s doubles in renovated tractor shed, 3 with showers, one with bath; 1 separate double with en/s bath and shower.
Price: Dinner, bed and breakfast from R390 – R590 pp sharing. Singles add R100.
Meals: Lunch and picnics on request from R40 pp. Dinner usually 3 courses (excluding wine).
Directions: Take exit 152 on the N3 signed Hidcote for 7km. At T-junction turn right towards Giant's Castle. After 14km turn right towards Moor Park onto dirt road. After 5.5km you will see The Antbear sign to the right. The thatched cottages are 2km up the farm road.

Cleopatra Mountain Farmhouse

Richard and Mouse Poynton

Kamberg Valley, Drakensberg
Tel: 033-267-7243 Fax: 033-267-7013
Email: cleopatramountain@telkomsa.net Web: www.cleomountain.com
Cell: 033-267-9900

Nowhere had come more highly recommended during my KZN travels than Cleopatra Mountain Farmhouse and its food-guru founders Richard and Mouse Poynton. And in retrospect, it was probably a good thing that I couldn't spend the night, as I never (ever) would have left. The setting is utterly magnificent, wedged into the Drakensberg and with superb walking and fishing. The rooms are destinations in themselves, facing the trout-stocked dam, the mountainside or ordered herb gardens. Each is unique and the largest has not only its own drawing room, fireplace and verandah, but his and hers bathrooms too! But as if all that wasn't enough, what you really come here for is the food. Richard is one of the top chefs in SA, and before starting their current venture, he and Mouse spent four years in Europe working alongside culinary legends in Ireland, England, France, Italy and, well, pretty much everywhere. All that learning is on show in their Cleopatra restaurant (and in their own cook-book). It's reserved for guests only and grub-lovers will go weak at the knees for Mozambique tiger prawns steamed in lemon grass or griddled springbok fillet on fondant potato. You don't get a midday meal but then, as Richard told me, "not a soul has ever asked for lunch."

Rooms: 11: 7 king/twins, 4 queens all with separate en/s baths and showers.
Price: R995 – R1,395 pp sharing for dinner, bed and breakfast. Singles plus 50%.
Meals: Dinner and full breakfast included. Snacks available all day.
Directions: From N3 take R103 at Nottingham Road (from Durban) or Mooi River (from Jo'burg) to Rosetta. There, turn L opposite Ugly Duckling onto Kamberg road for 30km until Cleopatra sign on L. Turn onto dirt road for 5.5km and Cleopatra is on R.

Stocklands Farm

Eve Mazery
4 Shafton Rd, Howick 3290
Tel: 033-330-5225 Fax: 033-330-5225
Email: edulink@iafrica.com Web: www.stocklandsfarm.co.za
Cell: 082-975-2298

The warm welcome that I received as I tumbled out of my car, late and weary, is undoubtedly typical of Stocklands. As my cognitive faculties jolted back to life over a restorative beverage, it became obvious that Eve and Roland are natural hosts; thoughtful, funny and relaxed. They have put a lot of love and plenty of style into the wonderful old house. The argument goes that half-measures are not really in keeping with Stocklands, and you can see their point. The walls of the original 1850s house, for example, are over 50 centimetres thick and the belhambra tree at the front of the house is no-less-than enormous. Birds come in droves – they love Roland's indigenous trees and bank upon bank of stunning flowers. I loved the fuchsia tree myself (it flowers in January). Down near the tennis court there is a koi pond and many guests like to savour a slow, hot afternoon in the thick shade on a blanket here after a picnic. The four rooms in the house, like the cottages, are meticulously decorated to individual themes. Eve has found hand-embroidered linen and original works by local artists to decorate and nothing is left out. Choose from a range of breakfasts including the Vegetarian, the Sunrise, the Decadent and… the Sensible! *Game can be viewed right next door, by the way.*

Rooms: 6: 2 suites & 2 bedrooms, 1 with en/s bath, 3 with en/s shower. Also 2 cottages: 1 with 3 bedrooms & 2 bathrooms, 1 w/ 2 bedrooms, 1 shower.

Price: R230 – R260 pp sharing. Singles on request.

Meals: Full breakfast included or you can self-cater in the cottages. An excellent café next door and more in the area.

Directions: From Jo'burg take N3 to Durban. Take 1st exit to Howick signed Howick/Tweedie. At Stop sign turn L to Howick. Thru' lights to bottom of hill, turn L to Karkloof. 100m turn R into Shafton Rd. Stocklands is 1km. From Durban take N3 to Jo'burg. Take 3rd Howick turn-off as above.

Entry Number: 227

Map Number: 14

Inversanda

Tom and Lucinda Bate
PO Box 1339, Howick 3290
Tel: 033-234-4321 Fax: 033-234-4751
Email: bate@nitrosoft.co.za Web: www.inversanda.co.za
Cell: 082-781-3875

I have to admit, I cut a pretty ungainly figure on an early morning ride through forest and field with Tom and Lucinda – my fourth-ever horse-back experience. Holding on for dear life, I was undoubtedly passenger rather than driver as I bounced up and down on Dablamanzi (unnervingly translated as the "wave parter") but, as with my entire stay here, I loved it. Hemmed in by mountains and a meander of the Mgeni River, Inversanda is in a world of its own but in easy reach of the major routes. All four Bates (plus assorted hounds) are utterly charming and you're encouraged to participate in their farm and life as much or as little as you like. Being their lone visitor, I joined the family and neighbours for dinner and was soon involved in a hard-fought game of after-supper "Articulate". When not farming cattle, buried in chartered surveying or battling to conserve their stunning surroundings, Tom and Lucinda are serious horse-lovers and breed and school polo ponies. Polophiles are more than welcome for a weekend knock-about on the makeshift, riverside pitch. Otherwise you can fish, walk or swim pretty much anywhere you want. The farmhouse itself (1800s) goes on forever and guests have their own wing, a pot-planted patio with stunning views across the valley, two enormous twin rooms and a basic kitchen. I loved the drawing room, where there's a hearthside, bottomless red sofa for the saddle-sore and enough firewood to spit-roast an elephant.

Rooms: 1 self-catering wing of the house with two twin rooms and shared bath and shower.
Price: R200 pp self-catering.
Meals: Meals available on request.
Directions: Faxed or emailed on booking.

Duma Manzi Safari River Lodge

Gerhard Le Roux

20 Ridge Road, Kloof 3610
Tel: 033-212-2055 Fax: 033-212-2055
Email: info@dumamanzi.co.za Web: www.duma-africa.co.za
Cell: 082-900-6504

If I get married (any volunteers?), I want to come to Duma Manzi on my honeymoon. For a romantic getaway and game lodge experience in easy reach of Durban you just can't do better. Gerhard is an architect and started on this project after designing Thonga Beach Lodge (another GG gem). He spent countless weekends camping on the 5,000-hectare reserve in search of the perfect spot on the banks of the Mkomazi River. His perseverance saw the lodge built on its present site, looking across to a forested kloof that rises some 500m to the grasslands that this valley divides. With just four riverside chalets and a handful of staff including Stephan – guide, handyman and chef extraordinaire – this represents a truly personalised experience. He'll collect you on arrival for a 4x4 rumble past zebra and antelope, down through riverine forest to the water's edge. I had the thatched honeymoon suite, an open-plan affair with an extra-large king-sized bed (I could comfortably sleep cross-ways in it) and open shower with its own balcony. I wasted gallons of hot water, staring through the steam at rich green acacia trees and paradise flycatchers. The plant and bird life are highlights of the game drives and there's plenty of riding, clay-pigeon shooting, rafting and bushmen visits to keep you busy. That just leaves time for candles, champagne and dinner by the duma manzi (thundering waters) of its name… pretty perfect actually.

Rooms: 4: 1 king and 3 king/twin chalets all with separate bath and shower.
Price: R750 – R900 pp sharing. Singles plus 25%.
Meals: All meals included.
Directions: Duma Manzi is about 100km from Durban. Directions faxed or emailed on booking.

Penwarn Country Lodge

Peta Parker

PO Box 253, Southern Drakensberg, Underberg 3257
Tel: 033-701-1777 or 1341 or 1342   Fax: 033-701-1341
Email: info@penwarn.com Web: www.penwarn.com
Cell: 083-305-3009

Penwarn is simply fantastic. There are two places to stay here (I'm afraid that the cave is no longer an option). The main lodge was converted from an old dairy and fertilizer shed into colourful sitting rooms, a bar and wonderfully comfortable bedrooms. And then there is magnificent Mthini Lodge complete with wooden deck overlooking the main dam, grazing game, horses, cattle and the mountains beyond. I stayed here and was up fishing at the crack of dawn (well, before breakfast at least). You can try your luck pretty much anywhere and kit and lessons are provided. In fact, the list of activities at Penwarn is exhaustive (and exhausting!): tubing on fast-flowing rivers or swimming in pools fed by waterfalls; bird-watching (lammerguyers may join you at the Vulture Restaurant); mountaineering or abseiling (tricky cliffs everywhere); and game drives where tame eland will approach you. I headed out on horseback after a pile of scrambled eggs and rode through herds of zebra and wildebeest before trotting off to inspect 1,500 year-old bushman art. Peta and her staff (or family, I couldn't tell) are great fun but all too-often overshadowed by TV celebrity Nimrod, a (very) tame otter partial to sausages, dog wrestling and baths (close the door or he'll be in yours!). Penwarn is a magical and brilliant place, run by the best.

Rooms: 11: 7 suites at Indabushe Lodge, 4 suites at Mthini lodge. All have en-suite bath and/or shower. (No cave dwelling anymore – sorry!).
Price: Full board is R750 – R950 pp sharing.
Meals: Full breakfast, lunch, 4-course dinner and all snacks are included. Wine is not. Canoeing is free.
Directions: Take Exit 99 off N3 marked Underberg, Howick South and travel 110km west to Underberg, going through Boston and Bulwer en route. Take the Swartberg Road out of Underberg and after 5km turn right onto Bushmansnek Road (dirt track). After 16km turn L to Penwarn (drive is 4km long.)

Map Number: 14

Entry Number: 230

Valemount Country Lodge

Dalene and Lance Bailey

PO Box 45, Underberg 3257
Tel: 033-701-1686 Fax: 033-701-1687
Email: info@valemountafrica.com Web: www.valemountafrica.com
Cell: 082-828-8921

The Sani Pass is as thrilling/hair-raising a drive as you'll enjoy/undergo in SA, so thank goodness Lance and Dalene are on hand to put a stiff drink in your hand at the bottom. The Baileys came here from Johannesburg just a year or two ago and they couldn't look more at home in their new surroundings. Their home is a thatched, sunny-yellow slice of tranquillity that spreads out across a regimented English country garden, between pin and English oaks and stunning copper beeches. The rooms all have bags of space, working fireplaces and patios facing the garden or surrounding woodland. You can wander wherever you like, ambling along winding, wooded footpaths, fishing for trout in the lake or bobbing about in the heated pool. That's the latest addition and Lance proudly showed me the three separate 'Martini seats' and jacuzzi jets. He and Dalene have a real eye for detail (they even cut the grass in the forest for you!) and have all sorts of plans for paths here and gazebos there, while quietly harbouring romantic visions of a mini-cheese-factory, although "we've got to learn to make cheese first," he acknowledges. If you've spent the day clattering around the dirt roads, I can't think of anywhere better to rub the dust from your eyes and relax.

Rooms: 6: 2 luxury kings, 2 standard twins, all with en-suite bath and shower; 2 double self-catering units with en-suite bath and hand-shower.
Price: From R245 pp sharing. Singles on request.
Meals: Full breakfast included. Dinner (R110) on request.
Directions: From N3 off-ramp 99 take R617 110km to Underberg. Continue for 8km towards Swartberg and Valemount is signed on the left.

Entry Number: 231

Map Number: 14

Free State & Lesotho

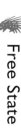

Die Ou Stal

Piet and Zenobia Labuchagné

38 George Street, Zastron 9950
Tel: 051-673-1268 Fax: 051-673-1268
Email: dieoustal@tiscali.co.za
Cell: 082-416-7832

In a place like Zastron, it's vital to find yourself a guide to show you the unknown gems that lurk around every corner and to recount the astonishing tales of yesteryear. Look no further than Piet. His enthusiasm for the geology and pre-history of Africa is infectious. After the whistle-stop tour of intriguing local rock formations, spiced up with ancient bushman legends, I'll never look at a cliff face in the same way again. Had I stayed longer, I'd have been begging him to take me on a day trip to nearby Lesotho, but alas I had to leave even before one of Zen's sumptuous suppers of bobotie or chicken pie. At least I had time to sit on the stoep outside the converted stables that are now the guest rooms and watch a lightning storm hammer away at the Lesotho mountains – a majestic sight indeed. The bedrooms are simple, cosy affairs with whitewashed walls and doors that open into a small kitchen. Breakfast, however, is served at the large dining table in the main house, atop wooden floorboards and next to a fridge surely dating from before fridges were invented (also wood): this intriguing feature is now a drinks cabinet. In a town that's won awards for its friendliness (driving around with Piet, the whole town and his uncle Joe came out to give us a wave) Zen is champion of champions.

Rooms: 2: 1 double with en-suite bath and shower; 1 twin with en-suite shower.
Price: R250 – R350 pp sharing.
Meals: Full breakfast included. Dinner on request, R50.
Directions: From N6 turn onto R26 and follow signs to Zastron. In town, turn right opposite the corner of the church into Mathee Street, then take third left into Berg Strat and see signs.

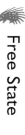

Pula House

Barbara and John von Ahlefeldt

PO Box 88, Smithfield 9966
Tel: 051-683-0032 Fax: 051-683-0032
Email: pula@acenet.co.za Web: www.pula-house.com
Cell: 083-272-3001

Sophistication and jaunty modernity mix eclectically and effectively in this Karoo-style house, which boasts one of the most beautiful drawing rooms I saw on my trip. It was built over 120 years ago for the local magistrate but was sadly neglected before journalists John and Barbara retired from their Devonshire inns in England and got their hands on it. Life has now been breathed back into the old place, and with interest, the exterior of the house revealing little of the drama within. Exotic rugs and pine floors are separated from 15-foot-high pressed metal ceilings by brightly-coloured walls; original South African art and conservative hunting prints hang peaceably next to a highly decorative carpet coat – a relic of '60s London; handsome antique furniture enjoys the presence of modern Africana. 'Juxtaposition' is a word that keeps coming to mind. With precious little water (this is almost the Karoo after all), Barbara has worked a minor miracle in the garden with lush lawns, interesting nooks and crannies to explore, rashes of vivid colour, and the quirky plunge pool is a summer godsend. The sun disappears behind a koppie and sunset on the terrace is a special time at Pula. Finally the von Ahlefeldt recipe of hospitality, humour and style is second to none and the home-made breads and creamy scrambled eggs make breakfasts truly excellent.

Rooms: 4: 2 doubles and 2 twins, all with en-suite bathrooms, 2 with baths, 2 with showers.
Price: R220 – R250 pp sharing. Singles on request.
Meals: Full breakfast included.
Directions: Pula House is on Douglas Street which comes off the N6 directly opposite the police station on the Bloemfontein side of town.

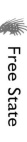

Free State

Springfontein House

Graeme Wedgwood
32 van Riebeeck Street, Springfontein 9917
Tel: 051-783-0076 Fax: 051-783-0425
Email: wedgie@icon.co.za Web: www.springfontein-guest-house.com
Cell: 082-450-6779

Graeme used to run Smithfield House, which he brought to life with cultivated, Epicurean zeal. Well, the same applies here at his new home. Those with a taste for fine living will find a kindred spirit in Graeme, a man whose love of house and garden, countryside, good company, food and wine now sets the tone at Springfontein House. He was once a gallery owner in Johannesburg – a far cry from his first, 26-year career as a London stockbroker – and his personal art collection includes a rather racy Battiss, an inky Sekoto and other originals by South African artists, both established and emerging. African rugs, powdery sofas, bowls of dried rose petals and side tables proffering porcelain complete the sandy-coloured sitting room. Through glass doors is a slate-floored, frond-filled sunroom and an incarnadine dining room, with Georgian tables and silver candelabras. In the bedrooms the curtains are silk, the towels soft and the comfy beds have crisp linen, plump pillows and mohair throws. Outside, white walls dazzle and creepers climb above the stoep; there's a bricked patio and colourful flower-beds, a pool and a series of fishponds. But the reason you come here is to be looked after, and arriving from the biscuity veld, you'll feel lucky indeed. *Graeme will explain about biking, hiking, rare bird-watching, fishing, sailing on Gariep Dam. And he regrets that the house is not suitable to children under 12 .*

Rooms: 3: 2 twins and 1 double, 2 with en-suite bath and 1 with en-suite shower.
Price: R200 pp sharing. Singles on request.
Meals: Full breakfast included. 3-course dinner available on request R70, excluding wine.
Directions: Heading north on the N1 turn off at Springfontein South sign. Follow road, becoming Settler St. Van Riebeeck St is on your left, and Springfontein House is at the end on right.

De Oude Kraal Country Estate

Gerhard and Marie Lombard

Nr. Bloemfontein 9300
Tel: 051-564-0636
Fax: 051-564-0635
Email: info@oudekraal.co.za
Web: www.oudekraal.co.za
Cell: 082-413-1798

Sprawled over 2,400 hectares of flat veld, the farm at De Oude Kraal was a hive of Boer War activity. British officers lived here in the final stages of the conflict as the countryside was swept clean between the infamous blockhouses, one of which can be found in a secluded corner. As I arrived, guests were saddling up for a riding tour to study the history, see the ostriches and check the sheep. By the time you read this, the observatory will be finished – the perfect star-gazing site beneath clear, unpolluted night skies. But not before enjoying one of Marie's fabulous traditional six-course dinners in the pine-floored dining room, complemented by a fine wine from Gerhard's award-winning cellar (and it's well worth asking him for a guided tour). With wider waists and tickled taste buds, guests waddle back to their rooms to make some space for the traditional 'boere' (farm) breakfast awaiting them the following morning. Rooms range from simple but cosy stone-floored affairs in the converted shearing shed to luxurious four-poster suites with private patios overlooking the smooth, tree-lined lawn. Some of the bathrooms are features in themselves, my favourite boasting an open shower in the centre of a bare-rock room, the spa-bath sunken into a rock bed and filled via a mini-waterfall. A word of warning: don't wear your best tie in the old railway sleeper-wood bar. Gerhard's collection numbers 779 and counting.

Rooms: 10: 4 standard, 2 with en-suite bath, 2 with en-suite bath and shower; 2 luxury, both with en-suite bath and shower; 4 executive, all with en-suite bath and shower.
Price: R350 – R450 pp sharing. Singles R410 – R510.
Meals: Full breakfast included. 6-course gourmet dinner R165 excluding drinks. Light lunches on request.
Directions: From Bloemfontein, travel 35km south on the N1. Take off-ramp 153, and then follow the signs (7km from N1).

Bishop's Glen

Ted and Bits Quin
PO Box 9, Glen 9360
Tel: 051-861-2210 Fax: 051-861-2210
Email: bishopsglen@connix.co.za
Cell: 082-374-4986

It's a particular pleasure to stay in a place where the owners give of themselves as unstintingly as Ted and Bits do. I love the fact that they join you (you join them?) for both dinner and breakfast – this is what staying in somebody's home is all about. Nine of us sat down to a sumptuous dinner in the evening and added new resonance to the word 'convivial'. The house dates back to 1813, and the dining room still has some of the original yellowwood timbers. All is lived-in yet elegant, with beautiful wooden furniture and family portraits in abundance. Earlier we had gathered on the plant-encrusted verandah, looking out over the lush garden and its 200-plus bird species, before moving to the sitting room where Ted's 27 (I counted) cattle trophies fill up one wall. My bedroom was impressively large and timbered, with pretty linen and a substantial array of novels. No old travel magazines here! Bits (a childhood friend called Pieces is out there somewhere) does not take last-minute bookings – she likes to be prepared – so make sure you ring well in advance to reserve a night in one of the Free State's finest, homeliest bolt-holes. *There is also a game farm, with many different antelopes.*

Rooms: 3: 1 double and 2 twins; all with en-suite shower, 1 with shower and bath.
Price: Dinner, bed and breakfast: R360 – R380 pp sharing. Singles R430 – R450.
Meals: Full breakfast included. Also dinner: 3 courses with pre-dinner drinks and wine at table.
Directions: Faxed or emailed on booking. Bishop's Glen is 20km north of Bloemfontein off ramp 213 from N1.

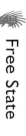

St Fort Country House

Ernestine Goldblatt
Clarens 9707
Tel: 058-256-1345 Fax: 058-256-1250
Email: info@stfort.co.za Web: www.stfort.co.za

Scrape the mud off the old walking boots and start limbering up. St Fort is a hiker's dream with trails leading through fields of bleating sheep that surround the house, up craggy koppies and jutting overhangs to Mushroom Rock (a rock, you will be surprised to learn, that is shaped like a mushroom). Or, for those with excess energy to burn, there's a day hike to caves decorated with bushman paintings. Rolling up the drive past the trout-fishing dam and towards the kaleidoscopic garden, dominated by purple larkspurs, I noticed guests sheltering from the afternoon sun on the brick-pillared verandah, locked in a game of bridge, too weary to walk or fish. Inside, Oregon pine floors creak underfoot, and framed photos chart the history of the farm from when a stern-faced Mr. Walker moved here from his St Fort estate in Scotland during the Boer War. Light floods into the lounge through a sprawling bay window, as in the cavernous master bedroom, and both rooms are kept snug in those harsh Free State winters with thick Persian rugs. Self-caterers are have a small kitchen, or use the original farm kitchen, with a table big enough for all-comers. Otherwise, Ernestine will zip over in the morning to prepare a breakfast feast, but with the option of haddock or even 'uitsmyter' – ham on toast, topped with tomato, scrambled egg and cheese, for those who didn't know.

Rooms: 5: all doubles or twins on request, 1 with en-suite bath and shower, 4 with en-suite showers.
Price: R210 – R240 pp sharing. Singles R230.
Meals: Full breakfast included. Self-catering option available or restaurants in Clarens.
Directions: From the N5 take the R712 signed to Clarens. Continue past Clarens for approx 5km, and St Fort is on the left.

Map Number: 13

Entry Number: 237

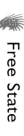

The View

Ryk and Bea and Sasha Becker

20 Bell Street, Harrismith 9880
Tel: 058-623-0961 Fax: 058-622-1442 Email: rmbecker@internext.co.za
Web: www.harrismithaccommodation.co.za
Cell: 082-775-7381 (Bea) 082-921-3624 (Ryk)

How better to while away a sticky afternoon than by nesting in a rocking chair behind teak pillars on a shady verandah, overlooking a lush garden, slowly draining a pot of tea? Bea and Ryk have found a magic formula simply by being themselves at home! The actual view of the title is now interrupted by an abundance of verdure, but I for one was glad of the green shade and the peaceful sounds of twittering birds hidden among the branches. Inside, a portrait of Bea's big-bearded great-grandfather, President of the Free State (deceased, of course), overlooks the social epicentre of this family home. The lounge, complete with creaking wooden floorboards, vibrant rugs and daringly bright sofas, sweeps through folded-back doors into the dining room where the heavy table awaits those staying in for dinner. And I thoroughly recommend you are among them. You would travel a long way to find a better meal and you'll miss out on Ryk spilling the beans on what to do in this area where he grew up. Before heading up to my goose-feathered bed for my best night's sleep in years, no visit to The View would be complete without being introduced to the rest of the family: four springer and two cocker spaniels. Son-in-law Simon can arrange stargazing visits to his farm and other local activities.

Rooms: 5: 4 doubles, 2 with en-suite bath and/or shower; 1 single. Rooms without en-suites have exclusive access to a private bathroom.
Price: R200 – R250 pp sharing. Singles R280 – R350.
Meals: Full breakfast included. Dinners on request from R95 pp.
Directions: From Jo'burg side into Warden Street (main street) go around church. 7 blocks from church turn right into Bell Street. From Durban and Bloem, on entering Harrismith turn away from Spur/Engen garage into King Street. Turn left into Warden Street at 1st stop-street. Bell Street is about 10 blocks from here on the left.

Malealea Lodge and Pony Trek Centre

Mick and Di Jones
Malealea, Brandhof 9324
Tel: 051-436-6766 Fax: 051-436-6766
Email: malealea@mweb.co.za Web: www.malealea.co.ls
Cell: 082-552-4215

You shouldn't need an excuse to go to the kingdom of Lesotho, but if you do, look no further than Malealea Lodge. Here in the country's heartland – no phones, no mains electricity – Mick and Di have created a fascinating environment through a combination of their own personal warmth, native knowledge and a wealth of natural and cultural attractions. Malealea thrives on its interaction with the neighbouring village, but this is no plasticky 'Cultural Village' experience. The lodge is entered via the area's trading station, horses for treks of up to six days are hired locally (you stay in the villages you visit), and children will guide you on hikes. In the evenings, you listen to a local choir, before a band plays with home-made instruments. It's worth travelling off the high roads to experience moments such as these! Communal suppers are served canteen style – backpackers and ambassadors rub comradely shoulders – before the pub and firelit stoep drag you away. Later your torch guides you back to thatched rondavel or farmhouse-style accommodation – try to stay as near to the front as possible. I arrived in the afternoon rain but woke up to the most stunning of mornings, with the mist lying low down in the valley, and the peacocks crowing arrogantly at everyone. I loved this place. Two nights are an absolute minimum. *Best visited between December and May.*

Rooms: 40: 8 doubles and 32 twins all with en-suite shower.
Price: Rondavels R220 pp sharing, farmhouses R175 pp sharing. Single supplement 50%.
Meals: Full breakfast included. Lunch R45. Dinner R65 for as much as you want. Horse treks R200 pp per day. Village accommodation R45 pp. Day rides from R100 p.p.
Directions: Faxed or emailed on booking.

Northern Cape

Papkuilsfontein Farmhouse

Willem and Mariëtte van Wyk, Jaco and Alrie

Nieuwoudtville 8180
Tel: 027-218-1246 Fax: 027-218-1246
Email: info@papkuilsfontein.com Web: www.papkuilsfontein.com

I'm going to stick my neck out and say that this is my favourite place to stay in South Africa! And here are my reasons…. You stay in an old stone cottage, surrounded by rock, gum tree and wildlife, not another human in sight. The quality of peace and stillness defeats description. Gas-fired plumbing for baths, hurricane lamps for light – many guests have refused to come back if Willem installs electricity. Then there's the small matter of the gorge and waterfall, which I would have kept secret if I wasn't insistent on your visiting the farm. Your jaw will drop 180 metres into the canyon. Take a picnic to the deep rock pools for swimming above the waterfall (or there's a pool next to the cottages) and you can climb down into the gorge in an hour and a half. The wild flowers in season are sensational even by Namaqualand standards; the plantlife, divided between Cape fynbos and Karoo succulent, a botanist's dream; steenbok, klipspringer, porcupine and dassie love the terrain and have NOT been specially introduced. Alrie is an excellent cook (breakfast a string of surprises). It's a magical place that not many know about and the van Wyks are all lovely, friendly people who seem unable to put a proper price on what they have to offer! You should stay at least two nights. There's also a restored corrugated-iron cottage for those who need their electricity!

Rooms: 2 stone cottages sleeping 4 and 6: one with bath and outdoor shower and the other with shower. 1 cottage with one twin and one double, one with en/s bath and one with en/s shower.
Price: R225 – R270 pp sharing. Single rates +R50.
Meals: Full breakfast included. 3-course dinners R110.
Directions: From CT take N1 then N7 to Vanrhynsdorp. Turn off onto R27 to Nieuwoudtville. Turn right into town, and straight through onto dirt road for 22km. The farm signed to the right.

Map Number: 4

Entry Number: 240

Naries Guest Farm

Johan and Denise Heydenrych

Route R355, Postal: PO Box 6315, Uniedal, 7612, Springbok/Kleinsee 8240
Tel: 021-882-9493 Fax: 021-882-9493
Email: reservations@naries.co.za Web: www.naries.co.za

It's a long and dusty drive to this remote corner of South Africa, but as always with remote corners, it's well worth the effort. Big barren hills march off in a vast and dramatic landscape to the sea 70km away at Kleinzee. The land is sun-scorched and dry except for the few spring weeks when it bursts into life during the Namaqualand wild flower extravaganza – one of the wonders of the world for which you'll need to book very early. The colours in the house can be equally flamboyant, and whatever you think of the seventies-inspired décor, I guarantee you will love the place before leaving! Johan and Denise gave up life in the Western Cape to come and be your hosts and you'll quickly see why. By day you can read by the swimming pool, go hiking, or visit the Richtersveld National Park and De Beers diamond mines. Guests are taken by tractor up to a hillside lapa for an almost surreal glass of sherry at sunset. The view to the distant sea from the 700-metre Southern African Escarpment is spectacular and you might see oryx, springbok or baboons on the way. Then it's all back to the farmhouse for some great home cooking shared with your hosts in a long, candle-lit dining room. Naries offers warm, involving hosting in the midst of a forbidding but fascinating landscape. *Customized tours to various local attractions are also available.*

Rooms: 5: 3 doubles and a twin, 3 with showers, 1 with bath; a self-catering cottage sleeping five.
Price: Dinner, B&B R435 – R605 pp. Self-catering cottage from R495 – R545 a night.
Meals: Full breakfast and dinner provided.
Directions: In Springbok take van der Stel Road west of Springbok – becomes the Kleinzee Road. Follow the dirt road for 15 km. Road is then tarred and the farm signed on the right, 12km on before you go down the mountain.

Riviera Garden B&B

Anneke Malan

16 Budler Street, Upington 8801
Tel: 054-332-6554 Fax: 054-332-6554
Email: ariviera@upington.co.za Web: www.upington.co.za/ariviera
Cell: 072-447-6750

Riviera is a true patch of paradise on the banks of the impressive Orange River, a patch it's taken Anneke a lifetime to find. It was the garden that I loved above all, a lush parade of palm trees, roses and agapanthus and racing-green grass that cools even the most overheated of travellers (as I certainly was when I visited). The lawn flows like a tributary past the pool, right to the water's edge and a secluded, white bench at the end of the garden, the perfect spot to sit and contemplate the river's flowing depths. It's from here that guests hop onto a cruise boat at six o'clock for evening river trips, bobbing downstream, washing down the sunset with a G&T before ambling into town for some dinner. The evenings can be as hot as the days in this part of the world and you'll be glad to find the two cool garden rooms hidden among the greenery with their hefty beds and bags of cupboard space for longer stays. From national parks (Upington is a gateway to the Kalahari Desert and Namibia) to vineyards there's plenty to keep you busy here and it's a must-do stop on any tour of the unspoiled Northern Cape.

Rooms: 2: 1 twin with bath and shower, 1 double with extra single and bath.
Price: R195 pp.
Meals: Breakfast R35. Dinner on request.
Directions: Follow main roads right into the centre of Upington. From Schroeder St turn onto River St towards the river, that leads into Budler St and Riviera is number 16 on the right about half way down.

Map Number: 11

Entry Number: 242

Guest House La Boheme

Evelyne Meier
Post Net Suite 101, Private Bag X5879, 172 Groenepunt Rd, Upington 8800
Tel: 054-338-0660 Fax: 054-338-0661
Email: laboheme@mweb.co.za Web: www.labohem.com
Cell: 083-383-8288

La Boheme claims its rightful place in this book on many counts: its fantastic view from a green, green lawn over the Orange River flood plain; its cool-blue pool; its palm trees that rustle in the hot breeze; and the fantastic dinners served on the verandah at a candle-lit, communal table (undoubtedly one of the best meals I have had in South Africa!). But all of these things play second fiddle to Evelyne herself, who is hugely friendly and energetic and a wholly exceptional host. A cultural blend herself, half-Hungarian and half-Swiss, her guest-house also melds various ethnic styles. There are only three rooms here, guaranteeing the personal touch and each offering something different. I had a trendy-Africa, honeymooners' room with a huge bed of sculpted 'decocrete' and its own patch of outside with iron chairs. Next door has a private patio too, but more of a Caribbean feel and for those wanting a little more space and a touch of Asia there's a separate garden cottage with its own kitchenette and gravel garden surrounded by lush plants. I highly recommend you find your way to Upington, which is an Orange River oasis in the middle of the Kalahari Desert. Not many do. The Kalahari-Gemsbok National Park is just a couple of hours away, Augrabies Falls less than that, and local vineyards and river cruises closer still. Languages spoken: French, German, Italian, English and Hungarian.

Rooms: 3: 1 king with en/s bath and shower, 1 queen with separate bath and shower, 1 cottage with queen and twin sharing a shower.
Price: R250 – R490 pp sharing. Singles R350 – R715.
Meals: Continental breakfast included. Full English breakfast an extra R16. 3-course dinners with 24hrs notice only: R150 (incl coffee and tea). Drinks are extra.
Directions: In Upington take Schröder St towards Olifantshoek, N14, under railway bridge and past Gordonia hospital. 1.7 km after hospital, turn R to Engen garage. Turn immediately L (Groenpunt Rd). Continue 2.5km to red & white Telkom tower and guest house is on right.

Witsand Nature Reserve

Bertus Bester

R64 Kimberley to Witsand, Postmastburg 8420
Tel: 053-313-1061/2   Fax: 053-313-1061/2
Email: witsandkalahari@telkomsa.net Web: www.witsandkalahari.co.za
Cell: 083-234-7573

There are few places beautiful enough to get me out of bed before seven – at Witsand, in the southern Kalahari, I sprang into action at five. It was distant roaring that woke me, not the call of big cats, but the rumble of vast waves of sand, shifting in the wind. At the foot of the Langberg Mountains, this national park is a 3,500ha gem, dominated by a 65 million-year-old dune system. The sky-scraping, grass-dotted ridges of sand vary in colour from blinding white to golden tones and tanned reds, dwarfing the six-man chalets that are hidden in the bush below. Ten spots offer plenty of air-conditioned comfort, fully-equipped kitchens and a huge, tree-shaded braai area with ancient railway-sleeper dining tables for jolly star-lit nights. I spent an afternoon soaking up the scenery, guided by resident expert Jeanene, who has a fascination for creepy-crawlies and pointed out springbok, oryx, and desert birds galore (there's a great bird hide). Bertus and Yvette run the show and very kindly welcomed a lone GGer into their home for supper. Self-catering is usually the order of the day, but I'd recommend opting for the Kalahari Experience which includes hearty meals, wine and guided walks. This is a truly spectacular place and my solo, crack-of-dawn walk through dunes ruffled only by wind and animal tracks, is a memory that will last as long as I do.

Rooms: 10: all family chalets with a double, 2 twins and shared bath, shower and toilet.
Price: Dinner, B&B plus guided walk for R825 pp. R210 pp self catering. Minimum R630 per night for chalets at weekends.
Meals: Dinner, B&B available. On-site shop sells basic foods.
Directions: From Kimberley travel 230km on R64 towards Groblershoop. At Witsand Nature Reserve sign turn R and follow dirt road 45km to the reserve gates on L.

Gauteng

Ordo Tours

Suzanne and Amos Ordo

PO Box 78220, Sandton, Johannesburg 2146
Tel: 011-883-0050 Fax: 011-883-0049
Email: ordotours@global.co.za Web: www.ordotours.co.za
Cell: 083-252-6776

This is an unusual one for us. But we've sat down to enough breakfasts with glassy-eyed travellers determined to see all that South Africa has to offer in as few days as possible to know that some of us – particularly first-time visitors – could do with a little help when it comes to planning. Let's face it, if you're rushing off to catch a plane or to drive five hours to tick off the next sight before the last crumb of toast has hit the breakfast table, you're not really giving yourself enough time to savour South Africa. The key to an enjoyable holiday is to make it manageable. Which is where Ordo Tours come in. Of all the tour operators we've seen, they come closest to our philosophy in their selection of places to stay and will happily help plan your holiday, exclusively using the places in the book. Suzi and Amos will put together a personalised itinerary that will suit your budget and pace, based on your preferences and their local knowledge. They'll take care of as little or as much as you want, be it booking the odd night or commission-free flight-arranging, car and mobile phone hire or piecing together guided tours that usher you round the country in air-conditioned micro-buses. Off-the-shelf packages cover Cape Town and the Winelands, the Garden Route, Johannesburg and Pretoria, Kruger National Park and Vic Falls.

Rooms: n/a
Price: Prices according to itinerary. Package tours from R3,875 for 3 days in Kruger Park to R12,125 for 9-day South Africa Highlights trip. Prices are pp sharing & may change after Oct '05.
Meals: n/a.
Directions: n/a.

Melrose Place Guest Lodge

Sue Truter

12a North St, Melrose 2196
Tel: 011-442-5231 Fax: 011-880-2371
Email: melroseplace@global.co.za Web: www.melroseplace.co.za
Cell: 083-457-4021

Once ensconced behind the electric gates at Melrose you have entered an Eden-in-the-city. The verandah overlooks a large flower garden and enormous swimming pool, all shaded by trees. Eight new rooms don't crowd it at all. It is such a pleasant environment that you may find yourself shelving projected tasks for a day's lounging about. My room was a suite attached to the main house, with mounted TV, huge bed (built up with cushions and pillows), a big bathroom and double doors onto the garden. The high levels of luxury in all the rooms are not reflected in the rates. Sue is the sweetest of hostesses, quick to smiles and reacting sensitively to the mood and wishes of each guest. On the night I stayed we had a braai with an amazing array of meat dishes and salads which appeared from nowhere, and Sue's team will cook dinner for anyone who wants it every evening. Her aim is to maximise the number of happy campers staying. This is her home after all, complete with kids, dachshund and a parrot in its 40s. While guest contentment is running at 100 per cent, it's difficult to see what else she can do. *Laundry provided on request. Nearby: Wanderers cricket ground, Rosebank and Sandton shopping precincts and many restaurants. Airport transfers arranged by Sue.*

Rooms: 14: all en-suite (1 bath only, 4 bath and shower, 9 shower only); includes two cottages.
Price: R360 – R390 pp sharing. Singles R545 – R595.
Meals: Full breakfast included. Lunches (R45) or dinners (R90) by arrangement.
Directions: Ask for a map when booking. Or a map is on the web site.

Johannesburg, Gauteng

North West Province

Dodona

Beresford Jobling

Dodona Farm, Hh 8-9, Hartebeesthoek, Skeerpoort, Magaliesberg 0232
Tel: 012-207-1320 Fax: 086-650-4818
Email: dodona@worldonline.co.za Web: www.hartbeespoortdam.com/dodona
Cell: 082-494-7568

I found the moments that slipped away sitting with Beres and his dog, in the shadow of the world's oldest mountains, listening to him recount local histories and call out the name of birds in the garden, amongst the most peaceful I've spent in Africa. Amonst other things Beres is an illuminating art historian, a vellophile and a direct descendant of Andries Pretorius, the Boer commander who led the massacre of the Zulus at Blood River, and who made his home on this farm. Battle has left an indelible mark on this area, and on Dodona. Beres's doughty grandmother built (with her own hands!) the thatched chapel here to commemorate family caught in conflict. A stone path leads to the Boathouse, a blushing colonial-style cottage housing two old-fashioned apartments, coir-carpeted, with delicate windows, Victorian furniture, fireplace and bookshelves. Days can be filled with ballooning, biking, hiking, riding and water-sports on Hartbeespoort Dam. Battlefields, game farms and the Cradle of Mankind are close by, too. But you may prefer to sit by the lake and spot high- and lowveld birdlife or wander round the sun-dappled garden. There's a freshwater plunge pool, a croquet lawn and a variety of conifers and gums, one of which Beres assures me becomes quite sensuous under moonlight. There's so much to recommend here… "except the nightlife," says Beres. But even so you can always dosi-do at the local square dance. *The Magaliesberg is a World Heritage site. Closed between Christmas and New Year.*

Rooms: 2 self-contained apartments, 1 king and 1 twin, both with en-suite bath and shower.
Price: R420 pp sharing.
Meals: Full breakfast included, eaten at the main house.
Directions: From Jo'burg, take R512 north, past N14 and Lanseria Airport. Turn left at T-jct, through Broederstroom and left, signed Cradle of Mankind, towards Hartebeesthoek.

Hideaway at the Farm

Mike and Sabine Manegold

Pelindaba Road 10, Broederstroom, Hartebeespoort 0240
Tel: 012-205-1309 Fax: 012-205-1309
Email: info@hideawayatthefarm.com Web: www.hideawayatthefarm.com
Cell: 083-476-0507

I couldn't imagine a less contrived and more relaxing place. Mike is a laid-back, nurturing soul (and reformed advertising executive) with a real commitment to and passion for South Africa and this spirit reigns at the farm. With views to the Hartbeespoort Dam and magical Magaliesberg – Johannesburg's playground and natural magnets for water-sport and hiking enthusiasts – the farm consists of a two-bedroom farmhouse and two conjoined rondavels backed by a koppie. The farmhouse has an open-plan kitchen and a large comfortable lounge whose sliding glass doors lead to a pool. Across the drive are the rondavels: slate floors, fleshy walls and towering, thatched ceilings. Though the farm no longer yields produce, it "farms people" instead. Charming Benjamin runs the place and chef George will serve you breakfast on your patio. There's a braai area marked out by Sabine's dream symbols while lower down Benjamin is busy building a bar, which will showcase George's fabulous fare. But the real reason to come to the farm is because it is filled with the optimism of the new South Africa. Swiss-born Mike has a wealth of knowledge about his adopted country but to listen to Benjamin's balanced tales of the Apartheid years is to witness the new hope for South Africa first hand. An enriching experience.

Rooms: 3: in farmhouse: 1 double with en/s bath/shower and 1 twin with en/s shower; 2 rondavels each with double and en/s bath/shower plus cooking facilities.
Price: R250 – R300 pp sharing. Singles on request. Weekly and monthly rates available.
Meals: Café restaurant on site for meals (including breakfast) and a good number of restaurants within a ten-minute drive.
Directions: From Johannesburg follow signs to Randburg and N1 heading north-west. Take R512 past Lanseria Airport toward Hartbeespoort Dam. At T-junction turn left and the farm is signed on the left.

Map Number: 13 & 17   Entry Number: 248

Mosetlha Bush Camp

Chris, June and Caroline Lucas
Madikwe Game Reserve
Tel: 011-444-9345 Fax: 011-444-9345
Email: info@thebushcamp.com Web: www.thebushcamp.com
Cell: 083-653-9869

Mosetlha puts the wild into wilderness; no doors or glass here as they would hinder the feel and dust of Africa permeating your very core; no electric fences surround the camp as there is no electricity; no worries either as you leave them at the gate. Facilities are basic but real; guests draw their own hot water from a donkey-boiler before proceeding to the shower. Recently the kitchen was extended and a new thatch and stone lapa has been added for guests to read, relax and compare sightings, but the authenticity remains untainted. The wooden cabins are comfortable, but used only for sleeping – you are here for the wilderness experience of the outdoors. Chris's passion for conservation and his environment shines through and is contagious (which reminds me to say that the area is malaria-free). His guests depart much the wiser, not only because of the game drives, but also because of the superb guided wilderness walks. Yes, the Madikwe Game Reserve (70,000 hectares) has the so-called 'Big Five', but a game lodge worth its salt (such as this) will fire your imagination about the whole food chain. Even the camp itself is an education – all sorts of birds, small mammals and antelopes venture in. Come for a genuine and memorable bush experience. Children welcome from 8 years old up.

Rooms: 8 twins sharing 3 shower/toilet complexes.
Price: All-inclusive from R895 per person. Alcoholic and fizzy drinks extra.
Meals: All meals and refreshments (tea, coffee, fruit juice) included.
Directions: Detailed written directions supplied on request or see website.

Jaci's Tree Lodge

Jan and Jaci van Heteren

Madikwe Game Reserve, PO Box 413, Movatedi 2838
Tel: 014-778-9900 Fax: 014-788-9901
Email: jaci@madikwe.com Web: www.madikwe.com
Cell: 083-447-7929, reservations 083-700-2071

"Hold on!" Joe Ranger hollers above walkie-talkie crackle and engine rattle. We're gunning through bush, bouncing along a sandy track, leaning in to avoid being whipped by thicket. Lion spoor's been spotted – a pride on the hunt – and we're in an adrenaline-pumping race to find them first. When we do, we watch in breathless awe as they saunter by less than a metre from us, senses fixed on their prey: an elephant, who charges and they scatter. We're still abuzz when we return to our already-run baths and chat animatedly around the boma fire at dinner. Jaci's has this effect on you. Wonderfully indulgent, this is one of Tatler's favourites. Beyond the foyer's tree-pierced, blonde-thatch roof lies an expansive restaurant overlooking riverine forest and separated from the chic bar by a four-sided open fire, which together keep you in long cocktails and gourmet food. Relax the excess off in a hammock; alternatively there's a pool and gym. Save your gasps of delight for the tree houses. Sitting six metres above ground and linked by a rosewood walkway, their glass doors concertina open onto private decks. Vibrant colours form a backdrop for a bed festooned with silk cushions, burnt-orange suede beanbag and swollen stone bath with handmade copper pipes. But Jaci's trump card is the rangers whose enthusiasm creates a wonderful, wild adventure. What a job they have – daily taking breath away. Further along the river bank you'll find Jaci's Safari Lodge, opulent canvas and stone suites. Kids of all ages specially catered for.

Rooms: 8 tree houses each with king-size bed and bath and outdoor "jungle" shower.
Price: R1,995 – R3,295 pp sharing.
Meals: All meals and game drives included.
Directions: Only 1.5 hours' drive from Sun City or a 3-hour drive from Johannesburg. Daily road and air transfers from JHB and Sun City. Ask for details when booking.

Mpumalanga

Chez Vincent Restaurant and Guesthouse

Vincent and Sara Martinez
56 Ferreira Street, Nelspruit 1200
Tel: 013-744-1146 Fax: 013-744-1147
Email: bookings@chezvincent.com Web: www.chezvincent.co.za
Cell: 082-331-1054

After weeks in the bush I was truly … well, bushed, but couldn't have been better looked after by Vincent and Sara. They are great people and theirs the perfect staging post during any journey through this part of the world (a must by the way). Nelspruit is a hub town, gateway to Mozambique and Swaziland, and also the Kruger National Park. Some guests come over from Maputo for shopping or even just for dinner chez Vincent, while others are international visitors stopping over before entering the park. All, including myself, go mad for Vincent's South-African-influenced French cuisine in the intimate restaurant, hung with paintings by local artists. He's originally from Toulouse and over an after-dinner bottle of wine he and Sara (a Liverpudlian) sympathetically listened to me prattle away in bad French gone rusty. Physically and grammatically exhausted I made a beeline for bed and one of the best nights' sleep I've had in South Africa. Rooms here are pretty much brand-new, all light-filled, air-conditioned and some opening out onto the swimming pool. Each has Sara's choice of funky colour splashes (lime green, turquoise, yellow, pink and orange) and I had one of the five family suites, complete with a full kitchen, sofa-bed and shower so spacious you could lie down in it… so I did. Delicious food, relaxed atmosphere, very nice hosts and an opportunity to do some shopping before disappearing into the bush.

Rooms: 11: 6 doubles with en/s showers and bath, 5 family rooms each with 1 double, bathroom with shower, sofa-bed, lounge and fully-equipped kitchen.
Price: R220 – R250 pp sharing. Singles R320 – R350.
Meals: Full breakfast included. A la carte restaurant on premises.
Directions: Take N4 to Nelspruit and turn right into Paul Kruger Street at Absa Square. This leads into Ferreira Street. At end turn right (still Ferreira St) and immediately left into service road, Chez Vincent is 4th house on the left.

Map Number: 18

Kavinga Guest House

Stuart and Ros Hulley-Miller

R37 Nelspruit/Sabie Rd, Nelspruit 1200
Tel: 013-755-3193 Fax: 013-755-3161
Email: kavinga@mpu.co.za
Cell: 083-625-7162

Thick orchards of avocados buffer Kavinga farmhouse and its green lake of lawn from the outside world. Ros assembles a country breakfast on the stone-tiled verandah, which is latticed with rare jade vine and camouflaged by plants and flowers. If you are like the majority of the Hulley-Millers' guests you will spend a good deal of time there, lying on wicker furniture and deck chairs or flopping indolently in the pool while Ros dispenses indispensable drinks. Spacious bedrooms dotted around the grounds are classily decorated and pander to the 21st century with satellite TV, bar fridges and sumptuous bathrooms (with both shower and free-standing bath). The family unit has its own sitting room with a sofa bed to unravel for extra bodies. French windows open onto small covered patios with broad views over the Lowveld. I think it was Walt Disney's Baloo the Bear who said: 'Float downstream, fall apart in my backyard'.... *Just 45km to the Kruger National Park.*

Rooms: 6: 3 twins, 2 doubles and 1 family unit with 1 double and 1 twin – all with en-suite baths and showers.
Price: R235 – R250 pp sharing. Singles R295 – R325.
Meals: Full breakfast included. Dinner by arrangement: R85 for 3 courses
Directions: 11.5km north from Nelspruit on R37 towards Sabie. Sign to right.

Entry Number: 252　　　　　　　　　　　　Map Number: 18

Ambience Inn

Hannes Scholtz and Issy de Lira

28 Wally Scott St, White River 1240
Tel: 013-751-1951 Fax: 013-751-1951
Email: ambience@lantic.net Web: www.ambienceinn.co.za
Cell: 082-928-0461

Lost again, I stopped at some traffic lights where I asked police officers for directions. I was escorted through a canopy of flamboyant trees – in full red-blossom livery – to the end of a quiet cul-de-sac where guinea fowl roam between properties. The house was built from scratch into an Aztec-style palladium. Terracotta-coloured columns and walls provide the entrance into a sub-tropical/indigenous garden of clivias, gingers, macadamias and a colossal kapok tree with cotton-wool flowers which Victorians apparently used to stuff their pillows. There is a refreshing and get-fit-worthy, fifteen-metre long lap swimming pool bordered by blue mosaic tiles. On the guests' stoep is a manicured garden of mosses, tropical staghorn ferns and orchids clinging to old tree stumps. Hannes is a qualified horticulturist and keen landscape gardener, and he delights in sharing his passion for the gardens with nature-lovers and bird-watchers alike. The bedrooms are comfortable with cool-for-the-summer screed floors, high ceilings and African bedspreads. All of the rooms have private outdoor courtyards with al fresco showers and imaginative breakfasts are served on the stoep with hessian curtains hanging from the high mantle and wind chimes singing in the breeze. Take-out picnic baskets can also be provided for early starts into the nearby Kruger Park. Come evening, sunset viewings with Issy and Hannes overlooking Legogote are also a possibility.

Rooms: 6: 4 doubles and 2 twins, all with en-suite showers and outside shower.
Price: R220 – R250 pp sharing.
Meals: Full breakfast or picnic basket. Dinners on request and restaurants nearby.
Directions: From Jo'burg take N4 to Nelspruit and turn left onto R40. When in White River turn first left after first traffic light into Henry Morey Rd, then right into Frank Townsend Rd, then left into Wally Scott St.

Map Number: 18

Jatinga Country Lodge

John and Lyn Davis

Jatinga Road, Plaston, White River 1240
Tel: 013-751-5059 /013-751-5108 Fax: 013-751-5119
Email: info@jatinga.co.za Web: www.jatinga.co.za
Cell: 082-456-1676

You know from the smile at the boom-gate and the cheerful greeting at the end of the gravel drive that all will be well at Jatinga. From the tiled foyer, you're led through an atrium hallway to a terracotta-tiled lounge. This is bathed in sunlight flooding through open French doors that lead onto a somnolent verandah. Here couples on cushioned wicker chairs take tea overlooking a glassy croquet lawn and a fabulous sub-tropical garden strewn with jacaranda petals. The large bedrooms, some modelled as modern rondavels, radiate from the 1920s homestead. Victorian rooms have outdoor showers, the Provençal house concrete baths so big they should come with a lifeguard. I stayed in the Colonial Suite and, clothes despatched for laundering, found I could enjoy my mini-bar ministrations from any number of positions: the oversized bed, the sofa, the claw-foot bath, the patio…. But the choices don't end there. You can browse safari journals in sofas like quicksand; perfect your heliotropic posturing by a pool shielded by ramrod palms; or sip sundowners on the deck above the White River. In the light-filled dining room with its cellar of top-notch wines I gleefully tackled the crab curry, my clean clothes preserved by a bib, the battle-scarred tablecloth not so lucky. You are so well looked after here you may forget that your safari adventure awaits.

Rooms: 14: 4 luxury suites and 10 superior rooms, all with en-suite bath and shower.
Price: R835 – R1,095 pp sharing. Singles R1,095 – R1,395.
Meals: Full breakfast included. A la carte restaurant serves breakfast, lunch and dinner daily. Gourmet picnic hampers on request.
Directions: From Nelspruit head to White River (approx. 20km) and proceed through town. Continue straight along the R538 to Karino/Plaston for 4.3km, from last traffic light, crossing over two railway lines. Turn right onto the Jatinga Road (dirt road). Travel for 1.9km to the Jatinga Gate.

Bushwise Safaris

Tim van Coller and Peter Winhall

Crocodile River, overlooking Kruger, Marloth Park, PO Box 909,
Komatipoort 1340 Tel: 083-651-7464 (Lodge)
Email: info@bushwisesafaris.com Web: www.bushwisesafaris.com
Cell: 083-555-0181 (Peter)

I defy you to find a more knowledgeable and enthusiastic raconteur on life in the African bush than Peter. I defy you to find anyone more insane than Tim, currently canoeing solo down the Zambezi, fending off hungry crocs. Bushwise seems an apt name. I'm certainly more bush-savvy after two action-packed days here and, cliché though it may have become, truly felt like I was leaving old friends when the time came to pack my bags. But charging rhino won't keep me from coming back. The lodge couldn't be better placed, on the portals to Swaziland and Mozambique, with the open-walled, thatch-roofed bar overlooking the Crocodile River and Kruger Park that stretches out beyond. It's here that hippos wallow and elephants drink (in the river, of course, not the bar). The distant roars of lion add sound effects to Peter's childhood tales from the Rhodesian bush as guests huddle around the boma fire to enjoy one of Donna's veritable feasts under the stars. With so much to do, I was up at three the next morning, grabbing my binos ready for a nerve-tingling walk in the Kruger. Turns out the binos were superfluous – another story for Peter to recount to future guests, or save for the latest chapter of his memoirs. I recommend at least three nights if you want to become as bush-wise as me.

Rooms: 5: all twins or doubles, 4 with en-suite showers, 1 with en-suite bath.
Price: R1,550 pp including all meals, full-day drives in open vehicles in Kruger, guided tours of Panorama Rte and day trips to Maputo/Swaziland, airport transfers (KMIA). R600 pp DB&B only.
Meals: All meals included, drinks extra.
Directions: Directions emailed on booking.

Numbela Exclusive Riverside Accommodatio.

Michael and Tamasine Johnson
White River 1240
Tel: 013-751-3356
Email: relax@numbela.co.za Web: www.numbela.co.za
Cell: 082-335-9528

I happened upon Numbela by chance on a day off and got lucky. Upon arrival I was met by a happy group of guests bringing the remnants of a picnic up from the river beach, and was soon joining them on the sandy bank for a drink. Just outside White River, the lodge is on a 200-acre wet-and-woodland wonderland that teems with bird life and which you are free to explore. Two cottages are separated by a converted mill-house. One has a raised stoep with a swing-seat piled with pillows and the interior is all about flair. The main room is enlivened by earthy red and orange paint-work, the bedroom is dressed with blushing fabrics and the washed-blue bathroom comes with an outdoor shower. The smaller thatched cottage near the river has chalky walls and claret-coloured floor with high ceilings, an Oregon pine kitchen, stable doors and an open fire. The bedroom is decorated with African artefacts, their origins explained in a thoughtful pamphlet. There's a welcome attention to detail, from the faultless design to the touches like refreshingly complimentary spirits and mixers and the delicious breakfast delivered to my patio. And you couldn't ask for more affable hosts than Michael and Tamasine. They are on hand to help with tasks great or small: organising Mozambique visas, balloon trips or spa treatments. These are people doing their own thing well. *Close to Casterbridge Farm shops and restaurants, golf courses and the Kruger gates.*

Rooms: 3: 2 self-catering/B&B cottages, 1 double with en-suite shower plus mezzanine single, 1 double & twin with en-suite bath and outdoor shower; 1 self-catering cottage with 4 twin bedrooms with en-suite showers, 1 private bath.
Price: B&B: from R380 pp sharing. Self-catering: from R660 for 2 people, R1,000 for 4. Singles on request.
Meals: Full breakfast included in B&B rate. Kitchen stocked with essentials including spirits and mixers (B&B only).
Directions: 20km north of White River on R40 Hazyview rd. Oval sign clearly visible on L. Turn L & follow signs down dirt road for approx 1km to gate.

Hops Hollow Country House

Theo and Sarie de Beer

PO Box 430, Lydenburg 1120
Tel: 013-235-2275 or 083-627-6940 Fax: 083-118-627-6940
Email: hops@hopshollow.com Web: www.hopshollow.com
Cell: 084-526-2721

The highest brewery in South Africa, Hops Hollow combines the warmest of welcomes with hand-crafted beers, scrumptious meals and a picturesque setting. There is something rather Scottish about the scenery surrounding this guest-house high on the Long Tom Pass, with its mountains, mist and crisp air. The area has many Boer War and gold-rush connections and Theo will tell you about both historical and natural wonders. Following a Damascene conversion one moonlit night he gave up clerical work for life in conservation and has never looked back. When not at his day job with the Mpumalanga Parks Board he's a proper microbrewer (supply your own 'De Beer' pun) and loves showing guests around his brewery. And once the theory is out of the way you can slide swiftly on to the practical in the smithy, a baronial drinking den with vast columns made from old railway sleepers. Sarie, meanwhile, is the force behind the guest house whose bedrooms have thick duvets and large cushions and, in some cases, views best appreciated from the pillow. She is also a wonderful cook (lots of beer in the recipes) and her breakfasts are super special, a 3-course meal in themselves. I defy you to leave Hops Hollow with your belt on the same notch. This small twin-pronged business is a delight, for ale-lovers and otherwise.

Rooms: 3: all twin/doubles with en-suite showers.
Price: R280 – R330 pp sharing. Singles from R330.
Meals: Full breakfast included. Dinner by prior arrangement: 3 courses R95 – R110.
Directions: On R37 between Sabie and Lydenburg, opposite milestone 22.2 on the Long Tom Pass (distance from Lydenburg).

Mpumalanga

Rissington Inn

Chris Harvie

PO Box 650, Hazyview 1242
Tel: 013-737-7700 Fax: 013-737-7112
Email: info@rissington.co.za Web: www.rissington.co.za
Cell: 082-327-6842

Informality and relaxation dictate at the Rissington Inn; you feel this even as you mount the broad steps to the verandah for the first time. Sun-lounging guests dazily contemplate the flower gardens full of frangipani; the swimming pool is a rectangle of cool aquamarine; the hazy valley shimmers beyond. In the evenings gourmet, incredibly good-value candlelit dinners are served by friendly staff. We have eaten with Chris on four separate occasions and never been disappointed, despite much creativity and daring in the dishes. High ceilings put the lid on well-designed rooms. The one I had was enormous with a Victorian bathroom and its own sitting area. But Rissington isn't the sort of place where you feel like hiding away or watching TV. Owner/mover/shaker Chris actually seems to LIKE seeing his guests doing what they want, dressed how they feel and making friends. When you arrive there is usually a gaggle of guests lined up at his wooden bar and you could easily mistake them for Chris's personal friends. They probably only arrived a few minutes before you. *Hazyview sits at the portals of the Kruger National Park.*

Rooms: 14: 2 queens, 3 with 2 queen beds, 3 queens with an extra single, 6 king/twins, all en-suite bathrooms. Garden rooms have outside showers.
Price: R295 – R495 pp sharing.
Meals: Full breakfast included and served till noon. Restaurant on-site for à la carte lunch and dinner.
Directions: 2km south of Hazyview on R40 White River Numbi Gate (KNP) Rd. On right coming from main Hazyview 4-way stop – see signs for Rissington and Kiaat Park.

Entry Number: 258

Map Number: 18

Timamoon

Maurice and Gaylyn Hammond
Sabie – Hazyview Road, Sabie 1242
Tel: 013-767-1740 Fax: 013-767-1889
Email: info@timamoonlodge.co.za Web: www.timamoonlodge.co.za
Cell: 082-445-3788

Through the entrance gate, down the forested slopes of the Sabie Valley, past peacocks and exotic birds whose names I can't pronounce (because I don't know them), I came at last to the Sabie River, straddled by a wooden bridge. Already the camera had been whipped out a dozen times and I hadn't even started the ascent to the lodges. On I pressed, past avocado and banana trees until the welcome sight of secluded thatched chalets, dotted over the hillside, signalled my arrival. If the views from up here don't win you over (and they will) the lodges will certainly knock you for six, especially when you consider that much of the handiwork – carved wooden four-poster beds, mosaicked floors – was crafted by Maurice's fair hand. Although slightly different in style, each lodge enjoys a small private pool from which to soak up the tranquillity that rises from the valley below, open log fires and the softest of soft leather sofas. Hardly surprising so many honeymooners find their way to Timamoon, and I didn't even catch a glimpse of the dedicated honeymoon lodge, so secluded is it. If nothing else entices the romantics from their idyll, the stilted, wall-less restaurant will. When I visited Jeannine, the chef, was busy preparing such delights as Smoked Trout and Cucumber Mousse and Venison Skukuza. Perhaps Gaylyn is right when she suggests Timamoon is the most seductive lodge on the planet. It certainly seduced me.

Rooms: 6 lodges: 3 with 2 bedrooms and 3 with 1 bedroom; full en-suite bathrooms and outside showers. All have private pools.
Price: R800 – R1,700 pp sharing DB&B.
Meals: Full breakfast included. 3-course dinner in the restaurant included (not drinks). Picnic lunch baskets R150.
Directions: From Jo'burg take N4. 25km before Nelspruit, turn left at Sabie sign (R539) which becomes R37. In Sabie take R536 towards Hazyview for 24km and sign is on left. 4km on dirt road.

Map Number: 18

Entry Number: 259

Mpumalanga

Böhms Zeederberg Country House

Marlene, Tina and Andrea Böhm

R536, Sabie 1260
Tel: 013-737-8101 Fax: 013-737-8193
Email: bohms@mweb.co.za Web: www.bohms.co.za
Cell: 083-29-3342

Böhms Zeederberg is a real institution in this part of the world, a large country house (in physical proportions rather than number of rooms), sitting pretty on one side of the Sabie River Valley. Your hosts are the extremely welcoming Böhms, mother Marlene and her daughters Tina and Andrea, and a cornucopia of indigenous bird-life. The large swimming pool, sauna, lapa and jacuzzi are pure indulgence and the temptation to slip into the latter with a glass (or bottle) of champagne overwhelming. The chalets are dotted around neatly-clipped lawns and each has its verandah, great view and personality. My favourite has an intricate wrought-iron bed-head and yellow painted walls. A walking trail to the river below guarantees many sightings of animals and birds, including the purple-crested turaco, a fan of the huge trees that dot the farm. You can admire the sunsets from the large stone verandah before hearty and delicious dinners in the main house. Also on the property is the Windmill Wine Shop, run by other members of the Böhm family, Thomas and his wife-chef Jacqui, who is a source of gastronomic delights. Come for luxury, pampering and peace. 20 mins to Kruger National Park, Blyde River Canyon et al. Hot-air ballooning, river rafting, game drives, riding and fishing all within easy reach.

Rooms: 10: 5 doubles and 5 twins, 8 with bath and shower, 2 with shower only.
Price: R370 – R420 pp sharing. Singles R420 – R470.
Meals: Full breakfast included. 4-course evening meal R100.
Directions: From Jo'burg take N4. At Belfast take R540 to Dullstroom and then to Lydenburg. Take R37 to Sabie and then turn left after 26.6km from the R536 towards Hazyview.

Entry Number: 260

Map Number: 18

Idube Private Game Reserve

Sally Kernick
Sabi Sand Game Reserve 1242
Tel: 011-888-3713 Fax: 011-888-2181
Email: info@idube.com Web: www.idube.com

There are few establishments where the staff seem to have as much fun working together as at Idube. Be they guides, trackers, managers or chefs, the Idube crew exude a delightful sense of goodwill to each other and to all mankind. And it's not difficult to see why. Warthog roam through the camp, elephants pass nearby; there is space and greenery, beauty and beast. The land was bought in 1983 by Louis and Marilyn Marais and Louis sensibly built the swimming pool before designing and constructing the rest of the camp himself. Guests sleep in chalets dotted around the sloping grounds, while the thatched seating and dining areas look out over the Sabi Sand Game Reserve. A rope bridge over the river bed takes you to a hide where you can admire the Shadulu dam and its regulars without being admired yourself. Two game drives per day plus guided walks give you the chance to see what's happening elsewhere in the reserve and tracker Titus amazed us with his ability to read bent grasses and droppings. We took time out for sundowners by a dam, accompanied by a bull elephant and a bull hippo. There was much posturing and manliness, not least from me, before a return to camp for dinner (which was excellent!) and conviviality under the stars.

Rooms: 10: 2 kings and 8 doubles all with en/s
bathrooms and outdoor shower.
Price: Winter (May to end Sept) R2,050 pp sharing.
Summer (October to end April) R2,950. Single
supplement +35%.
Meals: All 3 meals plus morning and evening drives
and a guided walk included. Drinks and transfers
extra.
Directions: 34.4km from Hazyview along R536
towards Kruger Gate. Follow signs off to the left.
19.5km along a dirt road.

Plains Camp

Nikki and Gerrit Mayer
Rhino Walking Safaris, Kruger National Park, Skukuza 1350
Tel: 011-467-1886 Fax: 011-467-4758
Email: info@rws.co.za Web: www.rws.co.za
Cell: 083-631-4956

This is where I fell for Africa: sitting outside my tent in the Kruger, sipping G&T (for the quinine, you understand) and watching game serenely traverse Timbitene Plain. This is the only private lodge where you can walk in pristine wilderness – nothing short of a privilege. From Rhino Post, the fabulous sister lodge on the Mutlumuvi river bank (where you can stay) you walk to Plains Camp. Here the refined, pioneer tents have dark wood furniture with brass hinges and leather straps, bathrooms with copper taps protruding from tree stumps and the largest, softest towels. During the day, you can doze on the chocolate-leather sofa or sip highball cocktails in the plunge pool. Pith helmets, surveying tools, maps and a gramophone add to the bygone feel and, to cap it all, the head ranger Gerrit is the sort over whom Karen Blixen might have swooned. Walking on rhino footpaths, the trails let you soak up both the scale and detail of the bush. No mad rush to tick off half-glimpsed Big Five, this – it's all about the quality of the sightings. That said, we encountered glowering buffalo, rampant rhino, lionesses on a hunt and had a pulse-quickening showdown with a bull elephant that I'll dine out on for ages. Afterwards we sent the sun down the sky and, wrapped in rugs, headed toward gas-lamp beacons for a never-ending feast. A safari fantasy come true.

Rooms: 4 twin-bed African-explorer style tents, each with en-suite loo, shower and overhead fan.
Price: R1,950 – R2,350 pp sharing. Ask about 3-, 4- or 5-night packages and single supplement.
Meals: All meals, activities, game drives, walks and optional sleep-outs included.
Directions: From the Paul Kruger Gate follow signs to Skukuza Rest Camp & Rhino Walking Safaris. Drive past Skukuza on H1-2 towards Tshokwane and Satara. Cross Sabie and Sand rivers and after second turning to Maroela Loop, turn left signed Rhino Walking Safaris. Meet at Rhino Post Safari Lodge.

Iketla Lodge

Albert and Hennielene Botha
off R555, Ohrigstad 1122
Tel: 013-238-0190 Fax: 013-238-0190
Email: relax@iketla.com Web: www.iketla.com

"Be relaxed… be peaceful' is Iketla's poetic English translation from the local Sotho dialect. Appropriately named, as it turns out. Surrounded on all sides by hills and rocky outcrops, Albert and Hennielene greeted me in the shebeen, where the late afternoon sun was gushing through the open sides, flooding the thatched, tiled dining area. For those that don't know, a shebeen is a drinking den and it's to this magnet that guests began to flock as they returned, brimming with exhilaration, from the day's adventures. Some had been exploring the Panorama Route, others had been walking guided trails through Iketla's 540 hectares of wilderness, inspecting all creatures great and small, and learning about the impressive range of bird life and traditional uses of indigenous plants. They regaled us with their new-found knowledge and enthusiasm, with Albert, a bushman at heart, chipping in with many jewels of profounder expertise. A faint drumbeat interrupted the banter to signal supper, though my acute senses had already picked up the aroma of something sensational on the air… ostrich strips in a sherry sauce as it turned out. At daybreak I inspected my chalet, similar in style to the main lodge with rugged stone walls, a thatched roof and a verandah outside sliding glass doors. There I read my book and rested my bones, listening to the morning wildlife bring this African wilderness alive.

Rooms: 6 chalets: 3 doubles and 3 twins, all with en-suite showers and outside showers.
Price: R670 pp sharing. Singles +R140. Under 12 half-price.
Meals: Full breakfast and dinner included.
Directions: From N4 turn off at Belfast and follow R540 through Dullstroom to Lydenburg. Follow R36 through Lydenburg to Ohrigstad. 4km past Ohrigstad turn left onto R555. Sign to Iketla 6km further on right.

Swaziland

Phophonyane Falls Lodge

Lungile de Vletter

PO Box 199, Pigg's Peak
Tel: +268-437-1429 Fax: +268-437-1319
Email: lungile@phophonyane.co.sz Web: www.phophonyane.co.sz
Cell: +268-604-2802

A South African visa is enough to see you popping over the border into the Kingdom of Swaziland and immersing yourself in 500 hectares of pristine nature. Phophonyane Lodge is perched high on a valleyside in thick indigenous forest with the constant background music of a thousand birds (230 species) and the rushing white water of the Phophonyane River cascading down the kloof below (waterfall-viewing walks are a must). You move between the main lodge and the various tents and cottages on cobbles and wooden walkways, past murals and rough wood sculptures, natural materials blending easily into the landscape. Some of the cottages have sitting rooms, private gardens, narrow wooden staircases up to bedrooms and balconies, big showers, kitchens et al. The safari tents with their private decks are simpler but more romantic. You are lost in the trees and I stayed in one of the two right down by the rushing water's edge, the best sleeping draught imaginable. The reserve is criss-crossed with hiking paths leading to natural rock pools for swimming, and guests congregate at the bar in the evenings to watch the sun go down. Family-owned and run, Phophonyane is perfect for outdoorsy nature lovers. Since the last edition a new salt-water swimming pool has been added in front of their newly-built restaurant. This has a small library and sitting area too. *4x4 drives to mountains and Bushman paintings available.*

Rooms: 4 cottages (1 sleeps 5, 2 sleep 4, 1 sleeps 2); 2 with shower, 1 with b, 1 with b and sh. 5 tents (4 sleep 3, 1 sleeps 2); 1 has en/s sh, others have nearby private b'room.
Price: Safari tents R330 – R350 pp sharing, singles R460 – R490; Cottages R420 – R560, singles R600 – R800.
Meals: Each unit is self-catering, except some tents. A la carte restaurant available and picnic lunches can be prepared.
Directions: 14km north of Pigg's Peak Town or 35km from Jeppe's Reef border post to sign posts then approx 4km of dirt road following the signs to the entrance.

Map Number: 14,15 & 18

Entry Number: 264

Limpopo

Gwalagwala

Dorian and Ann Harcourt-Baldwin

Guernsey Rd off the R40, PO Box 1499, Hoedspruit 1380
Tel: 015-793-3491 Fax: 015-793-0535
Email: gwala@netactive.co.za Web: www.gwala.co.za
Cell: 083-701-2490

Kitted out in khakis and walking boots I can't imagine Dorian as a Jo'burg banker, but that's what he was until a yearning for the bush got the better of him. This is a man who clearly loves every blade of grass on his 500ha reserve and his passion is easily understandable. Stocked with plains game, Gwalagwala is a stunning spot hidden away in the greenery of the Klaserie river and the most instantaneously peaceful retreat I found in this region. Deep (deep) in the bush, just yards from the gurgling waterway, Dorian and Ann have erected five huge tents, built onto raised decks, each with a tiled bathroom and reed walls. They're close enough to be friendly, but spaced enough for privacy, connected by shaded paths to the pool, boma and bar. And not just any old bar. Here drinks (and breakfast) are served 30 feet up in a circular tree house wrapped around a huge jackalberry tree. Why go to the birds when they can come to you? Purple-crested louries, the rare African finfoot ("not the prettiest thing since Sofia Loren, but beautiful in its own way," Dorian tells me)… the bird list takes hours to unscroll. Canoeing and croc-spotting, antelope and acacia, this is the sort of spot that ignites in me an urge to one day own my own piece of Africa (and preferably a big, noisy Landrover to go with it).

Rooms: 5: 2 doubles and 3 twins; 3 with shower, 1 with bath, 1 with bath and shower.
Price: From R995 pp full board, including 2 game activities, one of which is a "Big 5" game drive.
Meals: All meals included.
Directions: Faxed or emailed on booking or available on website.

Map Number: 18

Entry Number: 265

Pezulu Tree House Lodge

Gilly and West Mathewson

Guernsey, Hoedspruit 1380
Tel: 015-793-2724
Fax: 015-793-2253
Email: pezlodge@mweb.co.za
Web: www.pezulu.co.za
Cell: 083-376-3048

The sorry victim of a tree-house-free childhood, I was intrigued by the concept of Pezulu – six different reed-and-thatch constructions spread among the trees surrounding the central building, which is itself entwined around a large amarula. They are all hidden from view behind branch and leaf, and many have bits of tree growing up through the floor to provide the most natural of towel rails, stools and loo paper holders. The 'houses' are named after the trees in which they sit: 'False Thorn' has a magnificent shower with views over the Thornybush Reserve – be prepared for inquisitive giraffe; while 'Huilboerboom' is a honeymoon suite set eight metres above ground (privacy even from the giraffe). Gilly's husband West conjured Pezulu out of the Guernsey Conservancy on the edge of the Kruger Park. There are no predators in this area, only plains game, so you and the buck can wander around the property in perfect safety. Activities on offer include the usual two game drives a day and/or guided hikes. They can also arrange microlight flights and visits to rehabilitation centres and the white lion breeding project... assuming they can persuade you down from the trees.

Rooms: 6: 1 family unit (1 double and 1 twin) and 5 doubles; 1 with en/s shower, 2 with separate bath, 3 with separate shower.
Price: From R595 dinner, B&B to R995 all-inclusive. Microlight flights (R375), white-water rafting, Kruger visits and other activities also available.
Meals: Fully inclusive: all meals and game activities. Drinks extra.
Directions: Ask when booking.

Umlani Bushcamp

Marco Schiess
Timbavati Nature Reserve
Tel: 012-346-4028 Fax: 012-346-4023
Email: info@umlani.com Web: www.umlani.com
Cell: 083-468-2041

Rhino-tracking on foot; a rather exciting experience with a couple of bull elephants; sun-downers as the bush settles for the night... this is what safaris are supposed to be about. Umlani is set on a gentle slope above a dry river course (wet in spring) and no fence separates you from the Timbavati's more feral inhabitants. You do not, for example, leave your rondavel at night to investigate snuffling noises, and elephants regularly swing through the middle of the camp for a drink at the pool. You sleep in delightful reed-walled rondavels with thatched roofs (no bricks here), hurricane lamps (no electricity either), and you shower *au naturel*, but in complete privacy. Marco and his wife Marie ran the camp by themselves for a decade until the demands of a young family compelled them to find like-minded managers. After the evening game drive everyone sits out on the deck by the bar, or in the boma round the fire, mulling over what's just been seen, before sitting down to an excellent and often buzzy dinner at tables of 8. Thoughtful hosts and knowledgeable rangers provide the charming, human face of a full-on bush experience. I had many laughs during my stay, while another guest was in tears when she had to leave! Umlani is exceptionally personal and genuine and you live as close to nature as they dare let you.

Rooms: 8 doubles (2 sleeping 4); all with en-suite outside showers.
Price: R1,870 pp sharing. Singles R1,950. Children under 12 years old R1,400. Three-night special: R4,785 pp sharing or R6,250 for singles.
Meals: All meals, drinks and 2-3 game activities included.
Directions: You will get a map when you book.

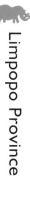

Gomo Gomo Game Lodge

Van Zijl Manktelow

Timbavati Game Reserve, PO Box 1696, Nelspruit 1200
Tel: 013-752-3954 (reservations) Fax: 013-752-3002 (reservations)
Email: gomo@netactive.co.za Web: www.gomogomo.co.za
Cell: 082-454-2571

How do they do that? Every time we visit Gomo Gomo they manage to produce spectacular game action. This year, out on drive with ace ranger Morné, we scored a stunning hatrick: two lions lying in the long grass, lazily eyeing the leopard they'd chased up a tree, with a bull elephant sloshing in the waterhole behind (and no doubt the rhino and buffalo keeping score). This bush is not for taming! And the camp's pretty wild too. Yes there's electricity, but fans and bedside lamps complement, rather than compromise, the bush atmosphere. You sleep in rondavels or safari tents (I prefer the latter), some of which are river-facing and have private decks. A day in camp usually contains morning and evening game drives and a bush walk before guests gather for dinner in the boma and sit round a fire in as much of a circle as numbers allow. Want to or not, you will find yourself telling big-game stories (or at least big stories about game). The camp sits right by the Nhlaralumi River (swimming is a mite hazardous – fewer crocs and hippos in the pool) and the sounds of the night will stay with you (in a good way) for a long time. To top it all, managers Rudi and Ancabé are an impressively enthusiastic couple, a vital element, which makes the camp stand taller than others.

Rooms: 9: 5 brick-and-thatch rondavels (3 with 2 bedrooms), 4 with shower, 1 with bath; 4 luxury safari tents, all with en/s shower.
Price: R850 – R1,230 pp sharing. Singles +R375. Prices may change from Dec '05. One-off vehicle entry fee is R75.
Meals: Full breakfast, lunch, dinner and game drives included. Extras are your bar bill and any curio purchases.
Directions: From Hoedspruit take the R40 south for 7km. Go left at Eastgate Airport sign. Follow to the gates – signed Gomo Gomo in the park.

Motswari Private Game Reserve

Kathy and Steve Bergs
Timbavati, Hoedspruit 1380
Tel: 015-793-1718 Fax: 015-793-2365
Email: motswari@webmail.co.za Web: www.motswari.co.za

Watching a leopard devour an impala at a distance of just a few yards is a special game viewing experience by anybody's book (except perhaps another impala's) – particularly when you're lucky to be there at all. It was late and I had been stood up for the night (the cheek of it), but like the stars that they are, Kathy and Steve came to my rescue. These two have been in the game game for years and are among the friendliest characters you'll meet in this book. They're bush-lovers through and through and they actually met at Motswari in the 1980s. After a brief stint away when Kathy ran an English school and Steve played with explosives (don't ask), they're back. And you can see why. The lodge is great, with a rocky pool, open bar and dining room all spread out across the green banks of the Sohebele river, deep in the Timbavati reserve. Along with a herd of bush-happy guests I ate supper under the stars at a long poolside table, talking cats with the rangers. Appropriately, each room's named after an animal and I was given "Cheetah", perhaps because of my lithe physique and feline cunning – or was it my searing pace? Anyway, they're all painted different shades of bush colours outside and whitewashed within with hefty mosquito-netted four-posters, satisfyingly chunky furniture and a plentiful supply of wildlife books and magazines to make yourself sound intelligent… just purrfect.

Rooms: 15: 1 king and 14 twins all with bath and shower.
Price: From R2,200 pp. Singles +R1,000. Price includes 2 game drives, game walks and meals.
Meals: All included.
Directions: From Hoedspruit take the R40 south towards Klaserie. Turn L at Timbavati and Hoedspruit Eastgate Airport signs. Continue straight to main gate (20km on tar/dirt road). Motswari is signed 40km in from the gate.

Map Number: 18

Phuza Moya Private Game Reserve

Steve and Hantie Topham
Hoedspruit 1380
Tel: 015-793-1971 Fax: 015-793-3313
Email: res@phuzamoya.co.za Web: www.phuzamoya.co.za
Cell: 082-894-2456

From Phuza Moya's breezy hilltop the panoramic view of the Drakensberg (yes, it does stretch this far north) is the best in the bush and after clattering along every dirt road available and swallowing half the dust of Limpopo Province I could happily have stood there all day. This is a legendary lodge with legendary hosts. The game reserves up here are less hectic than some of their Kruger Park cousins and after years working like wild dogs further south the Tophams have slotted into their new surroundings perfectly. Steve, ranger, husband and ecologist (in no particular order), was off wrestling hippo (or something), so Hantie gave me the grand tour. There are basically two sleeping options: decked, bush-feel tents, with enormous bathrooms (hardly camping!) and that fantastic view; or king-sized, stone–built suites. Three of these are set away from the lodge at an amazing look-out point above the Olifants and Blyde river confluence. These two waterways give the reserve its character and greenery, and provide a perfect riverside breakfast/swimming spot in the shade of an enormous jackalberry tree. There are loads of activities on offer and no shaggy-maned or spiky-tusked creatures to threaten a quick end to your trip when you head out game-viewing on one of the eight horses, a quad bike or on foot.

Rooms: 12: 4 luxury king/twin tents; 8 suites (2 kings and 6 king/twins). All rooms have bath and shower.
Price: R1,250 pp. Singles R1,875. Game drive and horse trails included.
Meals: All meals included.
Directions: From Jo'burg take the N4 west to Belfast, then the R540 north to Lydenburg and the R36 towards Tzaneen. After the Strijdom tunnel take the R526 R towards Phalaborwa. Phuza Moya is 16km further on, on R.

Garonga Safari Camp

Bernardo Smith
Greater Makalali Game Reserve, Hoedspruit 1380
Tel: Res: 011-537-4620 Fax: Res: 011-447-0993 Camp: 015-318-7902
Email: reservations@garonga.com Web: www.garonga.com
Cell: Camp: 082-440-3522

Garonga is as close to Heaven as most of us ever get. Bernardo has succeeded in creating a luxurious, yet completely relaxed, North African oasis in the middle of the South African bush: terracotta colours, thick earthen walls, cushions on low beds and billowing white fabrics. The pace is slow and unpressurised, the perfect relaxed environment for honeymooners, couples celebrating anniversaries – or for just about anyone who needs to make it up to someone else. Game drives are always available, but you may prefer to lie in under the high, white-tented canopy of your amazing room, dreaming of the candlelit bath taken under the stars on the previous evening with a bottle of wine; or of the sensational food you have enjoyed and hope still to enjoy. Alternately you can choose a more solitary, more exotic night's sleep twenty minutes from camp on a platform high above the water. Still stressed? Then return to Garonga and fall asleep in one of the hammocks or be pampered by the resident aromatherapist while gazing languidly over the nearby waterhole. Probably the most romantic place to stay in this book.

Rooms: 7: 4 king/twins and 2 doubles with indoor and outdoor shower; 1 bush suite with bath, shower, outdoor shower and air-conditioning.
Price: R1,595 – R6,500 pp.
Meals: Breakfast, lunch and dinner included, as well as picnics, sleep-outs and bush bath, house wines and beers, soft drinks and laundry.
Directions: Directions will be given to you when you book.

Mfubu Lodge & Gallery

Olga Kühnel and Jack Colenso

Balule Nature Reserve,Phalaborwa 1390
Tel: 015-769-6252 Fax: 015-769-6252
Email: olina@telkomsa.net or mfubulodge@hotmail.com
Web: http://travel.to/mfubu Cell: 073-416-0451

I've been deeper into the bush, but rarely has it seemed so penetrating. There are no fences here, just the guarantee of hot water, cold beer and animals that come to you. At dinner we ate the best Jansson's Temptation this side of the North Sea and awaited curtain-up. Silently hippos trotted onto centre stage, a brilliant moon silhouetting them against the white canvas of an alluvial beach. Nowadays the Olifants River eases like oil, so in the morning we ran the gauntlet, wading through its crocodile-infested waters. (Well, someone knew someone who thought they heard one here once). Safely on the other side, we clambered aboard a Land Rover, mingled with rhino, buffalo and giraffe and watched birds from a hide. On longer drives, Jack has been known to cook eggs on a shovel. Easy for a WW2 flying ace who's building himself a plane. "I've got all the parts," he says, "all I need is a miracle." The lodge itself sits on the riverbank, a trio of thatched cabins with fans, electric lights and tented fronts, connected by a walkway which weaves amongst trees. Further off, there are two cottages with kitchens, game-viewing platform and art gallery – Olga collects local art and encourages guests to paint, pen or ponder. It's not so much "shamrackle" (one of Olga's spoonerisms) as delightfully unrushed. Our friends in the bush.

Rooms: 5: 3 twin cabins sharing two bathrooms; 1 twin timber cottage and 1 double stone cottage, both with own showers.
Price: R490 pp. Single supplement R100.
Meals: Full breakfast and 3-course dinner included. Drinks not included. 3-hour game drive R160 pp including snacks and sundowners.
Directions: From Jo'burg N12, from Pretoria N4, through Witbank to Belfast. Left on R540 to Lydenburg, then R36 through Strijdom Tunnel following signs to Phalaborwa. Turn right onto R530 to Mica. 22km from Mica on R530 turn R on dirt road following Mfubu signs (about 9km).

Kings Walden Lodge

David and Tana Hilton-Barber

Agatha, Tzaneen 0850
Tel: 015-307-3262 Fax: 015-307-1548
Email: info@kingswalden.co.za Web: www.kingswalden.co.za
Cell: 083-380-3262

The famous garden at Kings Walden has been designed like a ship with terraces descending towards the prow – full of secret nooks and crannies. You never know what's round the next corner: a mirrored rose garden perhaps; a herb garden; an ornamental pond; lavender walks; bare-breasted sphinxes guarding a staircase leading to the next terrace up; a huge swimming pool or maybe Tana pottering in her straw hat? Found in the foothills of the northern Drakensberg Mountains the three-acre garden is a series of flower and foliage compositions each chosen for colour, texture and shape on land that's been in Tana's family since the turn of the last century. The house sits at the stern of the imaginary boat atop a plateau that drops away on three sides affording long and spectacular views across the lowveld Letsitele Valley to the Drakensberg escarpment. As morning mist clears you'll think you're on the roof of Africa. Decorated in the style of an English colonial homestead, rooms are full of antiques and feel homely – all with open fireplaces in their sitting rooms. You will eat well here too, by the way. Tana's *cordon bleu* cooking is delicious. From Kings Walden you can drive or hike in mountains or forests, visit waterfalls, go boating and fishing on dams, play golf or tennis. And it's one hour to the Kruger National Park.

Rooms: 5: 4 double suites and 1 family unit with double and bunk beds and its own kitchen.
Price: R320 pp sharing. Singles R395. Children up to 14 half price.
Meals: Full breakfast included. Lunches, picnics, scones and tea and 4-course dinner by arrangement.
Directions: From Johannesburg: N1 to Pietersburg then R71 to Tzaneen. Turn right onto the R36 just before Tzaneen. Stay on the R36; at first stop street, turn right to Agatha and sign to Kings Walden – approx 15km from Tzaneen – on the same road as the Coach House Hotel.

Coach House Hotel and Spa

Guy Matthews
Old Coach Rd, Agatha, near Tzaneen 0850
Tel: 015-306-8000; reservations: 015-306-8027 Fax: 015-306-8008
Email: info@coachhouse.co.za; reservations@coachhouse.co.za
Web: www.coachhouse.co.za Cell: 083-627-9999

The Coach House *is* a hotel, but it is a rare achievement in the genre to retain such a friendly and personal atmosphere; this is down to a dynamic Guy Matthews and his attentive team. You are encouraged to slow down, switch off, breathe in the air and maybe take a snooze on your own patio. The setting is spectacular, although the Drakensberg hid coyly behind the mist when I stayed. The food is also delicious and comes mostly from the surrounding farms. There is a floodlit croquet lawn (if you can muster the energy), a keyhole-shaped pool, a new spa with heated pool number two, a substantial gym and a variety of treatment rooms. You can also go hiking in the grounds (560 hectares, mostly dedicated to macadamia and pecan nut plantations) or sample the joys of the little nougat factory, the snooker room with views of the lowveld, the sitting room with roaring fires, and the oldest (109 years!) money jukebox in the world. Since the first edition people have continued to speak highly of the Coach House and it deserves its excellent reputation. *No children under 14. Kruger National Park is 100km away. Close to the Coach House: Rooikat Forest Trail, Debegeni waterfalls, and township and cultural tours.*

Rooms: 41 rooms, all with en-suite bathrooms.
Price: R675 – R975 pp sharing (B&B). Single room R950 – R1,250 (B&B). Includes use of the sensorium. Prices may change from Dec '05.
Meals: All meals available in the restaurant. Casual breakfasts R120. 5-course set-menu dinners R250 (wine extra) or à la carte. Dress smart-casual.
Directions: Ask when booking.

Kurisa Moya Nature Lodge

Ben De Boer and Lisa Martus

Houtbosdorp, near Magoebaskloof, PO Box 1965, Sovenga 0727
Tel: 015-276-1131 Fax: 015-276-1131
Email: info@krm.co.za Web: www.krm.co.za
Cell: 082-200-4596

Log cabins in an indigenous forest, a six-man cottage overlooking mile upon mile of mountains and veld, or a rustic, thick-walled farmhouse…. Ben and Lisa offer the lot and the hardest part of your stay will be choosing where to lay your head. For me it was just a stop-off sadly, with a lazy couple of hours on the verandah being filled in on available attractions (tea plantations, waterfall walks, Kruger expeditions…) and filled up with lunch and lime juice. All three destinations are self-cater-friendly, but homespun "meals on 4x4 wheels" are on hand and there are plans for a restaurant in an old barn. It's a family affair owned by Ben and assorted siblings and spouses. They've worked tirelessly to have as little impact on their mountainside environment as possible and that's what makes this such a tranquil place to stay. The stilted cabins (my favourite) are hidden by a dense canopy of afro-montane forest and their decks are the ideal spot for a lamp-lit braai or bino-less birding (Knysna loeries, long-crested eagles and some 300 others are on show when they choose to be). Ben, a former biology teacher (and so highly qualified nature guide) showed me the other spots too and pulling out of the drive I really wished I'd stayed the night. Ten minutes down the road one of my tyres exploded. I really, really wished I'd stayed the night. *Massages, fly-fishing, sunset 4x4 drives and bird walks available on site.*

Rooms: 4 venues: 2 forest cabins sleeping 2 adults and 2 kids each, sharing a shower; 1 cottage sleeping 6, sharing shower; 1 farmhouse with 5 twins, all en/s with bath and/or shower.
Price: R300 pp self-catering. Kids under 12 half price.
Meals: Breakfast R70, lunch R80, supper R120.
Directions: From Jo'burg take N1 north to Polokwane and then R71 to Tzaneen. After 20km turn L at first traffic lights, continue for 27km and turn R onto the farm.

Lesheba Wilderness

Peter and Kathryn Straughan & John and Gill Rosmarin

Louis Trichardt 0920
Tel: 015-593-0076
Fax: 015-593-0076
Email: magic@lesheba.co.za
Web: www.lesheba.co.za
Cell: 083-444-0456 / 083-266-9502

Kudu!" a shrill cry from pint-sized ranger Erinn as we bounce along to a family supper. Kathryn and Peter's daughter may be a mere nipper but she's an A-Z on the incredible array of life to be found in their mountaintop kingdom. And a kingdom it is. Creeping up to 4,400ft, I was amazed to reach not a rocky ridge but a huge plateau with its own mini-mountains, grassy plains and thick-bushed gorge. Kathy's parents own this 2,600ha game farm and over eleven years the family have rebuilt a dilapidated Venda village, created a secluded bush camp, started a traditional arts and crafts school, discovered seven rock art sites… and raised three kids. The village is stunning, a gaggle of clay-red rondavels regenerated with the help of Venda artist Noria Mabasa. She sculpted dozens of figures around the clustered bedrooms and huge kitchen/dining room that gazes across the bushy heights. In my room – one of two fabulous suites with inter-linked bedroom, bathroom and kitchen – a curvaceous mermaid stretched seductively around the bath. In the other, the outdoor shower springs from a standing man's ear. This is a magical, see-it-to-believe-it kind of place and a hiker's paradise. Come the morning we were back in the pick-up when Kai's voice crackled across the radio (daughter number 2). What was it? A rhino? A rarely-sighted leopard? "Mummy, Mummy, Erinn threw me off the bed." A false alarm.

Rooms: 4: exclusive bookings for Hamasha bushcamp (sleeps 8) and Venda village (sleeps 9): all rooms with en/s showers; 2 luxury kings both with bath and shower.
Price: From R280 pp self-catering to R1,250 pp full board.
Meals: All meals on request.
Directions: Take N1 north from Jo'burg to Louis Trichardt. At first crossroads in town turn L onto R522 towards Vivo. Continue for 36km and Lesheba is signed R down a gravel road.

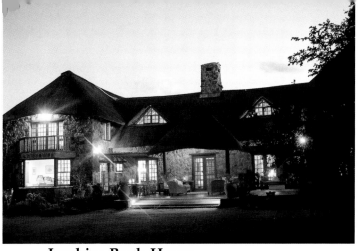

Jembisa Bush Home

Neil and Natasha Whyte

Vaalwater 0530
Tel: 014-755-4415 Fax: 014-755-4444
Email: info@jembisa.com Web: www.jembisa.com
Cell: 082-570-8474

Jembisa is simply the perfect family destination; a home from home kitted out for toddlers to teenagers and planted in some of the most spectacular bush you'll see. Despite palatial proportions the stone and thatch house could not feel more welcoming, its titanic living and dining room providing a central attraction, strewn with well-loved sofas and completed with a honky-tonk piano and vast fireplace. Rhodesian teak staircases sweep up each side to immense bedrooms and no less than five bathrooms, and whether you're flying solo (like me) or a team of ten, you'll enjoy cart-wheeling through them. It all feels reminiscently English, sipping tea on the verandah, swinging racquets on the floodlit tennis court and thumbing through the volumes of a snug library. But venture a little further and this is most certainly Africa. At the foot of the garden, beyond salt-water pool and shaven lawns, a huge deck juts from the hillside gazing proprietarily across the Palala River, a deep, snaking watercourse sliding through the forest far below (favoured spot for wallowing hippo and catchable yellowfish). You won't see the boundaries of the reserve from the deck – particularly when face-down, enjoying available massage treatment. It covers some 3,000ha (an awful lot of acres) and is packed with trackable game from rhino to leopard and hyena.

Rooms: 6: 1 king, 2 queens & 2 twins all en/s bath and shower. 1 twin bunk-bed sharing bath and shower.
Price: Bookings on an exclusive basis. R1,850 pp includes all activities. Kids under 12 half-price.
Meals: All meals included.
Directions: From Jo'burg take N1 north. After Warmbaths take R33 via Nylstroom to Vaalwater. In town turn R to Melk River. After exactly 40km turn L to Lapalala and Melk River school. 8km on turn R to rhino museum. Continue 4km and gates are on R.

Ant's Nest

Ant and Tessa Baber

Vaalwater, Waterberg 0530
Tel: 014-755-4296 / 014-755-3584 Fax: 014-755-4941
Email: antsnest@telkomsa.net Web: www.waterberg.net
Cell: 083-287-2885

Ant's (and Tessa's) Nest is a true bush home run by a truly great team. It's a one-party-a-go destination in the malaria-free Waterberg where the only rule is "do what you want". Built centre stage in a natural amphitheatre, bedrooms are arrayed in and around the farmhouse on Baber family land. There's a colonial feel to the Indian furniture and shaded verandah, but it's not in the least bit stuffy. In fact, it's one of the most relaxed and child-friendly places I've found, and there are activities galore. Top of the list are the horses, some 35 of them, from the novice's plodder – for those who still think them uncomfortable in the middle and dangerous at both ends – to the challengingly frisky. And horse-back is the best way to see the game (particularly the rare antelope like oryx and sable), while wallowing in the pool can also be pretty effective when Irwin the rhino and other animals come to munch the lawn or drink at the waterhole. Otherwise there are traditional game drives or walks, visits to meet Ant's dad Charles (a legend in these parts) and his cattle stud, tours of rock art sites or Iron Age villages… and always piles of gourmet food to come back to. Really, with so much on offer, why bother coming for less than a week?

Rooms: 4: 3 kings with en/s bath and shower, 1 family unit with 3 single beds and shared bath and shower.
Price: R2,000 – R3,000 pp. Kids from R1,300. Prices vary according to number of people and are fully inclusive of all activities whilst on the game reserve.
Meals: All meals and drinks included.
Directions: From Jo'burg take N1 north. After Warmbaths take R33 via Nylstroom to Vaalwater. Head through town and turn R opposite Total garage to Elisras/Lephalale. After 10km turn R to Dorset. Ant's Nest is signed on L 11km on.

Ant's Hill

Ant and Tessa Baber
Vaalwater 0530
Tel: 014-755-4296 / 014-755 3584 Fax: 014-755-4941
Email: antsnest@telkomsa.net Web: www.waterberg.net

And for those in search of a more classic lodge experience with all the same activities, there's Ant's Hill just up the road (and hill, obviously). This too is a family-friendly, exclusive-bookings venue and you're encouraged to use whichever of the five rooms you fancy. The troop staying when I visited were doing just that; Mum and Dad plus young twins in the huge family suite, a teenager above the lodge, overlooking the bush, and a ten-year-old in the hillside honeymoon suite! The main lodge, rooms and salt-water pool all teeter on the edge of a gorge that's a lush, green home to baboons and the ideal spot to watch the sun set over the Waterberg (G&T in hand, of course). All the stone and wood here comes from the farm, with twisted wild olive boughs hauled in to make door frames and fireplaces. The whole place has a truly homely feel, stuffed with Kenyan furniture, Ant's paintings, brightly-coloured cushions and royal-sized beds. Paul, your incredibly friendly host, runs the show with wife Daleen and baby Ruben. Activities in the game reserve are included in the rates. Other activities in the area are available at extra cost.

Rooms: One-group booking only. 5 rooms in total: 2 kings, 1 twin, 1 family cottage with 1 king & 1 twin room; all with bath and shower.
Price: R2,000 – R3,000 pp. Kids from R1,300. Prices vary according to number of people and are fully inclusive of all activities on the game reserve.
Meals: All meals and drinks included.
Directions: From Jo'burg take N1 north. After Warmbaths take R33 via Nylstroom to Vaalwater. Head through town and turn R opposite Total garage to Elisras/Lephalale. After 19km turn R at B11/13 sign onto dirt track heading uphill and follow Ant's Hill signs.

Map Number: 17

Limpopo Province

Zebras Crossing Private Game Lodge

Alice Zucchi
Nylstroom-Modimolle
Tel: 011-788-6658 Fax: 011-442-5990
Email: reservations@zebrascrossing.com Web: www.zebrascrossing.com

Alice is a German-Italian whirlwind, and her take on the game lodge is a real break from the norm. No feel-of-Africa furniture here. Inside, the earth-red thatched houses are whitewashed throughout – white furniture, white linen and white walls – and the immediate impact is one of calm and space. This is true of the whole reserve. Just an hour and a half's drive from the commotion of Johannesburg, this is the place "to let your soul relax" as Alice puts it. This she demonstrated by stretching out on the Bush Bed that's hidden among the trees, an imaginary glass of wine in her hand. The gravel drive is (was) perfectly raked (until I arrived), the deckchairs neatly lined and starched tablecloths always decorated with fresh flowers. Even the plains game here seems totally chilled out. A lone gemsbok was quietly munching the poolside lawn when I arrived and there are four zebra that often pop in for tea. Zulu manager Promise is great and always on hand to keep you topped up with fantastic South African/Italian fare – try game-drive nibbles of parmesan and rocket for a start. The kitchen is open to anyone who wants to look in and you can help yourself to drinks too. In fact, you'll soon feel so much a part of the place you'll want to adopt a zebra, and the best thing is – you can! *Children welcome on request.*

Rooms: 6: all king/twins with bath and shower. 2 have lofts. Each has additional 2 beds.
Price: R2,350 pp per day single or sharing (2005).
Meals: All meals included.
Directions: Faxed or emailed on booking.

Makweti Safari Lodge

Dawn and Alan Kisner

Welgevonden Game Reserve, Waterberg, Vaalwater 0530
Tel: Res: 011-837-6776 Lodge: 014-755-4948
Fax: Res: 011-837-4771 Lodge: 014-755-4950
Email: makweti@global.co.za Web: www.makweti.com Cell: 083-280-9801

Hosts Wayne and Vicky are the life and soul of this fantastic lodge and I just can't believe we didn't find them sooner. Not only has Wayne a sixth sense for game-finding, he also knows a lot about dung. At any given moment he'll leap off the game vehicle to explain the inner workings of an elephant or the mind-set of a dung beetle, and that's what stands out on his drives. Not only were our sundowners abruptly curtailed for an exciting lion hunt, but he also opened our minds to the full mosaic of bush life. From enormous browsers to tiny insects, it's a fascinating jigsaw that leaves you wondering only where we fit in. Makweti is buried in the Welgevonden private reserve on the undulating, malaria-free Waterberg range, and with fences dropping all the time there's an ever-expanding array of greenery and game on your doorstep. That doorstep overlooks a stunning gorge and summer waters tumble past the lodge, beneath a springy rope-bridge that leads to thatched chalets. Mine was sumptuously private, hidden in the bush with a well-decked-out deck peering through the undergrowth. Indoor and outdoor showers and a free-standing tub ensured I was clean as a whistle before moseying down to the main lodge, where a reed-filled fish pond divides the bar and bookshelves from the dining room. Here we spent much of our time, scoffing sweet potato, tomato tartlets and kudu loin with onion marmalade. Makweti is an unfenced camp — so expect the unexpected.

Rooms: 5: 4 doubles and 1 twin all with bath and shower.
Price: R1,750 – R2,950 pp sharing. Prices may change from January '06.
Meals: Meals, accommodation, safaris and local taxes included. Drinks extra.
Directions: 260km from Jo'burg. Directions faxed or emailed on booking, or on website. Car transfers available. Flight transfers can link to Mpumalanga airport for Kruger and Mozambique stays.

Map Number: 17

Mozambique

Casa Lisa Lodge

Bruce and Michelle Buckland
CP472, Maputo
Tel: +258-82-304-199
Email: buckland@teledata.mz

It was here, with a refreshing dry breeze wafting across the pineapple fields, that my Mozambican adventure began. I couldn't have chosen a more rustic destination, or such a charming, laid-back couple as Bruce and Michelle to launch me full stomached into an epic journey. At Casa Lisa you won't find luxuries like electricity points or glass in windows (a blessing as it turns out), but you will find comfort, friendliness and good cheer – far superior substitutes in the heat of Southern Africa. Built around a central tree trunk (where Bruce's hat with 'The Boss' emblazoned across the front dangles from a branch), it is the reed-walled, reed-roofed bar where the heart of Casa Lisa beats. Michelle can often be found ploughing her way through a paperback, waiting anxiously for the chicken delivery from Maputo to trundle up the long drive, while The Boss potters behind the reed and wood bar with the sheepdogs lolling at his feet. As fortune had it, the chicken-man arrived in the nick of time and I enjoyed the famous chicken supper I'd heard so much about. Washed down with the local brew, I retired to my reed and concrete chalet to snuggle up behind the mosquito net and read by candlelight. A perfect stopover to rest those weary driving legs.

Rooms: 15 chalets sleeping 1-11 people. 10 with en-suite showers, 5 with private bathrooms.
Price: $17 – $22 pp. Children under 12 half price.
Meals: Full breakfast $5; dinner $8.50 for 3 courses, $5 main course only. Lunch by arrangement.
Directions: On EN1, 48.5km from junction of EN4 onto EN1 (Xai Xai road, north of Maputo).

Casa Barry

Malcolm and Peggy Warrack
Tofo Beach, 4320
Tel: 082-808-5523 Fax: 031-762-3469
Email: peggy@dbnmail.co.za Web: www.casabarry.com
Cell: +258-232-9007 (Lodge)

Just what the doctor ordered after a seven-hour slog along the pot-holed roads of Mozambique. I couldn't wait to dump my bags and stretch my aching legs on the clear sands of Tofo Beach that arched away into the distance. In the lukewarm bay, a fleet of small (and rather rickety-looking) fishing boats were being hauled from the water's edge, overflowing with wriggling goodies from which 'executive chef' Johan makes his selection for the restaurant. Following my nose, I headed to the stilted wooden deck protruding from the reed-roofed bar, offering a birds-eye view of the comings and goings on the beach. This is clearly the place to be, with diners and drinkers soaking up the atmosphere as the sun goes down to the sound of some good ol' classics warbling in the background. Successful fishermen fired up the braais for a family feast on their verandah before sinking, satisfied, into a deep sleep under the reed roof of their wooden chalet. Seems these folk had an action-packed day behind them. Nevertheless, I rose early to find them strapping on scuba gear or untangling fishing lines as a couple of riders cantered along the deserted beach. Jon runs the scuba centre and is a Titan of knowledge on everything from reefs to whale sharks, so whether it's a boat trip or reel adventure, he's the catch of the day.

Rooms: 20: 12 chalets sleeping 4-6 with private shower rooms and kitchens; 8 casitas with en-suite showers.
Price: R900 per day for 4-sleeper chalet. R1,150 per day for 6-sleeper chalet. R180 pp for casitas.
Meals: Full breakfast R30. Self-catering or restaurant on premises specialising in local seafood.
Directions: Map on website, directions can be faxed.

Casa Rex

Melonie Glyn-Woods and Ray Monson
Bo. 19 Outubro, Vilanculos
Tel: +258-238-2048 Fax: +258-238-2048
Email: casarex@teledata.mz Web: www.casarex.co.zw

I've never met Rex, but you only have to stroll round his house to feel that you know him. He built it ten years ago, single-handed, with only a wheelbarrow to ease the strain, hand-crafting the furniture from heavy, mahogany-like local wood. He's dotted the house with flotsam and jetsam washed up on the beach below (not any old rubbish – a ship's wheel, lovingly restored, and a port-hole fitted into the front door were my favourites). A remarkable chap. And a remarkable place, run by the super-relaxed Ray and Mel… the most charming couple this side of Maputo? A few minutes sprawled on the deep black-slate verandah and, if you're anything like me, you'll quickly fall as deeply in love with the place as they have. And who can blame us? This shady haven plays host to the best restaurant in town (the thought of squid and stuffed crab as fresh as the ocean itself set my hunger pangs twanging), overlooking an oasis of a garden, drenched in colour, with views (and a path) down to the ocean. Pink bougainvilleas hide the garden rooms and palms, overflowing with coconuts, stretch skywards above the crystal pool. The rooms, scattered among the greenery, provide welcome relief from the African sun with their cool tiled floors and whitewashed or exposed walls. Rex may have built perfection.

Rooms: 7: 4 doubles, 1 with en-suite bath and shower, 3 with en-suite shower only; 1 triple (3 single beds) and 2 twins (family rooms) all with en-suite showers.
Price: $65 – $85 pp. Single supplement $20 in high season.
Meals: Full breakfast included. A la carte restaurant on the premises, approx $15 – $25.
Directions: 850 km north of Maputo on EN1, turn right at Vilanculos sign in Pambara. In Vilanculos turn left at the main T-junction and left again onto the sand road when you get to the sea (Casa Rex is signposted here). Casa Rex is 800m on right.

Dugong Lodge

Gavin Le Marque and Jane Golding

San Sebastian Peninsula, Vilanculos
Tel: 011-463-3551 (reservations) Fax: 011-463-2037 (res)
Email: reservations@dugonglodge.co.za Web: www.dugonglodge.co.za
Cell: +258-82-306-488 (lodge)

Clasping onto the handrails as the outboard roared into action, we were soon zipping across turquoise waves towards the horizon where a beach paradise awaited us: smooth, squeaky sand interrupted only by a jetty stretching into a perfect sea. It would appear that I had timed my arrival to perfection, for the tables on the deep wooden deck were being laid for lunch under the shade of the masasa tree. An afternoon of pottering around with a snorkel could wait – the chances of spotting the nearly extinct 'dugong' were minimal anyway. But as grinning guests returned from scuba diving with stories of reefs, sailfish and manta ray, and a dolphin glimpsed en-route, my afternoon was sealed and I spent hours basking in warm Indian Ocean water, flippering about, head down, eyes peeled. But Dugong Lodge has more to offer than a pristine beach and the unrivalled nature of the Vilanculos Coastal Wildlife Sanctuary in which it sits. My framed, tented room with its jekka-thatched grass canopy offered a deep stone bath and a hardwood deck from which to laze in a hammock watching the sun set over the horizon. A delightful dinner of local crab was served under the African stars on the deck – but for über-romance there's the gazebo at the end of the jetty.

Rooms: 6 twins or doubles, & 2 family units of 2 rooms sharing a lounge. All have bathrooms with outside showers.
Price: $250 pp sharing. Singles $350. Children 3-12 $125 sharing with 2 adults.
Meals: All meals included. Drinks extra.
Directions: Transfers to lodge arranged on booking.

Quilalea Island

Marjolaine Hewlett

PO Box 323, Pemba
Tel: +258-72-21808 Fax: +258-72-21808
Email: quirimbas@plexusmoz.com Web: www.quilalea.com
Cell: +258-82-317891

Such is the remoteness and idyllic-tropical-islandness of Quilalea Island that I felt compelled (ah poor me) to turn business into pleasure and I stayed for four days. The resort is the island. Apart from the next-door villa some 40 yards away, all I could see from my verandah were white sand, clear, sandy-bottomed Indian Ocean, mangrove-topped coral outcrops that grew and sank with the tides, and other (equally lovely, I'm sure) islands of the archipelago. The villas themselves are exquisitely constructed from natural materials (no glass, but rattan blinds in seaward-gazing windows) and manage to be both deeply luxurious as well as perfectly suited to their tropical environment. I was not long in the borrowing of snorkelling equipment and spent hours each day finning around the island, examining coral. I did my first-ever scuba dive here. A coral cliff and its surreal world of wild-looking fish are found just a fifteen-metre underwater stroll down the gently sloping beach. Other activities include a dhow trip around the bay at sunset, propped up on cushions, glass of wine in hand; kayaking up mangrove creeks, deep-sea fishing trips, walking round the island (maybe 3 kilometres). The food was simply fantastic morning, noon and night. And so it goes on. On top of everything, the island is still managed in a humorous, friendly and fun way. This takes Quilalea into the stratosphere of GG recommendations. Find a way…!

Rooms: 9 villas: all king-sized beds with en-suite showers with swing-doors out to verandah. Villas are serviced each day. No biting insects presented themselves for extermination while I was there.
Price: US$375 – US$450 p.p.
Meals: All meals included in the rates.
Directions: Ask about this when booking. Basically you need to get to Pemba in Northern Mozambique, flights from Maputo, Joburg or Dar es Salaam. You are picked up at the airport and either driven (US$90 pp, 2.5 hours) or flown to the island (US$180 pp, 20 minutes).

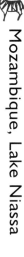

Nkwichi Lodge

Patrick Simkin
Manda Wilderness, Lake Niassa
Email: mdw01@bushmail.net Web: www.mandawilderness.org
Cell: 082-709-792

Ed's petrol crisis in Vilanculos made visiting Nkwichi (several tanks further north) impossible, so trusted friend of the firm Dorothy McLaren took up the baton and told us all we needed to know. Bewitching stuff. When we talk about venues being destinations in themselves, this is what we mean: Lake Malawi (or Niassa as it's known in Mozambique), hundreds of miles of gin-clear water, bound in by thick, indigenous forest. This really is true wilderness and the adventure starts with the transfer, buzzing in on a charter flight, chugging in on the M.V. Ilala steamer or sailing to a squeaky, white sand beach on the Nkwichi dhow. This is the only lodge on the Manda Wilderness Reserve and with beds for just fourteen guests you'll cross paths with nothing but the wildlife – otters, zebra, monkeys and eagles included. There are endless snorkelling spots, waterfall walks or sailing and canoeing expeditions available while hammocks are on hand for the readers, snoozers and lunch-time boozers. All six chalets are built of natural materials, artfully dotted within Nkwichi's invisible boundaries. Massive beds, great big armchairs and deckchairs at every turn invite you to relax and absorb the surrounding beauty, before digging into wholesome meals, heaped with locally-grown veg. The only tricky bit is deciding where to eat: the waterside deck, the lofty dining room or will it be in the shade of a 2,000 year old baobab tree…?

Rooms: 6 chalets: 5 dbles & 1 x 1 dble & 1 twin. All en-s/outside bathr'ms & 'eco-loos' (soon flush toilets).
Price: African residents: US$180 pn per couple. Internationals: US$360 per couple. Singles (African res'ts) from $90 to (peak season international) £150.
Meals: Transfers each way: from Likoma Island = $25 pp. From Cobue $20 pp. From Mbueca $10 pp. All meals and activities included in the rates.
Directions: From Malawi, charter plane from Lilongwe to Likoma Island (45 mins) & then by boat (40 mins). Or take Ilala ferry from Chipoka on Fri, arrive Sat. From Lichinga 4 hrs by road to Mbueca & then 15 mins by boat to lodge. 4X4 is needed. Lodge can organise vehicles & drivers.

Indexes

Index by town name

For our rural properties, we have listed the nearest town.

Index by house name

Index of Activities

Here is a simple way to find entries within the book catering for specialist interests. The numbers under each category represent the entry numbers of places where the owners/managers are themselves interested in the subject or can organise for these activities to take place on or near their property.

Gardens
Places with lovely gardens and owners who are enthusiastic gardeners.
1, 8, 9, 10, 12, 16, 17, 18, 19, 21, 26, 28, 31, 34, 36, 37, 39, 40, 41, 43, 44, 45, 46, 47, 48, 49, 50, 51, 52, 53, 54, 55, 56, 58, 59, 64, 65, 66, 68, 69, 70, 72, 73, 75, 78, 80, 82, 85, 86, 88, 90, 91, 92, 93, 94, 95, 96, 98, 100, 102, 104, 108, 109, 112, 113, 117, 118, 120, 123, 126, 127, 128, 129, 130, 132, 135, 137, 140, 141, 142, 143, 145, 146, 148, 149, 151, 153, 154, 155, 156, 160, 161, 162, 163, 164, 165, 166, 167, 168, 169, 173, 174, 176, 177, 178, 180, 182, 184, 187, 188, 189, 190, 191, 192, 193, 194, 195, 196, 197, 198, 199, 200, 203, 204, 205, 206, 207, 208, 210, 215, 218, 221, 224, 225, 226, 227, 231, 233, 234, 235, 237, 238, 239, 240, 241, 242, 243, 247, 248, 253, 254, 257, 259, 260, 263, 264, 273, 274, 275, 276, 284

Rock Art
Sites found either on the property or guests can be shown/guided to nearby sites.
60, 64, 65, 67, 118, 124, 149, 150, 155, 157, 160, 174, 177, 178, 184, 185, 186, 189, 195, 215, 218, 219, 220, 221, 222, 223, 226, 230, 232, 233, 237, 238, 239, 240, 258, 263, 264, 276, 277, 278, 279, 281

Culture
Township visits can be organised by owners or cultural experiences (e.g. Zulu dancing) available on site.
1, 2, 6, 8, 10, 11, 12, 16, 18, 19, 20, 21, 22, 23, 24, 25, 26, 29, 32, 33, 34, 35, 36, 39, 40, 41, 43, 45, 47, 48, 50, 51, 54, 55, 65, 69, 73, 74, 75, 78, 81, 84, 85, 91, 93, 94, 95, 97, 98, 102, 103, 104, 105, 106, 109, 111, 112, 115, 123, 126, 130, 132, 134, 136, 140, 144, 145, 146, 147, 152, 154, 156, 157, 161, 164, 165, 166, 168, 170, 172, 174, 175, 176, 177, 178, 179, 182, 186, 189, 193, 195, 200, 203, 204, 205, 206, 207, 208, 209, 210, 211, 212, 213, 214, 215, 216, 220, 232, 235, 236, 237, 238, 239, 248, 254, 255, 256, 258, 259, 260, 264, 269, 273, 274, 275, 276, 277, 279, 283, 286, 287

Wine-maker
Wine made on the property.
71, 72, 75, 82, 83, 95, 97, 110, 111, 260

Gourmet cuisine
Fine dining available at these properties.
2, 35, 41, 43, 45, 52, 53, 58, 61, 63, 70, 71, 72, 73, 74, 75, 77, 85, 86, 95, 97, 98, 102, 104, 107, 108, 109, 112, 113, 115, 116, 118, 122, 123, 124, 130, 138, 142, 145, 146, 147, 151, 153, 158, 161, 166, 170, 172, 174, 175, 184, 188, 190, 193, 197, 200, 204, 206, 208, 209, 210, 211, 212, 213, 214, 215, 216, 218, 219, 221, 225, 226, 229, 234, 235, 238, 243, 248, 250, 251, 252, 254, 259, 260, 261, 262, 267, 269, 270, 271, 273, 274, 277, 278, 279, 280, 281, 283, 284, 285, 286

Horse-riding
Available on site.
67, 80, 91, 96, 106, 110, 112, 118, 120, 129, 146, 149, 150, 155, 159, 161, 164, 168, 180, 186, 187, 188, 192, 202, 203, 208, 213, 214, 215, 218, 219, 221, 223, 224, 225, 226, 228, 229, 230, 235, 239, 259, 260, 270, 278, 279

Whale-watching
Available from the property or from so near by that it makes little difference.
1, 2, 3, 4, 5, 7, 18, 36, 59, 60, 61, 62, 63, 94, 98, 99, 100, 101, 102, 103, 104, 105, 106, 122, 125, 133, 138, 139, 140, 143, 161, 179, 197, 198, 201, 202, 204, 208, 211, 283, 286

Boat Charter
Property owns boats or can organise charters.
1, 2, 3, 4, 5, 6, 8, 9, 10, 11, 13, 14, 16, 17, 18, 19, 20, 22, 24, 29, 32, 34, 36, 39, 43, 48, 55, 57, 59, 60, 62, 63, 91, 93, 94, 97, 98, 100, 102, 103, 104, 105, 106, 107, 108, 109, 111, 122, 126, 127, 134, 137, 138, 139, 141, 142, 145, 152, 161, 162, 163, 164, 165, 170, 171, 173, 174, 176, 179, 181, 182, 183, 196, 197, 198, 201, 203, 204, 207, 208, 209, 211, 212, 213, 214, 232, 242, 243, 266, 275, 282, 283, 284, 285, 286, 287

Canoeing
Canoes owned or organised by the property.
1, 2, 3, 4, 5, 8, 10, 11, 16, 17, 18, 20, 22, 24, 29, 32, 34, 39, 43, 57, 58, 59, 60, 61, 62, 63, 64, 67, 70, 91, 94, 95, 97, 98, 99, 100, 102, 103, 104, 106, 107, 108, 111, 115, 121, 122, 123, 126, 127, 129, 130, 131, 134, 136, 137, 139, 140, 141, 142, 144, 145, 152, 162, 163, 164, 166, 170, 171, 172, 173, 174, 176, 177, 180, 181, 182, 183, 185, 186, 189, 207, 208, 209, 210, 211, 212, 213, 214, 220, 221, 222, 223, 230, 231, 232, 234, 236, 254, 258, 265, 283, 284, 285, 286, 287

Historic house
These places are historic buildings.
20, 24, 33, 34, 35, 37, 45, 54, 58, 69, 70, 71, 73, 74, 77, 80, 82, 84, 86, 87, 94, 95, 96, 97, 110, 112, 115, 123, 125, 128, 132, 143, 151, 153, 154, 155, 156, 157, 160, 166, 171, 172, 173, 175, 178, 180, 186, 188, 189, 190, 191, 192, 193, 195, 221, 224, 226, 227, 232, 233, 234, 235, 236, 238, 273, 274

History Tours
Organised here (including battlefields).
8, 20, 24, 33, 34, 36, 54, 69, 72, 96, 112, 123, 154, 155, 156, 160, 172, 174, 175, 176, 177, 178, 181, 182, 184, 186, 190, 193, 195, 205, 214, 215, 216, 217, 218, 220, 221, 222, 225, 232, 233, 236, 238, 241, 248, 263, 274, 278, 279, 286, 287

Self-Catering option available here.
1, 2, 3, 4, 5, 6, 7, 8, 9, 12, 15, 16, 17, 18, 19, 20, 22, 25, 27, 29, 32, 37, 38, 40, 41, 44, 46, 47, 48, 51, 52, 53, 54, 56, 58, 60, 64, 65, 66, 68, 69, 70, 71, 76, 80, 82, 84, 89, 91, 92, 96, 99, 101, 104, 108, 110, 115, 118, 119, 121, 123, 125, 129, 132, 133, 134, 137, 143, 148, 149, 150, 152, 158, 159, 160, 161, 162, 165, 176, 178, 181, 184, 185, 186, 187, 189, 194, 196, 197, 199, 201, 202, 203, 205, 210, 213, 214, 217, 218, 221, 224, 227, 228, 230, 231, 232, 237, 239, 240, 241, 243, 244, 247, 248, 251, 252, 256, 264, 270, 275, 276, 282, 283

Bird-Watching
Owners are enthusiasts.
1, 2, 3, 5, 8, 9, 12, 16, 17, 36, 39, 41, 47, 48, 50, 52, 55, 57, 58, 59, 60, 61, 62,
63, 64, 65, 66, 68, 70, 71, 80, 72, 75, 76, 82, 84, 90, 91, 93, 95, 96, 97, 98, 99,
100, 102, 103, 104, 105, 106, 107, 108, 109, 110, 111, 112, 117, 118, 120, 121,
122, 123, 124, 126, 127, 129, 130, 131, 132, 134, 135, 136, 137, 138, 140, 142,
143, 144, 145, 146, 148, 149, 150, 151, 152, 153, 154, 155, 156, 157, 158, 159,
160, 161, 162, 163, 164, 167, 168, 169, 170, 171, 172, 173, 174, 176, 177, 179,
180, 183, 185, 186, 188, 190, 191, 192, 194, 195, 196, 199, 202, 203, 204, 205,
206, 207, 208, 209, 210, 211, 212, 213, 214, 216, 217, 218, 219, 220, 221, 222,
223, 224, 227, 228, 229, 230, 232, 233, 234, 235, 236, 237, 238, 240, 241, 242,
244, 247, 248, 249, 250, 252, 254, 255, 256, 257, 258, 259, 260, 261, 262, 263,
264, 265, 266, 267, 268, 269, 271, 272, 273, 274, 275, 276, 277, 278, 279, 280,
281, 282, 284, 285, 286, 287

Beach House
2, 4, 7, 36, 57, 59, 60, 61, 62, 63, 99, 101, 102, 103, 105, 106, 125, 133, 139,
161, 162, 179, 183, 201, 202, 211, 283, 284, 285, 286, 287

White-water rafting
Can be arranged in-house.
24, 29, 78, 98, 99, 100, 145, 161, 163, 189, 216, 220, 221, 222, 223, 229, 231,
253, 254, 256, 258, 259, 260, 265, 266, 267

Fishing
Can be arranged.
1, 2, 3, 4, 5, 6, 8, 11, 12, 13, 16, 18, 19, 20, 22, 24, 29, 32, 34, 39, 43, 48, 50,
52, 55, 57, 59, 60, 61, 62, 63, 64, 65, 67, 68, 70, 72, 74, 75, 76, 77, 78, 79, 80,
81, 82, 85, 88, 89, 90, 91, 93, 94, 96, 97, 98, 100, 102, 103, 104, 105, 106, 107,
108, 109, 110, 111, 112, 115, 121, 122, 123, 124, 126, 127, 130, 134, 137, 139,
140, 141, 142, 144, 145, 146, 147, 148, 149, 152, 153, 154, 157, 158, 159, 161,
162, 163, 164, 166, 167, 172, 173, 174, 176, 179, 181, 182, 183, 184, 185, 186,
187, 188, 190, 196, 197, 198, 199, 201, 203, 204, 206, 207, 208, 211, 212, 213,
214, 215, 217, 218, 219, 220, 221, 222, 223, 224, 225, 226, 228, 229, 230, 231,
232, 236, 237, 238, 242, 254, 255, 258, 260, 270, 273, 274, 275, 277, 278, 279,
282, 283, 284, 285, 286, 287

Fully Child-friendly
Places where children will be particularly well looked after.
2, 5, 9, 11, 15, 17, 18, 20, 24, 26, 29, 31, 32, 35, 50, 52,55, 58, 62, 64, 72, 81,
82, 88, 96, 99, 102, 104, 108, 119, 122, 124, 129, 137, 143, 145, 147, 150, 152,
157, 158, 159, 164, 168, 172, 173, 174, 178, 183, 184, 186, 187, 189, 192, 201,
202, 203, 205, 207, 209, 211, 212, 213, 214, 218, 220, 221, 222, 223, 228, 230,
231, 232, 233, 235, 237, 238, 239, 240, 244, 246, 248, 250, 251, 261, 268, 270,
272, 273, 275, 277, 278, 279, 283

THE GREENWOOD GUIDE TO
SOUTH AFRICA
Hand-picked
Things to Do and Places to Eat

First edition to be published at the end of 2005

This is a brand-new Greenwood Guide, detailing those places to eat and things to do across the whole of South Africa that sit most cosily with our professed likes and dislikes, i.e. a strong leaning towards the small, family-run, unusual, off-the-beaten track, and, above all, friendly and charming.

This book is designed for holiday-makers, both South African and overseas, who want to travel independently, avoid mass tourism and meet friendly, humorous and hospitable people. To this end we have chosen small wineries, family-run restaurants where natural friendliness and character are as important as the food itself; wonderful walks and bird-watching excursions; small, even one-man or woman, tour operators to lend expertise if you want it; we have included the best things to do with kids; we have found the best gardens, both private and municipal. Among establishments or activities that are already well known we have only included the truly worthy.

Basically if you like the sort of accommodation we have chosen, then you will find the new book a treat!

To order a copy

The Greenwood Guide to South Africa, Hand-Picked Things to Do and Places to Eat is due for publication in late 2005. If you would like to order a copy of this or any of our books, please fill in the coupon and send it with payment to Greenwood Guides, 46 Lillie Rd, London SW6 1TN. Payment can be made by UK cheque made out to 'Greenwood Guides', or by Visa/Mastercard. We will not process payments until the book is sent out.

Order form

	copy(ies)	price (each)	subtotal
THE GREENWOOD GUIDE TO SOUTH AFRICA **Hand-picked things to do and places to eat** (1ST EDITION)		£13.95	
THE GREENWOOD GUIDE TO SOUTH AFRICA **Hand-picked accommodation** (4TH EDITION)		£13.95	
THE GREENWOOD GUIDE TO AUSTRALIA **Hand-picked accommodation** (2ND EDITION)		£9.95	
THE GREENWOOD GUIDE TO NEW ZEALAND **Hand-picked accommodation** (3RD EDITION - OCT /05)		£9.95	
THE GREENWOOD GUIDE TO CANADA **Hand-picked accommodation** (1ST EDITION)		£9.95	

post and packing costs ....

   £2 per order in the UK or South Africa
   £3 per order within Europe   **Total**
   £4 per order elsewhere

Name ....

Address to send the book to ....

....

....

Payment is by UK sterling cheque made out to 'Greenwood Guides' or by VISA/Mastercard (only)

Card number

Expiry date

CCV number

Please send this coupon to
46 Lillie Road, Fulham, London, SW6 1TN, UK

simon@greenwoodguides.com

THE GREENWOOD GUIDE TO

AUSTRALIA

special hand-picked accommodation

Second Edition

Following advanced and extremely delicate surgical procedures, we have managed to split Australia and New Zealand into two completely separate books. Both are alive and doing very well. The Greenwood Guide to Australia (2nd edition) contains 120 lodges, B&Bs, small hotels, inns and self-catering cottages.

For more information or to order any of our guides see our web site at
www.greenwoodguides.com
or email us at
simon@greenwoodguides.com.

THE GREENWOOD GUIDE TO
NEW ZEALAND

special hand-picked accommodation

Second Edition, 2004/5

The Greenwood Guide to New Zealand (2nd edition) contains 100 B&Bs, lodges, farms and self-catering cottages. We are in the process of researching the third edition and this will be due for publication in October 2005.

For more information or to order any of our guides see our web site at
www.greenwoodguides.com
or email us at
simon@greenwoodguides.com

THE GREENWOOD GUIDE TO
CANADA

special hand-picked accommodation

First Edition

This is the latest addition to the Greenwood Guides series. 87 great B&Bs, inns, lodges, self-catering cottages... and even lighthouses and boats.

For more information or to order any of our guides see our web site at
www.greenwoodguides.com
or email us at
editor@greenwoodguides.com.

Notes

Notes

Notes

Notes